The Way of Abū Madyan

The Way of Abū Madyan

Doctrinal and Poetic Works of Abū Madyan Shuʿayb ibn al-Ḥusayn al-Anṣārī (*c.* 509/1115-16—594/1198)

*

EDITED AND TRANSLATED
WITH INTRODUCTION AND NOTES BY
VINCENT J. CORNELL

THE ISLAMIC TEXTS SOCIETY
GOLDEN PALM SERIES

This edition published 1996 by
The Islamic Texts Society
22a, Brooklands Avenue
Cambridge, CB2 2DQ, U.K.

ISBN 0 946621 34 9 *cloth*
ISBN 0 946621 35 7 *paper*

British Library Cataloguing in Publication Data
A catalogue record for this book is available from
the British Library

English typesetting by Goodfellow & Egan, Cambridge
Arabic typesetting by Decotype, Amsterdam, Holland
Printed in Great Britain by St Edmundsbury Press Ltd,
Bury St Edmunds, Suffolk.

To Rkia and Sakina

For the kind of loyalty and support that can never be repaid

CONTENTS

Acknowledgements

A work such as that which follows could never have been written without the cooperation and efforts of numerous individuals in several countries. First of all, it is necessary to thank both my wife, Rkia Elaroui Cornell, and Jamil Diab, Ph.D., founder of the Islamic Cultural Center at Tempe, Arizona, for their assistance in editing the Arabic texts reproduced in this volume. For all the time spent in helping me decipher badly copied and partially incomplete manuscripts, as well as arguing and rearguing possible renderings of the texts contained therein, I owe them a particular debt of gratitude. Special acknowledgements must also be given to Professors John O. Hunwick of Northwestern University and Ismail Poonawala of the University of California, Los Angeles for their detailed proofreading of the final version of the edited Arabic texts and their comments and suggestions concerning the translations. The late Professor Victor Danner of Indiana University and Dr. Muhammad S. Eissa of Northwestern University also made useful suggestions. The contributions of all four were greatly appreciated and were included in the final product whenever possible.

I must also extend my appreciation to those who assisted me in finding, collecting, and copying the Arabic manuscripts of Shaykh Abū Madyan's works. These include Dr. Alan Godlas, of the University of Georgia, who not only spent considerable time trying to gain access to a number of manuscript copies in Istanbul but also provided great assistance in locating sources of 'weak' hadith, as well as Mr. Muṣṭafā an-Nājī of Rabat, Morocco, who generously provided me with a second manuscript of *Bidāyat al-murīd*. Special thanks must go as well to al-Ḥājj al-Kāmil al-Qādirī and his unnamed brethren in the Qādiriyya zāwiya of Marrakesh, Morocco, for their kind help in verifying the text of *al-Qaṣīda an-Nūniyya*.

Appreciation is also due to the staffs and directors of several Arabic manuscript libraries for aiding me in this effort. These include the Bibliothèque Générale (*al-Khizāna al-ʿĀmma*) of Rabat, Morocco and its Director, His Excellency ʿAbd ar-Raḥmān al-Fāsī; the Bibliothèque Royale (*al-Khizāna al-Ḥasaniyya*), also of Rabat, Morocco, and its Director, His

Excellency Muḥammad al-ʿArabī al-Khaṭṭābī; the British Library, London; the Bibliothèque Nationale, Paris; and the Biblioteca Nacional, Madrid. A particular note of thanks must go to the late Moroccan patriot and scholar Muḥammad Ibrāhīm al-Kattānī, who acted as an intellectual guide and mentor during my stay in Morocco. It is earnestly hoped that God will reward him for his contributions to Islamic scholarship and his service to his country.

I would also be remiss in not acknowledging the support and general assistance of the G. E. von Grunebaum Center for Near Eastern Studies at the University of California, Los Angeles, especially that given by its Director, Professor Georges Sabagh, and Administrative Analyst, Mary Murrell. In addition, I would like to thank Professors Michael Morony and Thomas Penchoen, also of the University of California, Los Angeles, for providing advice and guidance while this project was underway.

Finally, it is necessary to mention that some of the manuscripts edited and translated below were collected in the course of an unrelated research project funded by the Social Science Research Council and the Fulbright-Hayes program of the U. S. Department of Education. The opinions expressed in the following pages are entirely those of the present author and are not representative of these institutions.

بسم الله الرحمن الرحيم

INTRODUCTION

THE 'JUNAYD OF THE WEST' AND THE WORLD OF MAGHRIBI SUFISM IN THE TWELFTH CENTURY AD.

'And to Madyan (Midian) We sent their brother Shuʿayb, who said: "Oh my people, worship God! You have no other god but Him. A clear sign has come to you from your Lord, so give just measure and weight, do not withhold from people that which is their due, and do not commit perversions upon the Earth after it has been set right. That is best for you if you are believers.

'"And do not sit beside every road, uttering threats, hindering from the Path of God those who believe in Him, and seeking in it something that is deviant. Remember instead how you were small in number and He increased you, and think deeply about the end of those who were perverse.

'"If there is a faction among you who believes in that with which I have been sent, and a faction who does not believe, then keep patient until God decides between us, for He is the best to judge."

'The leaders, the arrogant ones among his people said: "Oh Shuʿayb! We shall surely drive you out of our city, along with those who believe as you do, unless you return to the ways of our religion."

'He said: "What? Even though we detest it? We should indeed invent a lie against God if we returned to your ways after God has rescued us from them. Nor could we return to them unless God Our Lord so wills. Our Lord encompasses everything with His Knowledge. In God we have put our complete trust. Oh Lord, decide in truth between us and our people, for You are the best to decide!"

'The leaders, those who rejected the Truth among his people, said: "If you follow Shuʿayb you will surely be ruined!"

'But the earthquake took them without warning and they found themselves prostrate in their homes. Those who rejected Shuʿayb were as if they had never flourished—those who rejected Shuʿayb were the ones who were ruined!

'So Shuʿayb left them, saying: "Oh my people, I have conveyed to you my

Lord's messages and have given you good counsel. How, then, shall I feel remorse for a people who refuse to believe?"'[1]

THE CAREER OF ABŪ MADYAN

The man who was to become the most influential figure of the developmental period of North African Sufism, Abū Madyan Shuᶜayb ibn al-Ḥusayn al-Anṣārī, who was called by later biographers the 'Shaykh of Shaykhs, Imam of the Ascetics and the Pious, Lord of the Gnostics, and Exemplar of the Seekers,'[2] and who remains known to posterity as 'Abū Madyan the Nurturer' (*al-Ghawth*), entered the world in inauspicious circumstances. Born around the year 509/1115–16 at the fortress of Cantillana in the region of Seville (Ishbīliya) in Muslim Spain, the future shaykh was orphaned early in life by the unexpected death of his father and suffered cruel treatment and exploitation at the hands of his elder brothers. Fortunately, Abū Madyan's own account of the often difficult, formative period of his intellectual development is available to the modern student of Sufism via the efforts of a near contemporary, the Moroccan biographer Abū Yaᶜqūb Yūsuf ibn Yaḥyā at-Tādilī (d. 627/1229–30), who reproduced many of the shaykh's autobiographical comments in his *Kitāb at-tashawwuf ilā rijāl at-taṣawwuf*, written a short time after the latter's death:

> I was an orphan in al-Andalus. My brothers made me a shepherd for their flocks, but whenever I saw someone praying or reciting [the Qur'ān], it pleased me. I would come near to him and found a sadness in my soul because I had not memorized anything from the Qur'ān and did not know how to pray. So I resolved to run away in order to learn how to read and pray.
>
> I ran away, but my brother caught up with me, spear in hand, and said, 'By God, if you do not return I will kill you!' So I returned and remained for a short time. Then I strengthened my resolve to flee by night. I slipped away at night and took another road [from that which I had originally followed]. My brother [again] caught up with me after sunrise. He drew his sword against me and said, 'By God, I will kill you and be rid of you!' Then he raised his sword over me in order to strike me. I parried him with a piece of wood that was in my hand and his

1. Qur'ān, VII (*al-Aᶜrāf*), 85–93. Translation by the present author.
2. Muḥammad ibn Jaᶜfar ibn Idrīs al-Kattānī (d. 1355/1926), *Salwat al-anfās wa muḥādathāt al-akyās bi man uqbira min al-ᶜulamā' wa'ṣ-ṣulaḥā' bi Fās* (Fez: Lithograph, 1318/1900), (1), p. 364.

sword broke and flew into pieces. When he saw [what had happened] he said to me, 'Oh my brother, go wherever you wish'.[3]

Upon leaving the region of Seville, the young Abū Madyan traveled south for three or four days, until he reached a hillock near the sea, upon which he found a tent. An old man (*shaykh*), wearing nothing except what was necessary to cover his nakedness, emerged from the tent and walked toward him. Thinking that the younger man was a captive who had fled from a Christian raiding party, he asked Abū Madyan about his situation. When told of the young man's desire to learn the fundamentals of Islam, the shaykh allowed him to remain in his company for a few days.

Then he took a rope, tied a nail to its end, threw it into the sea, and pulled out a fish, which he cooked so that I could eat it. I stayed with him for three days, and whenever I was hungry he would throw that rope and nail into the sea and pull out a fish. Then he would cook it and I would eat it. After [three days had passed] he said to me, 'I see that you covet honor (*amr*). Return to the city, for God is not [properly] worshipped except with knowledge.'[4]

Heeding his ascetic companion's advice, Abū Madyan returned to Seville, from whence he proceeded to Jérez (Sharīsh) and Algeciras (al-Jazīra al-Khaḍrā'). From Algeciras he crossed the Straits of Gibraltar to Tangier (Ṭanja) and went from there to Ceuta (Sabta), where he labored for a time in the employ of local fishermen. Impatient to gain the knowledge he so earnestly desired, with the little money he had earned Abū Madyan next traveled to Marrakesh (Marrākush), then the rapidly growing capital of the Almoravid state. Founded in the second third of the fifth/eleventh century by ʿAbdallāh ibn Yāsīn (d. 451/1059), an exoteric religious reformer who was

3. Abū Yaʿqūb Yūsuf at-Tādilī (d. 627/1229–30), *Kitāb at-tashawwuf ilā rijāl at-taṣawwuf*, Ahmed Toufiq, ed. (Rabat: Université Mohammed V, Faculté des Lettres et des Sciences Humaines, 1984), p. 320. Parallels with scenes and incidents from the lives of several prophets recur throughout the accounts of Abū Madyan's life. Note in this story that the shaykh, like all Islamic prophets, was originally a shepherd. Note also the apparent congruence of effect between Abū Madyan's 'piece of wood' (*ʿūd*) and Moses' staff. A number of later biographers have strongly implied that Abū Madyan himself was aware of and freely utilized such symbolism. In one account reported by at-Tādilī, the shaykh was visited at his zāwiya in Bijāya by a Berber disciple, Abū ʿImrān Mūsā ibn Idrāsen al-Ḥallāj, who complained of being persecuted in Fez. To this Abū Madyan replied: 'My name is Shuʿayb and you are safe. Moses (Mūsā) was not safe until he met Shuʿayb.' (Ibid., p. 331.) This account also appears to indicate that Abū Madyan equated the Prophet Shuʿayb of the Qur'ān with the priest of the people of Midian who befriended Moses and took him in out of the wilderness. Biblical scholars are in dispute over whether the man's actual name was Jethro, Reuel, or Hobab.

4. Ibid., p. 322.

influenced by the social and ethical doctrines of North African and eastern Iranian Sufism, the *Dawla al-Murābiṭiyya* had ruled the western part of North Africa and Islamic Spain for over fifty years by relying heavily on an alliance of Mālikī legal scholars and veiled Ṣanhāja Berber tribesmen from the Sahara desert, who formed the nucleus of the Almoravid military garrisons stationed in most major cities. To supplement these Berber contingents, which were spread quite thinly throughout the vast expanse of the western Maghrib, the Almoravid rulers often hired additional Andalusian troops, both Christian and Muslim, who, for reasons of internal security, were most commonly assigned garrison duties in Morocco, far from their Iberian homelands.

Upon arriving in Marrakesh, Abū Madyan was recruited by these mercenaries and drafted into the regiment of Andalusians that was charged with defending the Almoravid capital. The shaykh apparently suffered further exploitation during the period of his military service, for he mentions that other, more experienced soldiers would regularly steal his wages, leaving him only a little with which to provide for his needs. Finally, someone said to him, 'If you want to devote yourself to religion, go to the city of Fez (Fās).'

> So I turned toward [Fez] and attached myself to its mosque-university (the famous *Jāmiᶜ al-Qarawiyyīn*), where I learned to make the ablution and the prayer and sat in the study circles of legists and hadith specialists. I retained nothing of their words, however, until I sat at the feet of a shaykh whose words were retained firmly within my heart. I asked whom he was and was told, 'Abu'l-Ḥasan [ᶜAlī] ibn Ḥirzihim'. [I went to this shaykh] and told him that I could memorize only what I had learned from him alone and he said to me, 'These [others] speak with parts of their tongues, but their words are not worthy [even] to call the prayer. Since I seek [only] God with my words, they come from the heart and enter the heart.'[5]

Abū Madyan attached himself to the study circle and zāwiya of ᶜAlī ibn Ḥirzihim[6] (d. 559/1162) for a number of years, where he was required to read and memorize the *Kitāb ar-riᶜāya li ḥuqūq Allāh* of the famous Sufi of Baghdad, Ḥārith ibn Asad al-Muḥāsibī (d. 243/857), and the *Iḥyā' ᶜulūm*

5. Ibid., p. 320.

6. ᶜAlī ibn Ḥirzihim is the famous Moroccan shaykh 'Sīdī Ḥarāzim' who was considered the patron of Fez until the 'rediscovery' of the tomb of Idris II in the ninth/fifteenth century. His tomb remains venerated in the Bāb Futūḥ cemetery outside of the present walls of Fez.

ad-dīn of the Sufi and Ashʿarī theologian Abū Ḥāmid al-Ghazālī (d. 505/1111), which he would later make obligatory for his own disciples. The twelfth/eighteenth-century Algerian biographer Ibn Maryam tells us that Abū Madyan was especially fond of al-Ghazālī's *Iḥyā'*—so much so, in fact, that he would spend hours reading it in seclusion and often used the book as a source for religious advice and in answering the objections put to him by exoteric scholars who were critical of his doctrines.[7]

During the period in which he was attached to the Ibn Ḥirzihim zāwiya, Abū Madyan also attended the study circle of Abu'l-Ḥasan ʿAlī ibn Khalaf ibn Ghālib al-Qurashī (d. 568/1172–73), one of the foremost disciples of the Andalusian Sufi master Abu'l-ʿAbbās Aḥmad ibn al-ʿArīf (d. 536/1141) and principal teacher in Morocco of the *Sunan*, or collection of hadith compiled by Abū ʿĪsā at-Tirmidhī (d. 279/892–93).[8] To aid in his memorization of the traditions contained in this large work, the shaykh lived for a time in seclusion amid the ruins of an abandoned mosque on the outskirts of Fez. The account left by Abū Madyan of one of his experiences while staying among these ruins reflects, even in this early period of his life, how much the shaykh was influenced by the method of ascetic scrupulousness advocated in the writings of the eastern Sufi al-Muḥāsibī—an attitude which was eventually to become a cornerstone of Abū Madyan's own concept of Islamic chivalry, or *futuwwa*:

> While staying in Fez I used to take a verse from the Qur'ān and a hadith and go to an empty place on the edge of the cultivated land. When I had fully understood [and memorized] the verse and the hadith, I would return to Fez, learn another verse and hadith, and do the same with them. The place on Jabal ʿImrānā where I secluded myself was ruined, and out of all its buildings only the *maqṣūra* [a protective screen placed before the mihrab] of the mosque remained. While I sat there [in thought and contemplation] a gazelle would come up to me. I do not know whether it used to come to the people who had lived in that place and when they left continued to visit it, or whether it came to me in particular. When I went to that place it would come to me, sniff me from my head to my toes, and then lie down in front of me.

7. Abū ʿAbdallāh Muḥammad ibn Muḥammad ibn Aḥmad Ibn Maryam, *al-Bustān fī dhikr al-awliyā' wa'l-ʿulamā' bi Tilimsān* (Algiers: al-Maṭbaʿa ath-Thaʿālabiyya, 1326/1908), p. 108.

8. Abu'l-ʿAbbās Aḥmad al-Khaṭīb Ibn Qunfudh al-Qusanṭīnī (d. 810/1407–8), *Uns al-faqīr wa ʿizz al-ḥaqīr* (Rabat: al-Markaz al-Jāmiʿī li'l-Baḥth al-ʿIlmī, 1965), p. 14. Abu'l-Ḥasan ʿAlī ibn Ghālib is buried at al-Qaṣr al-Kabīr (El Ksar El Kebir) in northwestern Morocco, where he is regarded as the patron saint of that city and is presently known as 'Sīdī ʿAlī Bū Ghālib'. Ibn al-ʿArīf, now called 'Sīdī Bel ʿArīf', is buried in Marrakesh.

One Thursday I went to Fez and stayed there that night. I met a man whom I had known from al-Andalus and asked Abū ʿAbdallāh ibn Abī Ḥājj about some cloth that he was holding [for me]. 'What do you want to do with it?' he asked. 'I wish to sell it and give its price to that man as his welcome (*ḍiyāfa*),' I replied. 'Take ten dirhams,' he said, 'and give it to him.'

I took [the money] and looked for the man, but could not find him. So I placed it in a purse, put it in my apron, and went to the hill. On my way there I would pass by a village full of dogs, who would come to me, wagging their tails, and surround me. But [this time], when I neared the village, the dogs attacked me and barked at me, and I could not escape until the people of the village placed themselves between the dogs and me. When I arrived at my place on the hill the gazelle came to me, sniffed at me, and then pushed me away. It then looked at me with a hateful glance and butted me a second and a third time with its horns, such that I had to grab them with my hands. I pondered this and the hatred of the village dogs for me and knew that it was because of the dirhams I had put into the purse. So I ripped it out [of my garment] and threw it to the side. Then [the gazelle] looked at me and lay down in front of me as was its custom.

I slept in that place and in the morning I took the purse to Fez, found the man I had hoped to welcome, gave it to him, and returned to the hill, as I used to do. I passed through the village on my way and the dogs wagged their tails as they used to and did not bark at me. I then returned to my place on the hill. The gazelle came and sniffed at my cape (*silhām*) from my head to my feet and then lay down in front of me, as it had done before.[9]

By studying under ʿAlī ibn Ḥirzihim and Abu'l-Ḥasan ibn Ghālib in Fez, Abū Madyan found himself perfectly situated to assimilate most of the traditions of 'orthodox', or *sharʿī* mysticism that were then current in the western Maghrib and Muslim Spain. Especially significant in this regard was his extensive study of al-Ghazālī's *Iḥyā'*, for by the mid-sixth/twelfth century hardly any North African Sufi of note was not familiar in one way or another with the works of the so-called 'Proof of Islam' (*Ḥujjat al-Islām*) and many could claim to be students of his followers (see Figure 1, p. 21). Almost as important as his concentration upon the teachings of al-Ghazālī was Abū Madyan's interest in the *Sunan* of at-Tirmidhī, which had begun to attain great popularity in the Maghrib through the influence of the noted Andalu-

9. at-Tādilī, *Tashawwuf*, pp. 322–30.

sian theologian and jurist, Abū Bakr ibn al-ʿArabī al-Maʿāfirī (d. 543/1149). In contrast to the method followed in utilizing other hadith compilations, Abū Bakr ibn al-ʿArabī's students used the *Sunan* of at-Tirmidhī more as a manual for pietistic behavior than as a book of precedent in making juridical decisions. According to at least one modern scholar, the fact that over half of this particular collection of traditions covered such non-juridical subjects as theology, asceticism, accounts of the lives of companions of the Prophet, and Qur'anic commentary meant that it was admirably suited to be employed by early religious reformers as a symbolic statement of protest against the preoccupation of conservative Andalusian legists with *furūʿ* (branches of jurisprudence and precedent based only on the doctrines of the Mālikī school of law) as opposed to *uṣūl* (Qur'anic and more broadly based hadith sources for theology and jurisprudence).[10]

Although a number of biographers, such as Aḥmad ibn Qunfudh al-Qusanṭīnī (d. 810/1407–8), have claimed that Abū Madyan was formally attached to the *ṭā'ifa*, or Sufi order, of ʿAlī ibn Ḥirzihim 'until God opened for him the Exalted Vocation and the Divine Secrets, as well as the correct orientation and work [until] he attained the rank desired for him,'[11] the Moroccan at-Tādilī, claiming to quote the shaykh himself, maintains that Abū Madyan also 'took the Sufi path' from two other mystics—Abū ʿAbdallāh ad-Daqqāq, from the caravan center of Sijilmāssa on the edge of the Sahara desert, and one Abu'l-Ḥasan as-Salāwī from Salé (Salā).[12] Little verifiable information is presently available about ad-Daqqāq, a famous *malāmatī* (follower of the Sufi 'Path of Blame') and political activist, who traveled regularly between Fez and Sijilmāssa in order to meet with his disciples, except that he was a stubborn opponent of the Almoravid state and was given to extravagant claims of his own sanctity. In the city of Fez, where he was eventually confined by the Almoravid authorities in order to be kept out of trouble, this enigmatic individual most likely instructed the still impressionable Abū Madyan in the subject of *ʿilm at-taṣawwuf*, or the formal aspects of Sufi doctrine. If so, his curriculum would have included some of the more famous Eastern handbooks and biographies of Sufism, such as as-Sulamī's *Ṭabaqāt aṣ-ṣūfiyya* and al-Qushayrī's *Risāla*, to which Abū Madyan may already have been exposed in the zāwiya of Ibn Ḥirzihim. So little is conclusively established about the career of Abū ʿAbdallāh ad-Daqqāq that even the date of his death (apparently more or less contemporaneous with that of Abū Madyan himself) remains unrecorded. In an article published in

10. Dominique Urvoy, *El mundo de los ulemas andaluces del siglo v/xi al vii/xiii* (Madrid: Ediciones Pegaso, 1983), p. 163. Abū Bakr ibn al-ʿArabī is also buried in the Bāb Futūḥ cemetery of Fez.
11. Ibn Qunfudh, *Uns al-faqīr*, p. 16.
12. at-Tādilī, *Tashawwuf*, p. 322.

1923, the French orientalist Alfred Bel reported that ad-Daqqāq's tombstone, long separated from his grave, was found preserved in a small mosque in Fez dedicated to his more famous student Abū Madyan.[13]

While still a student at Fez, Abū Madyan heard fabulous accounts about the miracles of the noted Berber illuminate and spiritual master Abū Yaᶜzā Yalannūr ibn Maymūn ad-Dukkālī (d. 572/1177), so he resolved to visit the latter's zāwiya in the Middle Atlas mountains in order to discover what the reputation of this charismatic shaykh was all about. Although at-Tādilī records, without comment, two separate accounts of the first meeting between these two great teaching masters of sixth/twelfth-century North Africa, the most widely accepted is the following:

> When we arrived at Jabal Īruggān and entered Abū Yaᶜzā's presence he greeted all of the group except me, and when food was brought he forbade me from eating it, so I sat in the corner of his house. Whenever food was brought and I got up to eat it, he rebuked me. I remained thus for three days, until I was tortured by hunger and humbled. After I had completed three days, Abū Yaᶜzā rose from his place. I went there and rubbed my face in [the spot where he had been sitting]. When I raised my head I found that I could not see anything and had become blind; so I remained, weeping, all night.
>
> In the morning [Shaykh Abū Yaᶜzā] called for me, saying, 'Come near, oh Andalusian!'[14] so I approached him. He wiped his hands over my eyes and my sight returned. Then he rubbed his hands on my chest and said to those who were present, 'This one will have great fame,' or words to that effect. Next he gave me permission to depart and said to me, 'You will meet a lion on your way, but it will not harm you. If fear of it overcomes you, then say to it, "By the sanctity of Yalannūr, depart from me!" Next you will encounter three thieves near a tree. You will admonish them [to change their ways] and two of them will repent at your hands, but the third will return, to be killed and crucified on that tree.'
>
> I promised [to do as he had said] and left. Soon a lion came upon me in the road. I swore at him by Abū Yaᶜzā that he should leave the road. He continued to follow me until I had left the forest, and then he turned

13. Alfred Bel, 'Sidî Bou Medyan et son maître Ed-Daqqâq à Fès', *Mélanges René Basset* (Paris: Editions Ernest Leroux, 1923), (1), pp. 31–68. A photograph of ad-Daqqāq's tombstone can be found in this article on p. 46.

14. According to Ibn Qunfudh, the Berber-speaking Abū Yaᶜzā would seldom address Abū Madyan by name, saying instead, '*Ā shigg, argāz al-Andalusī* (Oh you, the Andalusian man)!' See *Uns al-faqīr*, p. 16.

> away from me. Next, I came upon three thieves who were sitting at the base of a tree. They came upon me [to rob me] and I admonished them. The warning affected the hearts of two of them, who left, but the third remained, [lying in wait], at the base of the tree. The governor heard about him and sent someone to chop off his head and crucify him on that [very] tree. I then continued traveling until I arrived at Bijāya, where I settled.[15]

Perhaps because of the teachings he had learned from his Sufi masters in Fez, or because the experiences of his early life had so closely paralleled those of the illiterate and ascetic shepherd Abū Yaᶜzā, Abū Madyan was quickly able to overcome any prejudices that may have been instilled in him by his now considerable degree of learning and erudition and fully appreciated the intuitive wisdom of his newly acquired Berber shaykh:

> I stayed with [Abū Yaᶜzā] for some days, during which I saw him let a [different] man lead the prayer [at various times]. If the recitation [of the Qur'ān] was done well, he was pleased with him, but if it was sung [with a melody like that of popular singing] he would remove him. Now Abū Yaᶜzā was illiterate, but had been graced [by God] with an understanding of the science [of Qur'anic recitation].[16]

Eventually, Abū Madyan became a semi-official spokesman for Abū Yaᶜzā and head (*muqaddam*) of the latter's zāwiya in the city of Fez, where he strove to answer the objections of legal scholars and others by explaining his shaykh's seemingly scandalous habits and sayings in terms of formal Sufi doctrine and parallels drawn from Islamic jurisprudence:

> A group of scholars who had visited Abū Yaᶜzā said to me, 'The sanctity of Abū Yaᶜzā has been confirmed by us, yet we have seen him touch the breasts and stomachs of women and spit on them so that they may be healed. We consider this forbidden, yet if we spoke [these thoughts] we would be killed [by Abū Yaᶜzā's followers] and if we were silent we would feel guilty.'
>
> So I said to them, 'Do you consider that if one of your daughters or sisters had contracted a disease, no one could approach her except her husband, or that no one could help her other than a Jewish or a

15. at-Tādilī, *Tashawwuf*, pp. 320–21. At least two anecdotes are combined in this one account. The first concerns Abū Madyan's initial meeting with Abū Yaᶜzā, while the second tells of his departure for Bijāya after the completion of his discipleship.

16. Ibid., p. 323.

> Christian doctor? Would you then allow the supposed treatment of a Jew or a Christian and forbid the certain cure of Abū Yaᶜzā, while refraining from forbidding [the treatment of] one you doubt?'
>
> Abū Yaᶜzā was informed of my words and said, 'When you see Shuᶜayb tell him that perhaps he will free me from my bondage (*yaᶜtiqunī*). It was as if he had improved upon my own answers.'[17]

Closely related to stories describing the first meeting between Abū Yaᶜzā and Abū Madyan is one that appears in several variants which recounts a pilgrimage that the shaykh is supposed to have made to the holy city of Mecca, where he is said to have met and studied under the famous Sufi master of Baghdad, ᶜAbd al-Qādir al-Jīlānī (d. 563/1166), namesake of the influential Qādiriyya Sufi order, whose later adherents in the Maghrib were to posthumously adopt Abū Madyan as one of their own. A common version of this story can be found in Ibn Maryam's *al-Bustān fī dhikr al-awliyā' wa'l-ᶜulamā' bi Tilimsān*:

> Then the shaykh, the lights of sanctity apparent upon him, turned toward the East, where he studied under the most knowledgeable scholars and learned from the ascetics and saints (*awliyā'*). At ᶜArafa he came to know Shaykh ᶜAbd al-Qādir al-Jīlānī, under whom he studied many hadiths at the Noble Sanctuary (*al-Ḥaram ash-Sharīf*) and who bestowed the mantle of Sufism (*al-khirqa aṣ-ṣūfiyya*) upon him, imparted many of his secrets to him, and adorned him with the garments of his illumination. Abū Madyan took pride in his companionship with [ᶜAbd al-Qādir al-Jīlānī] and considered him the greatest and most excellent of his shaykhs.[18]

Although the story of an alleged meeting between these two great shaykhs, contemporaries, and systematizers of the Sufi Way has been taken as an undisputed fact since at least the tenth/sixteenth century, it is striking and highly significant that no mention of such a meeting appears in the works of Abū Madyan himself or in those of his two earliest biographers. At-Tādilī, writing in 617/1220, less than thirty years after the shaykh's death, mentions no pilgrimage to Mecca at all, but instead intimates that Abū Madyan proceeded directly toward Bijāya after leaving the zāwiya of Abū Yaᶜzā.[19] Ibn Qunfudh, writing more than a century and a half later, in 787/1385, mentions for his part that the shaykh attempted to travel to the Mashriq but

17. Ibid.
18. Ibn Maryam, *Bustān*, p. 110.
19. at-Tādilī, *Tashawwuf*, p. 321.

got no further than Ifrīqiyya (the region of modern-day Tunisia), where he eventually settled.[20] These early versions of Abū Madyan's biography appear to be supported, at least indirectly, by the shaykh's own writings, for the Rabat copy of the treatise *Bidāyat al-murīd* traces the transmission of the *muraqqaᶜa* (the traditional patched cloak of investiture) from the Prophet Muḥammad through the Caliphs Abū Bakr, ᶜUmar, and ᶜUthmān, as well as the Prophet's favorite wife ᶜĀ'isha, without mentioning the Prophet's son-in-law, nephew, and fourth Caliph, ᶜAlī ibn Abū Ṭālib. The elimination of ᶜAlī from this chain of transmission, not unexpected for a scholar raised in an Andalusian intellectual environment that had been heavily influenced by centuries of anti-ᶜAlid propaganda disseminated by apologists for the Umayyad Caliphs of Córdoba, would seem out of the question for a true follower of ᶜAbd al-Qādir al-Jīlānī, who was a proud descendant of ᶜAlī on both his mother's and his father's side.[21] It thus appears highly probable that later accounts of a meeting between Abū Madyan and ᶜAbd al-Qādir al-Jīlānī are apocryphal and were most likely concocted in succeeding generations to explain why so many members of the Qādiriyya brotherhood identified themselves with Abū Madyan's spiritual method. One may also speculate that this 'pious fiction' was additionally useful in allowing Qādiri Sufis living in Tlemcen (Tilimsān), where Abū Madyan is buried, to claim equal spiritual status with members of the increasingly popular Shādhilī Sufi order, whose founder, Abu'l-Ḥasan ash-Shādhilī (d.656/1258), was revered by both rulers and ruled alike as much for his Prophetic lineage as for his doctrinal innovations.

Upon completing his religious studies and spiritual training, Abū Madyan moved to Bijāya, then a city of more than 100,000 people located on the Algerian coast about halfway between the present-day cities of Algiers (al-Jazā'ir) and Annaba. In the sixth/twelfth century Bijāya, which had long served as the main port for the nearby Ṣanhāja Berber city-state of Qalᶜa Banī Ḥammād, was the premier urban center of the central Maghrib. The

20. Ibn Qunfudh, *Uns al-faqīr*, p. 16. Note that Bijāya, the eventual location of Abū Madyan's *rābiṭa*, is not in Ifrīqiyya but in *al-Maghrib al-Adnā*.

21. Abū Madyan Shuᶜayb ibn al-Ḥusayn al-Anṣārī, *Bidāyat al-murīd* (Rabat: Bibliothèque Générale [*al-Khizāna al-ᶜĀmma*, MS number 731 Q), folios 328–35. The quotation in question can be found reproduced below in the section entitled, 'On Wearing the *Muraqqaᶜa*, the *Shamriyya*, and the *Farajiyya*.' The earliest formally constituted Eastern Sufi ṭarīqa to become widely established in the western Maghrib appears to have been the Rifāᶜiyya, which attracted adherents in the Rīf mountains of northern Morocco as early as the first half of the seventh/thirteenth century, not long after the death of its founder, Aḥmad ar-Rifāᶜī (d. 578/1182–83). ᶜAbd al-Ḥaqq al-Bādisī, author of the biographical work *al-Maqṣad ash-sharīf*, written in 711/1311, mentions an account of a supposed meeting between Abū Madyan and Aḥmad ar-Rifāᶜī which could have served as the basis for later stories of a meeting between the shaykh and ᶜAbd al-Qādir al-Jīlānī. See, ᶜAbd al-Ḥaqq ibn Ismāᶜīl al-Bādisī, *al-Maqṣad ash-sharīf wa'l-manzaᶜ al-laṭīf fi't-taᶜrīf bi ṣulaḥā' ar-Rīf* (Rabat: al-Maṭbaᶜa al-Ḥasaniyya, 1402/1982), pp. 63–64.

geographer al-Idrīsī, writing during this period, mentions that Bijāya was an entrepôt for both Saharan caravans and sea-borne trade and that it served as a stopping point for ships traveling from the Far Maghrib and al-Andalus toward Egypt and the Muslim East.[22] At the time when Abū Madyan first entered the city, roughly one-fifth of the population of Bijāya consisted of Ṣanhāja Berber refugees from al-Qalᶜa, which had been destroyed by the Almohads (the Maṣmūda Berber reformist state that eventually succeeded the Almoravids) shortly before their conquest of Bijāya itself in 544/1151.[23]

Adding to the strategic importance that Bijāya held for its Almohad conquerors was the fact that the nearby mountainous region of Qabīliyya ('tribal' in Arabic) had ample supplies of both timber and iron, which allowed the city to maintain a naval arsenal.[24] The existence of this arsenal also made Bijāya a major objective of the Banū Ghāniyya, remnants of the former Almoravid ruling élite who had fled toward Ifrīqiyya after being expelled from Majorca by the Almohads. For a considerable part of Abū Madyan's sojourn there, Bijāya was under Banū Ghāniyya control and served as a base for Ṣanhāja Berber and pastoralist Arab opposition to the Almohad state in the central and eastern Maghrib.[25]

Apart from its geopolitical importance, a major reason for Abū Madyan's attraction to Bijāya may also have been the fact that the city was full of Andalusians—merchants and scholars from the Iberian Levant—who gave it an intellectual and cultural life more akin to that of Muslim Spain than to North Africa. Especially important to its intellectual life was the Almerian school of hadith study, which moved to Bijāya after that southern Andalusian city had been occupied for a time by Christian forces. Abū Madyan would naturally have gravitated toward this school, now headed by a *muḥaddith* named ᶜAbd al-Ḥāqq ibn ᶜAbd ar-Raḥmān al-Azdī, because his own teacher of hadith, Abu'l-Ḥasan ᶜAlī ibn Ghālib, had been a favorite student of the Almerian Sufi and hadith transmitter Abu'l-ᶜAbbās ibn al-ᶜArīf. Although extant biographical sources do not explicitly tell us what Abū Madyan thought of the Almohads, their 'Mahdī' Ibn Tūmart, or the state that they

22. Abū ᶜAbdallāh Muḥammad ash-Sharīf al-Idrīsī, *Nuzhat al-mushtāq fī ikhtirāq al-āfāq*, R. Dozy and M. J. De Goeje, eds. and trans. (Leiden: E. J. Brill, 1968), p. 90.

23. Abbé J. J. L. Barges, *Vie du célèbre marabout Cidi Abou-Médien* (Paris: Ernest Leroux, 1884), pp. 11–12. The Almohads, successors to the Almoravids as rulers of the Maghrib and Islamic Spain, comprised a religious reform movement opposed to many of the doctrines advocated by their predecessors. Because most members of the Almohad movement had Maṣmūda Berber origins, as opposed to the largely Ṣanhāja Berber Almoravids, the ensuing war between the two groups often took on an inter-tribal aspect.

24. al-Idrīsī, *Nuzhat al-mushtāq*, p. 91.

25. Muḥammad ar-Rashīd Mulīn, *ᶜAṣr al-Manṣūr al-Muwaḥḥidī* (Rabat: Maṭbaᶜa ash-Shamāl al-Ifrīqī, n.d.), p. 93.

founded, it is known that al-Azdī conspired with members of the Banū Ḥammād ruling family and Banū Ghāniyya rebels to drive Ibn Tūmart's followers out of the central Maghrib and Ifrīqiyya. After the Almohad caliph Yaᶜqūb al-Manṣūr finally defeated the Banū Ghāniyya in 581/1185, ᶜAbd al-Ḥaqq al-Azdī was imprisoned for treason and died under torture the following year, while the remnants of the Banū Ghāniyya family were sent to Salé, then a place of internal exile for enemies of the Almohad state.[26] Given the Almohad caliph's distrust of Bijāya and its religious scholars, who ardently opposed the theological and juridical innovations advocated by the adherents of Ibn Tūmart's doctrines, it is quite possible that Abū Madyan himself, when finally summoned by Yaᶜqūb al-Manṣūr to Marrakesh in 594/1198, was intended to end his days in Salé as well.

A frustratingly sparse amount of information is given in primary sources concerning Abū Madyan's activities in Bijāya. We know, for example, that his fame was great enough for him to be called 'Shaykh of Shaykhs' by the local populace and that more than one thousand individuals who assumed or later were accorded the rank of spiritual master were said to have been taught by him.[27] The shaykh's notoriety became so widespread that well before his death he had become famous throughout all of the Maghrib, from Ifrīqiyya in the east to his native Seville and the Atlantic coast of Morocco in the west. In *Uns al-faqīr wa ᶜizz al-ḥaqīr*, an eighth/fourteenth-century travel *memoire* dedicated to Abū Madyan and his followers, the jurist and biographer Aḥmad ibn Qunfudh al-Qusanṭīnī mentions that the shaykh's disciples came from every region of the western Islamic world. Many of these individuals first accepted the *khirqa* of Abū Madyan's *ṭā'ifa* after attending 'sessions of admonition' (*majālis al-waᶜẓ*) that were regularly held at his zāwiya, known locally under the name of 'Rābiṭa az-Zayyāt'.[28] At these sessions people from all walks of life would come before the shaykh for advice on personal, legal, or even political matters and large numbers of Sufis would also be present to ask questions about doctrine, many of which the shaykh answered by using quotations from either al-Ghazālī's *Iḥyā'* or al-Qushayrī's *Risāla*.[29] Ibn Qunfudh reports that, following the example of his own shaykh Abū Yaᶜzā, Abū Madyan saw his primary role to be that of teaching master, or *shaykh at-tarbiya*. This meant that he concentrated his efforts on 'the spiritual tutelage (*tarbiya*) of his disciples, supervising their personal development (*ifāda*), imparting religious education, stimulating the practice of piety, and

26. Ibid., pp. 94–96.
27. Ibn Maryam, *Bustān*, p. 108.
28. Ibid. See also, Ibn Qunfudh, *Uns al-faqīr*, p. 37.
29. Ibn Qunfudh, *Uns al-faqīr*, pp. 16–17.

attending to God both inwardly and outwardly.'[30] Even more importantly, the shaykh would prepare short, to-the-point instructions and lessons that were specifically suited to the needs of each individual who asked him for advice. These sayings and aphorisms (*ḥikam*), stylistic forerunners of the more famous aphorisms of the Shādhilī Sufi Ibn ʿAṭā'illāh as-Skandarī (d. 709/1309), were noted for their brevity and effectiveness in stimulating the spiritual awareness of those who memorized and meditated upon them.[31]

Abū Madyan's personal habits, like those of his teachers, were austere and ascetic. He apparently practiced celibacy for most of his life as well, for in at-Tādilī's *Tashawwuf* we find that his only known female partner was a black concubine whom he kept for a short time at the request of Abū Yaʿzā:

> Abū Madyan used to tell his companions that Shaykh Abū Yaʿzā informed him that he would be given an 'Abyssinian' (*ḥabashiyya*—i.e., black African) slave girl as a gift and that she would bear him a son who, if he lived, would be great. A merchant gave him a black slave girl and she bore him a son, whom he named Muḥammad. Then Abū Madyan ceased having sexual relations with her and signs of distress appeared upon him. He was asked about this [by his disciples] and said, 'I have no desire for this slave girl. If Shaykh Abū Yaʿzā had not told me that I would have a son by her I would never have approached her. No desire for her is left in me. Yet if I abandoned her I would be committing a sin and if I married her I would be embarrassed at having a son by her.'
>
> 'Then [said Abū Madyan] ʿAbd ar-Razzāq [al-Jazūlī] said to me, "I will marry her and care for your son".'
>
> Abū Madyan replied, 'Would you do that, even though marriage with a black woman is shameful among the Maṣmūda [Berbers]?'
>
> 'I would do it for your sake,' said ʿAbd ar-Razzāq.
>
> So he married her and cared for the son of Abū Madyan, who memorized the Qur'ān in a very short period of time and began to give evidence of clairvoyance (*firāsāt*). But death carried him off while he was still young and ʿAbd ar-Razzāq moved to the East.[32]

30. Ibid., p. 17.

31. Ibid., pp. 17–19. These aphorisms, collected under the title, *Uns al-waḥīd wa nuzhat al-murīd*, are reproduced and translated below.

32. at-Tādilī, *Tashawwuf*, p. 328. Prejudice against subsaharan Africans appears to have been prevalent among many North African Berbers from the early Islamic period to the end of the sixth/twelfth century. While the greatest discrimination was apparently suffered by those black clients and sharecroppers who served the oasis gardens of Ṣanhāja pastoralists, neither Maṣmūda nor Zanāta peoples could claim to be free of such prejudice either, as this passage conclusively demonstrates. Interestingly, examples of color prejudice mentioned in the hagiographical literature of the western Maghrib seem to decline rather precipitously in direct proportion to the extent of Arabization in the region as a whole.

Abū Madyan's strong opinions about social justice and personal integrity, often expressed publicly during his sessions of admonition, caused him to make numerous enemies, especially among those powerful members of the Bijāyan religious élite whom he considered to be especially ignorant or hypocritical. The popularity of the shaykh's public lectures, many of which appear to have been at least implicitly political in nature, eventually began to attract the notice of the Almohad Caliph Yaᶜqūb al-Manṣūr, who, constantly mindful of his prior experiences with the hadith scholar al-Azdī and the Banū Ghāniyya, could never bring himself to fully trust the inhabitants of Bijāya. It was perhaps inevitable, then, that Almohad religious leaders and the caliph's agents in that city would send provocative reports about the activities of the great Andalusian shaykh, and that he would eventually be summoned to Marrakesh in order to answer a large number of suspicions and accusations. According to biographical sources, these accusations mostly concerned the shaykh's explicitly expressed opinion that his followers and other Sufis were the Qur'anically mandated 'Party of God' (Qur'ān LVIII [*al-Mujādila*], 22) and the fact that, following the chivalric practice of the *fityān* of Khurāsān in the Muslim East, he often called his disciples 'sultans'. The inevitable summons to the Almohad capital finally came in 594/1198, when Abū Madyan was around eighty-five years of age.[33] Although he was accompanied and cared for on his journey by a number of close disciples, the shaykh succumbed to old age and illness not far from the city of Tlemcen and was buried at al-ᶜUbbād, a graveyard situated in the hills above the city that was reserved for the local pious and revered *awliyā'*. According to his companions, the last words uttered by Abū Madyan were enunciated in a clear and precise manner and reflected the preoccupation with the Real that characterized so much of his life. Looking up at them, he said in a soft whisper, 'God is the Truth,' and peacefully closed his eyes for the last time.[34]

ABŪ MADYAN AND SUFISM IN THE WESTERN MAGHRIB

The basis for calling Abū Madyan the 'Junayd of the West' in the title of this introduction rests on the fact, to which we have alluded in the preceding

33. al-Kattānī, *Salwat al-anfās*, (1), p. 366.

34. Ibid. It is interesting to note that Tlemcen, the city for which Abū Madyan is now the patron, did not figure at all in the life of the shaykh and served only as the resting-place for his remains. For those inhabitants of the Maghrib who were not residents of Tlemcen, Abū Madyan was regarded as a patron for all Muslims who lived between Tripolitania and the Atlantic Ocean—an attitude confirmed by the fact that rulers, princes, scholars, Sufis, and even common folk from the Maghrib as a whole continued to visit his tomb for centuries. For residents of Morocco or Muslim Spain in particular, a visit to the shrine of Abū Madyan was practically obligatory for anyone who desired a successful completion of his pilgrimage to Mecca.

pages, that like his illustrious third/ninth-century predecessor in Baghdad, he was uniquely situated in both time and space to synthesize and transcend the Sufi traditions of his era within one formally articulated doctrine. He thus became the Spiritual Axis, or *Quṭb* of his age, in that his teachings on the subjects of doctrine, methodology, and ethics were to influence, centuries after his death, western Islamic Sufism in general and especially the teachings of later Maghribi spiritual masters, such as Abu'l-Ḥasan ash-Shādhilī (d. 656/1258) and Muḥammad ibn Sulaymān al-Jazūlī (d. 869/1465).[35]

The period during which Abū Madyan attained his intellectual and spiritual maturity was characterized in the western Maghrib (the area from the western part of present-day Algeria to the Atlantic coasts of Morocco and southern Portugal) by political instability and profound social change. Nowhere was this more the case than in Muslim Spain, where a combination of disastrous military defeats at the hands of Christian forces and an increasing sense of rebelliousness among disaffected ethnic groups within Umayyad

35. The question of Abū Madyan's influence on the Sufi doctrines of Muḥyī'd-Dīn ibn al-ʿArabī (560/1165–638/1240) has recently been raised by Claude Addas in her excellent and groundbreaking biographical study, *Ibn ʿArabī ou La quête du Soufre Rouge* (Paris: Gallimard, 1989). Noting that Ibn al-ʿArabī mentions Abū Madyan more often than any other shaykh in the text of his *Futūḥāt al-Makkiyya* (p. 83), and that no fewer than six spiritual masters frequented by Ibn al-ʿArabī were either disciples or companions of Abū Madyan (Appendix II), she concludes that, despite the fact that these two great masters of western Sufism never met, Abū Madyan stood symbolically as Ibn al-ʿArabī's 'maître *par excellence*' (p. 66).

Although it is undeniable that the widespread fame of Abū Madyan in the Maghrib ensured that his way influenced the doctrines of many Sufis in the generations subsequent to his death, it remains prudent for the modern scholar to exercise caution before assuming the extent of this influence over any single individual. The most important pause for reflection in Ibn al-ʿArabī's case is provided by Addas herself, who mentions that the future *Shaykh al-Akbar* visited the cities of Tlemcen and Tunis in 590/1194, a full four years before Abū Madyan's death. If the latter were indeed Ibn al-ʿArabī's 'master', it seems inconceivable that the younger Sufi would have failed to pay a visit to so great and important a shaykh in the city of Bijāya–especially since Bijāya lay as a natural stopping place on both the land and sea routes between Tlemcen and Ifrīqiyya. Apparently, the text of the *Futūḥāt* gives no information as to why its author failed to take the step that would have been required by proper Sufi *adab*. Is it also just a coincidence that Ibn al-ʿArabī, then far away in Fez, was vouchsafed the 'divine secret' and hence the successorship to Abū Madyan in the very year of the latter's death? Could this behaviour have been a sign that Ibn al-ʿArabī was the originator of an entirely new approach to Sufism in the Maghrib, and not a systematizer of what had gone before? The answer to these questions may never be conclusively known. For our own purposes, perhaps, it is better to practice *ḥusn aẓ-ẓann* and quote the following verses of Ibn al-ʿArīf, whose own influence extended to both Abū Madyan and Ibn al-ʿArabī:

> Oh you of Muḍar who have attained to the Chosen One,
> You visited [him] in body, while we visited in spirit.
>
> Verily, we stand excused by circumstance,
> And he who stands excused is like one who has [actually] gone!

(Muḥammad ibn al-Muwaqqit (d. 1376/1956), *as Saʿāda al-abadiyya fī't-taʿrīf bi mashāhīr al-ḥaḍara al-Marrākushiyya* [Lithograph, n.d.], vol. 1, p. 10.)

society had combined to force major transformations in both the social and intellectual makeup of the region. By the middle of the fifth/eleventh century, as a result of clientship, intermarriage, and political accomodation, significant numbers of North African Berber immigrants and Iberian converts to Islam had been assimilated into local 'Arab' society.[36] This gradual yet inexorable process of integration had diffused the ethnic makeup of the southern and eastern regions of al-Andalus to the point at which the 'Syrian' and 'Yemenite' families that had long monopolized political and religious authority under the now defunct Umayyad Caliphate began to perceive that their hold on political and intellectual dominance was slipping away from them. To rectify this crisis, many members of the more 'purely' Arab scholarly élite sought to preserve their privileges by adhering to increasingly outmoded forms of social stratification and juridical methodology. In doing so, they perpetuated a tradition-bound and intellectually insular form of pre-Ashʿarī theology and Mālikī jurisprudence that upheld the *status quo ante* by downplaying the egalitarian nature of Islamic society and rejecting any attempt to make Andalusian theology and jurisprudence conform to developments that were already prevalent in the eastern Islamic world.

Just as in the East, however, the force that ultimately overcame the intellectual reactionism then characteristic of Muslim Spain was a new reliance upon 'sources of jurisprudence' (*uṣūl al-fiqh*), which highlighted the systematic study of hadith. The practitioners of this revisionist approach to Islamic *praxis*, although also coming from the ranks of formal legal scholars, were often the descendents of the very same assimilated Berbers and Iberian converts who had just begun to penetrate Andalusian Arab society. As such, they had no particular interest in perpetuating the monopoly of power held by their former masters and were more likely than the latter to be open to the influence of other reformist and socially active forms of religious expression, such as Sufism and the related *futuwwa* 'youth' movements that had recently been introduced into the region by Maghribi mystics who had studied in the Middle East.[37]

36. A vivid picture of the socio-ethnic make-up of Andalusian society just prior to the birth of Abū Madyan can be found in Ismāʿīl ibn al-Aḥmar, *Buyūtāt Fās al-kubrā* (Rabat: Dār al-Manṣūr, 1972) pp. 23–25. This work, an updated version of the originally entitled *Dhikr mashāhīr Fās fi'l-qadīm*, is both a description of the major families of Fez and an eighth/fourteenth-century Andalusian scholar's view of his society during the late Umayyad and Ṭā'ifa periods. See also, Maya Schatzmiller, 'Professions and Ethnic Origins of Urban Labourers in Muslim Spain: Evidence From a Moroccan Source,' *Awrāq*, 5–6 (1982–83). For a first-hand account of the confused and chaotic political situation in al-Andalus at the end of the Ṭā'ifa period see E. Lévi-Provençal and Emilio García Gómez, eds. and trans., *El siglo XI en Iª persona: las 'Memorias' de ʿAbd Allāh último rey zīrī de Granada, destronado por los Almorávides (1090)* (Madrid: Alianza Editorial, 1982).

37. For a detailed account of the social and intellectual ties linking Andalusian scholars during this period see Urvoy, *El mundo de los ulemas andaluces*.

While the first representatives of this new juridico-theological trend were adherents of the Shāfiᶜī school of jurisprudence who had begun to enter al-Andalus as early as the late third/ninth century, the most influential were Mālikī scholars who attempted to use Shāfiᶜī analytical methods in order to reform their own school of law from within. Significantly, a large proportion of these individuals adhered to the doctrines of Sufism as well. One of the earliest was a social reformer from the region of Madrid named Aḥmad ibn Muḥammad ibn Qarlumān aṭ-Ṭalamankī (d. 429/1038), who spent his formative years in Córdoba (Qurṭuba), where he studied under the noted mystic and hadith scholar Abū Jaᶜfar ibn ᶜAwn Allāh. Later he traveled to the Mashriq and studied in Medina under Abu'l-Qāsim al-Jawharī, an Egyptian shaykh whose family appears to have had connections with the illuminationist Nūriyya Sufi tradition. Upon his return to Spain he taught the principles of *ḥisba* (the correction of Islamically inappropriate behavior) in Córdoba, after which he fought beside and exhorted the defenders of the faith (*mujāhidūn*) who battled Christian forces along the Northern Marches, finally ending his days in Talamanca, the town of his birth.[38]

A contemporary of aṭ-Ṭalamankī and another apparent teacher of both theology and Sufi doctrines was Abu'l-ᶜAbbās Aḥmad al-Ilbīrī (d. 429/1037–38). Originally from the town of Elvira, this scholar spent most of his life in Granada, where he was noted as a poet, a philosophically-minded theologian, and an important spokesman for the lower classes. His school was one of the first to introduce Ḥārith ibn Asad al-Muḥāsibī's *ar-Riᶜāya li ḥuqūq Allāh* into Muslim Spain.[39]

Ashᶜarī theology, long popular in the Muslim East, first began to enter al-Andalus under the influence of the Moroccan legist and moral crusader Abū ᶜImrān Mūsā ibn ᶜĪsā al-Ghafjūmī al-Fāsī (d.430/1039), who distinguished himself as a student of the famous Eastern theologian Abū Bakr al-Bāqillānī (d. 403/1012-13). This influential figure, who was born as a member of an important 'Arabized' Berber family in the city of Fez, mixed his teachings of theology and jurisprudence with strong doses of ascetic Sufism and the politics of social reform. The most famous of al-Fāsī's followers in Muslim Spain was Muḥammad ibn Saᶜdūn al-Qayrawānī, who died in Morocco at Aghmāt Ūrīka, south of Marrakesh, in the year 485/1092. A native of Ifrīqiyya who also studied Sufism in Mecca, he was instrumental in

38. Abu'l-Qāsim Khalaf ibn ᶜAbd al-Mālik ibn Bashkwāl (d. 578/1183), *Kitāb aṣ-ṣila fī tārīkh a'immat al-Andalus* (Cairo: 1374/1955), (1), pp. 48–49.

39. Ibid., p. 48. See also, Urvoy, *El mundo*, pp. 127, 153. The eventual importance given to the *Riᶜāya* as a manual for Abū Madyan and other Sufis in Morocco and Muslim Spain appears to stem from al-Ilbīrī's use of this text.

disseminating both Ashʿarī theology and the study of 'sources of religion' (*uṣūl ad-dīn*) in the Andalusian Levant.[40]

Clearly, a new theological and juridical consensus had begun to form in Muslim Spain that was largely based on the contributions of reform-minded legists and Ashʿarī theologians. The movement giving rise to this consensus was also supported by many Sufis, who, desirous of conforming to the all-inclusive model of Islamic orthodoxy advocated by the *Ahl as-Sunna wa'l-Jamāʿa*, now preferred to use hadith-based rather than philosophical arguments for their doctrines. The development of this trend paralleled a gradual decentralization of religious learning in al-Andalus following the breakup of the Umayyad Caliphate, which allowed a number of *Ṭā'ifa* ('Sectarian') city-states, such as Seville, Valencia, and Almería, to replace the former capital of Córdoba as centers for the study of jurisprudence, Qur'anic exegesis, Sufism, and hadith. The increased interest by hadith scholars from these cities in developing legal and theological principles based on the prophetic example and the behavioral precedent of the first generations of pious Muslims led in turn to a secondary interest in ascetic and pietistic forms of religious expression that were thought to be in accord with the original, 'pristine' Islam of the prophetic community. This new-found interest in the essential forms of piety and asceticism, a concern shared by Sufis and exoteric scholars alike, caused many of the latter for the first time to regard mysticism as a legitimate interpretation of Qur'anic teachings. The limited approval given by these scholars to the doctrines of Sufism stimulated the development of an ascetic, action-oriented, socially conscious, and *sharʿī* (legally legitimized) form of 'orthodox' mysticism in the Muslim West that was strongly influenced by contemporary developments as far away as eastern Iran. Just as in the Muslim East, this new 'Sunni' or *sharʿī* Sufism now developing in Muslim Spain owed much to the teachings of Abū Ḥāmid al-Ghazālī (d. 505/1111) and his encyclopedic theological work, *Ihyā' ʿulūm ad-dīn*.[41]

Both al-Andalus and North Africa in the sixth/twelfth century could boast a number of students of the famous *Ḥujjat al-Islām* (Figure 1). It has already been noted that during his stay in Fez Abū Madyan assimilated many of al-Ghazālī's doctrines from his shaykh ʿAlī ibn Ḥirzihim, whose most famous teacher, Abū Bakr ibn al-ʿArabī, had been a disciple of the noted Iranian

40. Urvoy, *El mundo*, pp. 125, 127 n. 113. See also, at-Tādilī, *Tashawwuf*, pp. 83–85. The 'Blessed Creed' (*al-ʿAqīda al-mubāraka*) of Abū Madyan, reproduced below, shows unmistakable Ashʿarī influence.

41. On the concept of 'Sunni Sufism' see Muḥammad al-Manūnī, 'at-Tayyārāt al-fikriyya fi'l-Maghrib al-Marīnī,' in his *Waraqāʿan al-ḥaḍāra al-Maghribiyya fī ʿaṣr Banī Marīn* (Rabat: College of Letters and Human Sciences, Muḥammad V University, 1979), pp. 236–47.

theologian, and whose uncle, Abū Muḥammad Ṣāliḥ ibn Ḥirzihim, had apparently studied under al-Ghazālī in Syria.[42] As for Muslim Spain, primary sources mention the existence of at least three students of al-Ghazālī. One of the most noted of these individuals, ʿAbd ar-Raḥmān ibn Abī'r-Rajā' al-Balawī (d. 545/1150–1), was a Sufi and reciter of the Qur'ān who started his career as a student of the school of reformist mysticism founded by Aḥmad al-Ilbīrī in Granada. He studied under al-Ghazālī in the year 497/1103–4 and later served as an influential leader of Friday prayers in Almería. While there, he taught the famous Sufi shaykh Aḥmad ibn al-ʿArīf, whose disciple, Abu'l-Ḥasan ibn Ghālib, was Abū Madyan's teacher of hadith.[43]

As the career of Abū Madyan admirably demonstrates, the transmission of knowledge across the Straits of Gibraltar in the eleventh and twelfth centuries of the Common Era was not unidirectional—from north to south—as many scholars of Andalusian history have assumed, but was instead bidirectional, and reflected long-established, reciprocal intellectual ties between Muslim Spain and the western part of North Africa. The increased importance of the Maghrib to the intellectual development of al-Andalus in this period can even be conceptualized goegraphically, since most of the famous Sufis, Ashʿarī theologians, and scholars of *uṣūl ad-dīn* and *uṣūl al-fiqh* were concentrated in the southern and eastern portions of the Iberian Peninsula—in cities such as Granada, Málaga, Valencia, Almería, Guadix, and Murcia—which were not far from the major sea routes to Morocco and the central Maghrib.

Furthermore, the data available in primary biographical sources present a strikingly different picture of Andalusian Sufism from that given by the Spanish orientalist Miguel Asín Palacios, who assumed, on the basis of highly fragmentary and apparently faulty evidence, that the Sufi tradition of Muslim Spain had little to do with the formal Islamic sciences and was instead a direct heir to the doctrines of the supposedly neo-Empedoclean mystical philosopher Ibn Masarra (d. 319/931), whose followers were prominent for several generations in the hinterlands of Córdoba and Almería.[44] On the contrary, with the exception of the Granadan theologian and reformer Aḥmad al-Ilbīrī,

42. at-Tādilī, *Tashawwuf*, p. 94.

43. Abū ʿAbdallāh Muḥammad ibn al-Abbār al-Balansī, *Kitāb at-takmila li kitāb aṣ-ṣila*, Francisco Codera, ed. (Madrid: 1887), p. 563.

44. Miguel Asín Palacios, *The Mystical Philosophy of Ibn Masarra and His Followers*, Elmer H. Douglas and Howard W. Yoder trans. (Leiden: E. J. Brill, 1978), pp. 120–23. The idea that Ibn Masarra adhered to the tenets of neo-Empedoclean philosophy was successfully challenged by the late Samuel Stern in 1968. See, S. M. Stern, 'Ibn Masarra, Follower of Pseudo-Empedocles—An Illusion,' in S. M. Stern, *Medieval Arabic and Hebrew Thought*, F. W. Zimmermann, ed. (London: Variorum Reprints, 1983), pp. 325–37.

FIGURE I

Ghazālian influences among Sufis in the western Maghrib

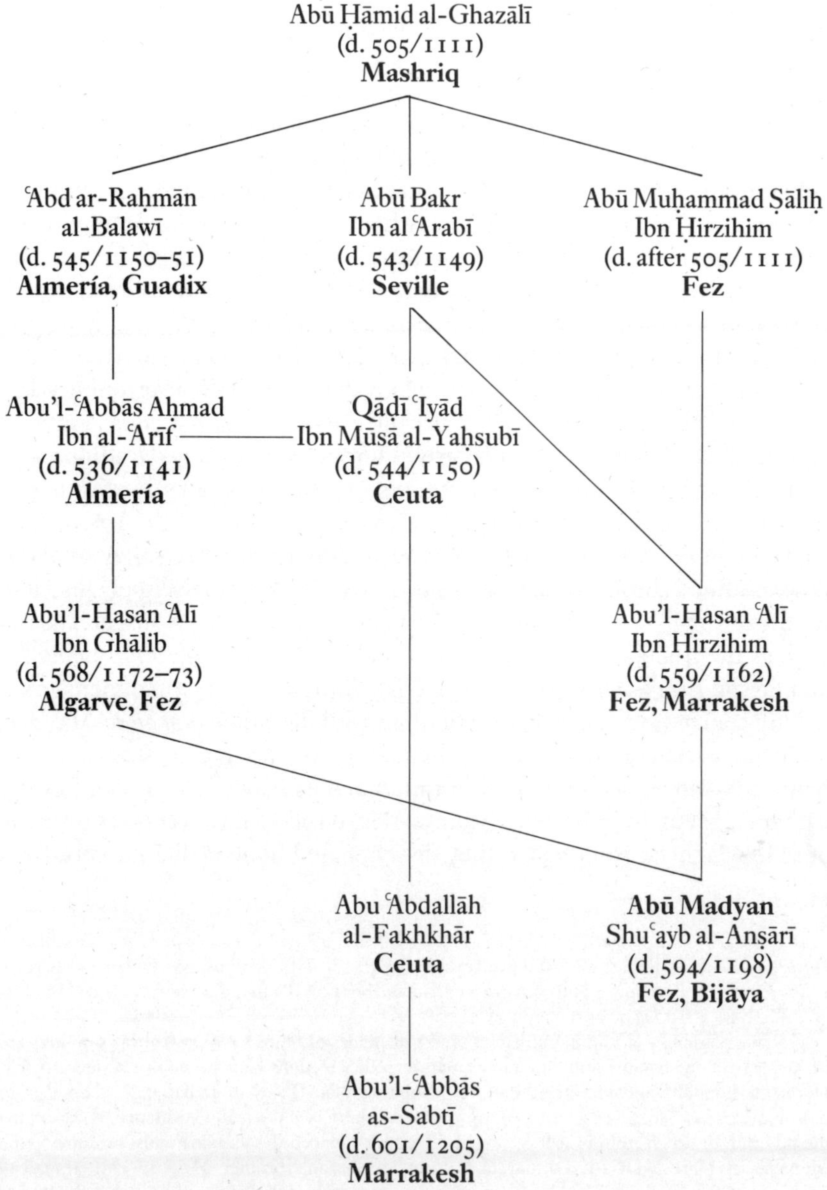

an interest in the Greek philosophical tradition (*falsafa*) does not figure prominently in the biographies of the individuals mentioned above. Indeed, the Almerian Sufi Ibn al-ʿArīf, himself an intellectual descendant of Aḥmad al-Ilbīrī, even went so far as to dismiss *falsafa* as a 'blameworthy method' (*madhhab madhmūm*).[45] Quite the opposite of what Asín Palacios and those who rely on his works have heretofore supposed, the study of *falsafa* appears to have been tangential to the wider tradition of *sharʿī* Andalusian Sufism and during Abū Madyan's lifetime was most prominent, not among orthodox mystics like those described above, but rather among mystically-minded adherents of Hellenistic 'naturalism' such as the famous Abū Bakr ibn Ṭufayl (d. 581/1185) of Guadix (Wādī Āsh), who sought their spiritual and intellectual guidance in the more purely apodictic works of Ibn Bājja, Ibn Sīna and other representatives of the Neoplatonic and Aristotelian traditions.[46]

An approach to Islamic mysticism that may indeed have been influenced by Neoplatonic ideas, however, perhaps via Fāṭimī Ismāʿīlī or even Manichaean antecedents, can be found in Abū Madyan's doctrinal background via an 'illuminationist' tradition that had already existed for more than a century in the still little-known world of early Moroccan Sufism—a tradition best represented by its most famous proponent, Abū Madyan's Berber master Abū Yaʿzā.[47] Sufism in the urban areas of western North Africa, from Tlemcen to the Atlantic coast of Morocco, developed in ways very similar to those outlined above for Islamic Spain. The city of Fez, for example, had long profited from its own complement of ascetic teachers, *sharʿī* Sufis, and jurists, such as the Mālikī Imām Darrās ibn Ismāʿīl (357/968), the *uṣūlī* theologian and mystic Abu'l-Faḍl Yūsuf ibn an-Naḥwī (d. 513/1115), the members of the Ghazālian zāwiya of ʿAlī ibn Ḥirzihim, and the Sufi *mutakallim* Abū ʿAmr ʿUthmān aṣ-Ṣalāljī (d. 564/1167). In addition to these, many students of the famous North African legist Abū ʿImrān al-Fāsī, coordinating their efforts with their brethren in Islamic Spain, settled at rural caravan centers throughout the Maghrib, from which they disseminated both Mālikī jurisprudence

45. Abu'l-ʿAbbās Aḥmad ibn Mūsā ibn ʿAṭā' illāh ibn al-ʿArīf aṣ-Ṣanhājī, *Miftāḥ as-saʿāda wa taḥqīq ṭarīq al-irāda* (Rabat: Bibliothèque Royale [*al-Khizāna al-Ḥasaniyya*], MS number 1562), p. 41.

46. On the philosophical and Sufi antecedents of Ibn Ṭufayl's thought see Lawrence I. Conrad ed., *The World of Ibn Ṭufayl* (forthcoming).

47. The possibility of Fāṭimī influences on the doctrines of Shihāb ad-Dīn Yaḥyā as-Suhrawardī (d. 587/1191), the famous Sufi illuminate and martyr, has recently been raised in a review article by Hermann Landolt. See Hermann Landolt, 'Suhrawardī's "Tales of Initiation"', *Journal of the American Oriental Society* (107), 3, 1987, pp. 475–86. There is at present no evidence, however, that the tradition to which Suhrawardī belonged directly influenced the illuminationist tradition within Morocco. A more likely source may have been al-Ghazālī's brother Majd ad-Dīn Aḥmad (d. 520/1126), whose followers in Morocco at this time may have included the philosopher Ibn Ṭufayl. See at-Tādilī, *Tashawwuf*, pp. 36–37.

and rudimentary Sufi doctrines to lowland bedouins and highland transhumants alike. The most famous of these missionaries was a Ṣanhāja Berber named Waggāg ibn Zallū al-Lamṭī (d. second half of the fifth/eleventh century), who, based at the famous *Dār al-Murābiṭīn* at Āglū on the southern Moroccan coast, attained lasting fame as the teacher of ʿAbdallāh ibn Yāsīn, founder of the Almoravid movement. Others included Abū Muḥammad ʿAbd al-ʿAzīz at-Tūnisī (d. 486/1088), who spread Islamic orthopraxy and Sufism among the Maṣmūda Berbers of the High Atlas mountains living near the trading center of Aghmāt Ūrīka, and his nephew Abū Muḥammad ʿAbd as-Salām at-Tūnisī (d. 537/1139), who introduced the principles of Sufi asceticism to the Almoravid rulers of Tlemcen.

Unique to Morocco, however, appears to have been an extensive network of hermitages, rural centers of religious instruction (*ribāṭs*), zāwiyas, and mosques, which were instrumental in effecting the spread of both Islam and Sufism throughout the countryside. One of the earliest and most famous of these rural centers of learning, so large that it was more of a town than a mere complex of buildings, was the *ribāṭ* of the Banū Amghār family at Tīṭ-n-Fiṭr, located on the Atlantic coast of Morocco just south of the present-day city of El Jedida (Mazīghan al-Jadīda). Arriving in the western Maghrib no later than the mid fifth/eleventh century, the founding family of this *ribāṭ*, descendants of the Prophet Muḥammad who apparently hailed from the Ḥijāz, soon intermarried with daughters of the élite families of local pastoralist Ṣanhāja Berbers and within a century became the de facto religious and political leaders of the entire coastal region between the Umm ar-Rabīʿ and Tansīft rivers. The greatest shaykh of this distinctly tribal zāwiya, Abū ʿAbdallāh Muḥammad ibn Isḥāq Amghār (d. before 550/1152), founded a Sufi order known to later generations as the Ṣanhājiyya, which was mentioned by the biographer Ibn Qunfudh as late as the eighth/fourteenth century as one of the five most important rural confraternities in all of North Africa.[48]

The little that is known about the doctrines of the Ṣanhājiyya indicates that it was oriented theologically toward the Ashʿarī model then becoming popular in the cities of North Africa and Muslim Spain. In terms of practice, it was strongly ascetic and pietistic: Abū ʿAbdallāh Amghār was known to have taught his followers the practices of spiritual retreat (*khalwa*), mortification of the carnal soul (*mujāhada*), frequent fasting (*ṣiyām*), and extreme care (*waraʿ*) in the amounts, types, and origins of foods taken into the body. Much like Abū Yaʿzā, who was a strict vegetarian, Abū ʿAbdallāh Amghār's practices

48. Ibn Qunfudh, *Uns al-faqīr*, p. 64.

apparently exceeded those of Abū Madyan and other urban Sufis in that he restricted his diet exclusively to the leaves of trees, 'allowable plants of the Earth,' and fish from the sea.[49]

In its approach to interpersonal behavior, the way of the Ṣanhājiyya closely followed the doctrines of Islamic chivalry (*futuwwa*) laid down by spiritual masters in the Muslim East more than two centuries earlier. From the son and successor of Abū ʿAbdallāh Amghār we learn that this great *murābiṭ* required his followers to adhere to ten 'Rules of Companionship' (*shurūṭ aṣ-ṣuḥba*): (1) the avoidance of controversy among disciples and the community of believers in general (2) justice (3) nobility of character (4) constancy and satisfaction with what God provides (5) forgiveness of the harmful acts of others (6) preservation of esoteric knowledge from the uninitiated (7) concealment of the sins of other Muslims (8) forgetfulness of the need to have the last answer in a dispute (9) satisfaction with the material necessities that come to one most easily (10) the eating of what is found close at hand.[50]

The Moroccan tradition of rural Sufism represented by *ribāṭs* like Tīṭ-n-Fiṭr appears to have first merged with formally established, eastern Sufi orders through the influence of the Nūriyya—a *ṭā'ifa* originally founded in Baghdad by the followers of al-Junayd's companion Abu'l-Ḥasan (or Abu'l-Ḥusayn) Aḥmad ibn Muḥammad an-Nūrī al-Khurāsānī (d. 295/907–8). The earliest followers of this tradition to appear in western Maghribi biographical sources are the Subsaharan African saint and butcher Abū Jabal Yaʿlā of Fez (d. 503/1109–10), and the noted shaykh and patron of the town of Aghmāt Ūrīka, ʿAbd al-Jalīl ibn Wayḥlān ad-Dukkālī (d. 541/1146). Both of these individuals were disciples of an Egyptian shaykh, Abu'l-Faḍl ʿAbdallāh ibn Bishr al-Jawharī, who was linked to the Nūriyya through his father and Abū Bakr ad-Dīnawārī, a disciple of an-Nūrī himself.[51]

The idea that a purified ascetic could partake in a divinely-inspired, illuminative wisdom, a doctrine that appears to have been characteristic of the Nūriyya since its inception, must have struck a responsive chord among the Ṣanhāja and Maṣmūda Berbers living along the Atlantic littoral of Morocco, for all prominent Maghribi adherents of the Nūriyya tradition up to the end of

49. Muḥammad ibn ʿAbd al-ʿAẓīm az-Zammūrī (d. early ninth/fifteenth century), *Bahjat an-nāẓirīn wa uns al-ʿārifīn wa wasīlat Rabb al-ʿĀlamīn fī manāqib rijāl Amghār aṣ-Ṣāliḥīn* (Rabat: Bibliothèque Royale [*al-Khizāna al-Ḥasaniyya*], MS number 1358), pp. 79, 108.

50. Ibid., p. 131.

51. al-ʿAbbās ibn Ibrāhīm, *al-Iʿlām bi man ḥalla Marrākush wa Aghmāt min al-aʿlām* (Rabat: al-Maṭbaʿa al-Malakiyya, 1976), (8), p. 32. See also, E. Michaux-Bellaire, ed., 'Les Confréries Religieuses au Maroc,' *Archives Marocaines* (Paris: Librairie Ancienne Honoré Champion, 1927), (27), p. 40.

the sixth/twelfth century originally came from this region.[52] The tombs of two of these saints, even today, remain important pilgrimage centers. The earlier of these individuals, Abū Īnnūr ʿAbdallāh u-Agrīs al-Mashanzāʾī, now called 'Sīdī Bennūr' (*Abū Nūr*, or 'Possessor of Light'), was a companion of ʿAbd al-Jalīl ibn Wayḥlān who died sometime during the first half of the sixth/twelfth century. Abū Īnnūr's main social function seemed to be that he acted as a champion and protector for the sedentary Maṣmūda Berbers of the coastal lowland region of Dukkāla, who were then sorely beset by incursions of Ṣanhāja pastoralists. Sīdī Bennūr's fame was soon eclipsed, however, by that of his disciple, Abū Shuʿayb Ayyūb ibn Saʿīd aṣ-Ṣanhājī (d. 561/1166), the famous 'Mūlay Būshʿayb' and patron of the town of Azemmour (Azammūr), who appears to have been able to synthesize the various strands of rural mysticism already present in Morocco within a single inclusive doctrine.

The *shaykh al-khirqa* (shaykh who formally bestows membership in a Sufi *ṭāʾifa*) of Abū Madyan's spiritual master Abū Yaʿzā, Abū Shuʿayb as-Ṣanhājī eventually inherited the leadership of the Nūriyya tradition in Morocco from ʿAbd al-Jalīl ibn Wayḥlān and until the end of his life divided his time equally between his own *ribāṭ* at Azemmour and that founded by the latter at Aghmāt Ūrīka.[53] It is clear that he closely followed the doctrines of *futuwwa* and social consciousness originally prescribed by Abu'l-Ḥasan an-Nūrī himself, for biographers recount a story in which Abū Shuʿayb, finding his cow grazing in a neighbor's garden, ran toward the beast, stuck his hand into its mouth, and forcibly pulled out all the plant matter that the animal had not swallowed. In order to make symbolic restitution for what his cow had eaten, the shaykh kept it at home for three days, until all of its food had been digested, and gave its milk to the poor as charity.[54]

Also like an-Nūrī, Abū Shuʿayb's advocacy of social justice created numerous problems with both local and regional authority figures. He initially directed his activities against the Almoravids, whose religious leaders disapproved of Sufism and whose political leaders forced the pastoralists and merchants of Dukkāla to pay unpopular and onerous taxes that were legitimized by neither the Qur'ān nor the corpus of Prophetic hadith. Despite his opposition to the oppresive ethnocentrism of the desert Ṣanhāja ruling élite, however, he was equally opposed to the massacre of the Almoravids that was carried out by Almohad forces when they conquered Marrakesh in

52. See, for example, Paul Nwyia, 'Textes Mystiques Inédits D'Abū'l-Ḥasan al-Nūrī' (m. 295/907), *Mélanges de l'Université Saint-Joseph* (Beirut: Imprimérie Catholique, 1968), (14), fasc. 9, p. 138. The illuminationist aspects of an-Nūrī's doctrines are apparent in the edited text provided by Nwyia.

53. Ibn Ibrāhīm, *Iʿlām*, (1), p. 397.

54. Ibid., p. 396.

541/1146. A dramatic account from at-Tādilī's *Tashawwuf* depicts Abū Shuʿayb's selflessness as extending even to the use of his own arrest and incarceration in Marrakesh as an opportunity to intercede for the Almoravid ruling family before the Almohad Caliph ʿAbd al-Mu'min ibn ʿAlī al-Gūmī.[55]

By far the most influential member of the Moroccan Nūriyya tradition was Abū Madyan's *shaykh at-tarqiya* ('shaykh of ascension' or master of the gnostic experience), the illiterate Maṣmūda Berber Abū Yaʿzā Yalannūr (also 'Possessor of Light') ibn Maymūn ad-Dukkālī. A disciple of Abū Shuʿayb as-Ṣanhajī and companion of scores of other North African saints, including Abū ʿAbdallāh Amghār of Ribāṭ Tīṭ-n-Fiṭr, in his long life of nearly one hundred and thirty years Abū Yaʿzā symbolized the culmination of the rural Sufi tradition of the western Maghrib that was to be absorbed and finally transcended by his even more famous Andalusian student. The two themes which most consistently appear as the pillars of this shaykh's spiritual method are *futuwwa* (defined in this case as humility and a total devotion to the service of others) and severe asceticism, which eventually led the shaykh to practice a regime of strict vegetarianism that included the avoidance of any domestic foodstuffs grown by a person other than himself. According to his biographers, Abū Yaʿzā wandered about the uninhabited regions of the Far Maghrib for more than twenty-five years, during which he subsisted on wild plants and was befriended by lions, beasts, and birds of the forest.[56] At one time he was even known by the Berber nickname, *Abū Wagartīl*, or 'Owner of the Prayer-Mat,' because, like the unknown saint that the young Abū Madyan met on the Andalusian seacoast, he was in the habit of wearing nothing but a woven mat to cover the nakedness of his body.[57]

Despite the undeniable influence exerted by Abū Yaʿzā in developing the methods employed by subsequent Moroccan Sufis in training their own disciples, little doctrinal material remains today that can clearly be attributed to this noted shaykh and *quṭb*. Much of this shortage of data is most likely due to Abū Yaʿzā's own illiteracy and inability to speak the Arabic language (his lessons were often translated from Berber into Arabic on the spot by a bilingual interpreter), as well as the tendency of rural Moroccans, even during his lifetime, to ignore the shaykh's doctrinal teachings in favor of the more dramatic accounts of his miracles. Thus far, all that appears to remain of these lessons are a few aphorisms transmitted by Abū Madyan and one short treatise preserved at the Bibliothèque Générale in Rabat.[58]

55. Ibid., pp. 396–97, 400.

56. Aḥmad ibn Abī'l-Qāsim aṣ-Ṣūmaʿī at-Tādilī (d. 1013/1604–5), *al-Muʿzā fī manāqib Abī Yaʿzā* (Rabat: Bibliothèque Générale [*al-Khizāna al-ʿĀmma*], MS number 299 K), folio 3.

57. at-Tādilī, *Tashawwuf*, p. 217.

58. This treatise is reproduced in Appendix II.

The text of this treatise, a few lines of which also appear in a poem attributed to Abū Madyan himself, recall in simpler form a number of themes commonly expressed by Abū Yaᶜzā's more sophisticated eastern contemporaries. As a whole, the text is a discourse on the illuminative aspects of *mushāhada*, or gnostic contemplation.[59] Among the concepts discussed by Abū Yaᶜzā are: (1) the idea that gnosis involves perceiving creation as a manifestation of the Divine attributes of beauty (*jamāl*) and majesty (*jalāl*) (2) the all-encompassing nature of gnostic knowledge (3) the concept of the 'Sun of Gnosis' (4) the reciprocal relationship between mystical annihilation (*fanā'*) and the eternal presence (*baqā'*) of the Divine, and (5) the spiritual alchemy which transforms the base metal of the soul into its opposite.

Given such a heterogeneous intellectual heritage as that described above, is it possible, in any meaningful sense, to ascertain exactly which aspects of Sufi doctrine Abū Madyan obtained from his Andalusian and Moroccan masters? This question is more difficult to answer than one might first suspect, since the sixth/twelfth century, although barely past dawn in the history of Sufism in the western Maghrib, was already well beyond mid-morning in the development of Islamic mysticism as a whole. Each shaykh who lived in the Muslim West already stood as the recipient of numerous eastern Islamic esoteric traditions, filtered down and transformed through time, that were often nearly as influential as the teachings of his or her own spiritual masters. Textual evidence clearly demonstrates that the western Maghrib, although far removed in distance from the heartland of the Islamic world, was privy, through the pilgrimage to Mecca and institutionalized scholarly contacts, to most of the intellectual developments that had recently occurred in the Muslim East. In the case of the writings of al-Ghazālī, for example, one finds that his *Iḥyā' ᶜulūm ad-dīn* had already attained widespread popularity in Fez and the Andalusian Levant a mere two decades after its author's death. As for al-Ghazālī's other, more philosophical writings, the text of the famous *Risāla Ḥayy ibn Yaqẓān* of Ibn Ṭufayl proves that many of these works were widely circulated in al-Andalus by at least the middle of the sixth/twelfth century.[60] The text of Abū Madyan's *Bidāyat al-murīd*, reproduced below, also clearly demonstrates how pervasive was the influence in the Maghrib of the doctrines of eastern Sufis, especially those from Khurāsān. Indeed, were it not for references to specifically Maghribi attitudes and practices, such as the clothing worn by members of his *ṭā'ifa* and the types of fasts the shaykh required his followers to perform, one would be hard put to

59. See Henri Corbin, *The Man of Light in Iranian Sufism* (London and Boulder Colorado: Shambhala Books, 1978), pp. 84–89, where some of the same themes are included in a discussion of what Corbin calls the 'Heavenly Witness', or 'suprasensory personal guide'.

60. Abū Bakr ibn Ṭufayl, *Ḥayy ibn Yaqẓān* (Beirut: Imprimérie Catholique, 1963), pp. 22–23.

distinguish Abū Madyan's treatise from those written in the Mashriq during the same era.

While it cannot be said, therefore, with complete exactitude and certainty, which individual elements of his doctrine Abū Madyan acquired from ʿAlī ibn Ḥirzihim, Abū ʿAbdallāh ad-Daqqāq, Abu'l-Ḥasan ibn Ghālib, or Abū Yaʿzā, it nevertheless remains possible to discern in his works the general outlines of a unique spiritual method that stands out from the larger tradition of Sufism as a whole. Much of the regional flavor that one finds in early works of Maghribi mysticism like those of Abū Madyan comes from the fact that North African shaykhs and most of their *sharʿī* Andalusian counterparts were raised and educated within the Mālikī jurisprudential tradition, which tends to judge the inner piety of an individual on the basis of one's outward acts. Consequently, while it shared many of the viewpoints, philosophies, and symbologies of eastern Sufism, the 'Way of Abū Madyan' also tended, on the whole, to be more orthoprax, pietistic, and less overtly metaphysical than one familiar with other Sufi traditions might at first be led to assume.

Like the spiritual methods employed by all great Sufis in the sixth/twelfth-century western Maghrib, the way of Abū Madyan, at least in its initial stages, was oriented as much toward *ʿamal*, or spiritual praxis, as it was to *ʿilm*, or esoteric doctrine—an emphasis which required a strong commitment on the part of the seeker to practice strict asceticism and the mortification of bodily desires. Included in Abū Madyan's doctrine of *ʿamal* was a complementary emphasis on absolute sincerity, a necessary requirement for the development of the purity of soul upon which one's spiritual development was based. Noting that 'the Folk of Truthfulness are rare among the pious',[61] Abū Madyan, much like Ḥārith al-Muḥāsibī three centuries earlier, used his public 'sessions of admonition' to impress upon his followers the need to eliminate all traces of hypocrisy from their character.

Significantly, the shaykh saw sincerity as being necessary not only for individual development but for the good of society as well. In one of the most famous of his aphorisms he states: 'With the corruption of the masses appears the rule of tyranny; with the corruption of the élite appear false prophets who seduce [the masses] away from religion.'[62] Because he saw the fully actualized Sufi master not only as a member of a spiritual élite, but also as an individual specifically charged with the responsibility of guiding human society in general, Abū Madyan was especially concerned that those who accepted spiritual leadership would be free from false pretensions. 'Beware,' he said, 'of [the preacher] whom you see advocating in the name of God a state which is not outwardly visible in [his behavior],' for 'the most harmful of

61. *Uns al-waḥīd*, aphorism 41.

62. Ibid, aphorism 83.

things is companionship with a heedless scholar, an ignorant Sufi, or an insincere preacher.'[63] From the ranks of these misguided individuals, Abū Madyan believed, arise the *Dajājila* (sing. *Dajjāl*)—the 'anti-Christs' or false prophets, who periodically lead the Muslim community into doctrinal error, fanaticism, and excessive sectarianism.

For Abū Madyan, as it was for both his shaykh Abū Yaᶜzā and al-Muḥāsibī centuries before him, the lower, passional soul was an adversary that had to be vanquished before a human being could attain the meritorious attributes that would lead to his salvation. Since it was in the nature of this adversary, like the human adversary faced by warriors on the battlefield, to take shelter behind the ramparts of a strong castle or redoubt, the defences of this redoubt had first to be reduced before the adversary itself could be decisively defeated. The redoubt of this inner adversary, the primary defense of the passional soul in the material world, was seen by the shaykh to be the human body, which stands as the physical manifestation of the ontologically insincere 'I'—the egoism and self-centeredness that habitually prevents man from actualizing his true, deiform nature. To reduce its stubborn defenses, the body must be subjected to the assault of its greatest fears—those of privation and death—so that it could become humbled and made malleable in the hands of the soul's physician. The key to this process, thought Abū Madyan, was hunger:

> He who is hungry arrives and he who is satiated is cut off. He who remembers [God] is moved to meditate, while he who forgets is himself forgotten. This is because hunger comprises ten qualities: the purification of the lower soul from lusts and doubts; remembrance; meditation; the shedding of blameworthy attributes and the acquisition of those that are praiseworthy; the emulation of spiritual masters who have gone before, as well as the Companions of the Prophet and those who succeeded them among the first generation of the pious; preoccupation with suppressing the lower soul; and preventing the lower soul from following its lusts.
>
> . . . Hunger is the vehicle of the worshippers, the way of the pious, the method of the gnostics, the key of those who are guided, and the goal of those who have arrived at the highest [level] of *ᶜIlliyyīn*.[64]

Essential to the practice of hunger as defined by the shaykh was the systematic practice of fasting. This included fasting every day of the months of Rajab and Shaᶜbān, the Ramaḍān fast required for every Muslim, and a

63. Ibid, aphorisms 12 and 11.

64. *Bidāyat al-murīd*, p. 58 below.

supplementary fast of three days per month done at an individual's personal discretion.[65] Even more praiseworthy, if the disciple could perform it, was the 'Fast of David,' advocated in a number of hadith collections, which, for Abū Madyan, meant fasting one day and eating the next.[66]

The most distinctive fast practiced by the followers of Abū Madyan, also mentioned in hadith collections but extended by the shaykh to a degree far beyond that prescribed for ordinary believers, was called *wiṣāl*, or *ṣawm al-wiṣāl*—the fast of intercession or 'intimate union'. Patterned after the fasts of Moses in the Egyptian desert and those practiced before the onset of revelation by the Prophet Muḥammad in the cave of Ḥirā' above Mecca, this fast entailed devoting oneself to a predetermined period of retreat, total abstention from food, and invocation. The *murīd* desiring union with God in this way would first enter into a state of repentance and remorse, after which he would make the major ablution and pray two prostrations. He would then embark upon a regime of strict seclusion, lasting as many as forty days, during which he would ingest nothing but water (even at night, when food is allowed during Ramaḍān), all the while repeating the formula, 'There is no deity but God' (*lā ilāha illā' llāh*), and stopping only to answer the call of nature, attend Friday prayers, or sleep when sleep overtook him. According to Abū Muḥammad Ṣāliḥ ibn Yanṣāren al-Māgirī (d. 631/1234), one of the greatest successors to Abū Madyan and a follower of the latter's disciple ʿAbd ar-Razzāq al-Jazūlī, the purpose of this strenuous exercise was to 'purify the heart, illuminate the quintessence, restrain evil impulses, sharpen insight, acquire the taste for intimate converse with God during sessions of *dhikr*, and enable one to explain esoteric mysteries.'[67] In a secondary sense it was designed to curb the tendency of the limbs to engage in unlawful acts, supress the desires that prevent the illumination of the heart and prevent one from practicing invocation, turn one away from habitual behavior, make the body healthier, and preserve religion.[68]

The ultimate purpose underlying the *ṣawm al-wiṣāl* and other ascetic practices required by Abū Madyan was to instill in his followers an attitude of

65. Ibid, p. 56 below. All of these fasts are based on the precedent of Prophetic hadith. See for example, Abū Zakariyyā Yaḥyā ibn Sharaf an-Nawawī, *Riyāḍ aṣ-ṣāliḥīn min kalām Sayyid al-Mursalīn* (Beirut/Kuwait: 1389/1970), pp. 367–70.

66. Ibid. The 'Fast of David' is more often thought of in the Muslim world as a practice that entails abstaining from food on Mondays and Thursdays only.

67. Abu'l-ʿAbbās Aḥmad ibn Ibrāhīm ibn Aḥmad ibn Abī Muḥammad Ṣāliḥ ibn Yanṣāren al-Māgirī, *al-Minhāj al-wāḍiḥ fī taḥqīq karāmāt Abī Muḥammad Ṣāliḥ* (Cairo: al-Maṭbaʿa al-Miṣriyya, 1352/1933), pp. 218–25. ʿAbd ar-Razzāq al-Jazūlī, now buried near Alexandria in Egypt, was one of the first major Moroccan Sufis to settle permanently in the Mashriq. It was he who married Abū Madyan's concubine despite the prejudice of his tribe. See above, p. 14.

68. Ibid.

complete and utter reliance upon the will of God (*tawakkul*)—so much so, in fact, that the shaykh urged his disciples to adhere to the unequivocal dictum of the early Iraqi mystic Ibrāhīm al-Khawwāṣ (d. 291/904): 'It is not part of Sufi conduct to have [financial] means upon which to rely in case of need, nor something that can be accepted by another [in payment], nor sight nor tongue with which to beg if one is hungry, nor a word by which to beseech humankind in case of misfortune.'[69]

Apart from his contributions to the development of Sufi methodology, Abū Madyan was best known by succeeding generations of Sufis in the western Maghrib as a master of the station of *tawakkul*. Indeed, among those aphorisms that have survived up to the present, the shaykh's sayings about reliance upon God are more numerous than those dealing with any other subject except asceticism. Closely related to the concept of *tawakkul* was that referred to by Abū Madyan under the terms *tawānī* or *sukūn*—the quiescence or deliberate 'slowness' of the soul that allows it to become aware of the Divine presence. 'One who adheres to the Expected Promise', says the shaykh, 'does not part company with quiescence. The seeker moves toward it while the gnostic moves within it.'[70] He also said: 'Complete reliance upon God means putting your trust in what is guaranteed and transforming activity into quiescence.'[71]

This quiescence, however, is not the mere physical inactivity or listlessness usually implied by the term in English. Instead, it involves the conscious effort of the *murīd* to cease all of the vain, world-inspired activity of the cognitive intelligence and replace it with a passive, empty mind prepared to receive the gift of eternal presence (*baqā'*) that follows the attainment of self-extinction (*fanā'*). 'The heart has no more than one aspect [at a time],' says the shaykh, 'such that when you are occupied with [a particular aspect] it is veiled from another. So take care that you are not drawn toward anything but God, lest He deprive you of the delights of intimate converse (*munājāt*) with Him.'[72] Once the desired quiescence is attained, the soul becomes like an empty cup, now fully prepared to receive an infusion of Divine light.

The attainment of quiescence in turn prepares the seeker to enter a further stage, which Sufis call 'fusion' (*jamᶜ*)—the ultimate merging of the human soul into the Divine plenitude. In *Bidāyat al-murīd* Abū Madyan describes fusion as '. . . that which abrogates your disunity and effaces your expression of self. Fusion is the total absorption of your attributes and the negation of the qualities [by which you were known].'[73] Of his own experience at this level of

69. *Bidāyat al-murīd*, p. 64 below.
70. *Uns al-waḥīd*, aphorism 19.
71. Ibid, aphorism 46.
72. Ibid, aphorism 9.
73. Ibid, aphorism 43.

spiritual awareness the shaykh once said: 'My station is slavery (*ʿubūdiyya*), my knowledge is Divinely-inspired (*ulūhiyya*), and my attributes are lordly (*rabbāniyya*). His knowledge has filled that which is hidden and manifest within me and my body and soul (literally, "my land and my sea"—*barrī wa baḥrī*) have been filled with His light.'[74]

Only a person fully able to undertake the rigors of this exacting spiritual method was considered by Abū Madyan worthy of bearing the honored title of *faqīr*, or 'Poor One.' After discussing, in *Bidāyat al-murīd*, a number of the sects of false mystics, charlatans, and inadequately-trained gnostics whom he regarded as being responsible for sullying the name of Sufism and leading believers into error, the shaykh stresses the need for reliance upon a normative religious tradition based on the Qur'ān and Sunna as well as the guidance of exoteric religious scholars. The Sufi and gnostic, he believed, must be no different from the ordinary believer in that he too must honor the religious figures of the Islamic community and uphold the Sunna of the Prophet Muḥammad in his outward practices and habits. Indeed, this adherence to formal religion served as one of the foundations of the *faqīr*'s role as a quintessential *muslim* or 'one who surrenders himself to the will of God':

> Among the signs of the true *faqīr* are his love for scholars, his service to the jurisprudents, his companionship with the *fuqarā'*, and his transformation [of self] by fasting and standing [in prayer]. His clothing is ragged and his food is coarse. When he sees [something] he reflects upon it, when he speaks he invokes [God], and when he is silent he meditates. He walks like one who is infirm and is immersed [in remembrance] when he sleeps. He resembles a bereaved mother in his ecstatic state, yet no one criticizes him and he criticizes no one; instead, he is the purest of mankind in his actions and in his speech. The Qur'ān is on his right, the Sunna is on his left, and the [Divine] threat and promise is his concern. He hopes for nothing but God, he does not fear the censure of critics, and his heart is attached to [the idea of] being cut off from [the material world]. His similitude is like the Earth, which bears everything that is repugnant. These are the attributes of the true *faqīr*, whom God ennobles and makes into one of the saints of God Most High. 'They are the Party of God (*Ḥizb Allāh*). Verily it is the Party of God who have attained felicity.'[75]

74. al-Kattānī, *Salwat al-anfās* (1), p. 365.
75. Abū Madyan, *Bidāyat al-murīd*, pp. 88–90 below.

Abū Madyan's characterization of Sufis as the 'Party of God'—those rightly-guided followers of the Islamic message who call mankind to the Truth and point the way to salvation—not only places the shaykh squarely within the politically charged Maghribi tradition of *futuwwa* and *īthār* (the practice of giving preference to others over oneself) advocated by earlier spiritual masters such as Ibn al-ʿArīf and Abū Yaʿzā, but also indicates a probable reason why he was viewed with so much suspicion by the Almohad religious élite, who also referred to their own followers as the 'Party of God'. For Abū Madyan as well as for the more exoteric followers of the 'Mahdī' Ibn Tūmart, an individual's ascetic or contemplative practices could never be separated from his social responsibility: 'Sufism is not the [mere] observance of rules, nor does it consist of degrees or stages. Instead, Sufism consists of personal integrity, generosity of spirit, the emulation of what has been revealed, knowledge of the Message, and following the Way of the Prophets. He who deviates from these sources finds himself grazing in the gardens of Satan, submerged in the ocean of lust, and wandering in the darkness of ignorance.'[76]

Anticipating a doctrine later made famous by the seventh/thirteenth-century Moroccan mystic Abu'l-Ḥasan ash-Shādhilī, Abū Madyan regards the true Sufi as not merely a withdrawn ascetic, who contemplates God and ignores all that transpires around him, but instead as a full and integral part of his social environment. He is an individual who may periodically detach himself from others for the purpose of personal development, but also maintains a constant vigilance over his own behavior and the actions of those around him for the sake of the Muslim community as a whole:

> The true *faqīr* must not be jealous, egotistical, or arrogant with his knowledge and should not be miserly with his money. On the contrary, he must act as a guide—cheerful, merciful of heart, and compassionate with [God's] creatures. To him [all human beings] are like one of his hands. [He is] ascetic; everything is equal to him, whether it be praise or blame, taking or giving, acceptance or rejection, wealth or poverty. He is neither joyful about what comes to him nor sad about what has been lost.[77]

On the same subject the shaykh adds: 'Among the attributes of the *faqīr* are five things: the keeping of secrets, love for the virtuous poor, the avoidance of fools and those who are evil, following the commands of [God] the Subduer,

76. Ibid, p. 90 below.

77. Ibid, p. 96 below.

and following the Sunna of the Chosen Prophet.'[78] It was further incumbent upon the true Sufi to look after his own kind and to correct deviant behavior when warranted: 'When you see a *murīd* or a *faqīr* who is obedient [only] to himself, who has abandoned his invocations, who goes [to women] without marrying them, and asks for things without any need for them, then whip him as a punishment.'[79]

Abū Madyan's disapproval of ignorant or deviant Sufism extended to many of the ecstatic practices and rituals that are still followed by certain Sufi orders and saint cults in the Maghrib today. It thus comes as somewhat of a surprise when we learn from the text of *Bidāyat al-murīd* that the shaykh and his disciples apparently practiced *samā*ᶜ, or ecstatic sessions of song and invocation, and that these sessions often included both flute music and emotional outbursts:

> The Folk of *Samā*ᶜ are a group of people who moan, do penance, and blame themselves. They spend their days fasting and their nights standing [in prayer]. Then they break into weeping, wailing, crying out, imploring and sobbing. They completely renounce the material world and devote their hearts to their Beloved, irrevocably divorcing the material world . . .. When they hear a teaching, the lights of love are kindled in their hearts, which clothe their external bodies with the onset of ecstasy. In their ecstasy they occupy the station of the possessed—they become agitated and lose their senses, but they bear no blame.[80]

Participation in these ecstatic sessions, however, was strictly forbidden to the general public. '*Samā*ᶜ is a private thing,' said Abū Madyan. 'No one but its folk should know of it. When [Sufis] are present for ecstatic sessions they should lock the doors of their homes and when the food is brought they should open them again.'[81] By maintaining this attitude Abū Madyan puts himself unequivocally at variance with the practices of many lower class and rural Sufi orders of his day as well as the present, such as the Ḥamādsha, Jilāla, and ᶜIsāwa of Morocco, who continue to hold large public gatherings, attended by both men and women, during which participants often enter into trance-like states, speak to demons, eat insects and other vermin, and cut themselves with knives and axes. Especially important to Abū Madyan's gatherings was the exclusion of all who were spiritually unprepared to take part in them: 'The most serious impediment [to *samā*ᶜ] is the Sufi who is selfish. Holding ecstatic sessions with those who are not suited for them is

78. Ibid, p. 94 below.
79. Ibid, p. 94 below.
80. Ibid, p. 80 below.
81. Ibid, p. 82 below.

also forbidden. Being present and taking part in them is permissible only for those who are their folk.'[82]

Before a beginner could participate in a session of *samāʿ* at Rābiṭa az-Zayyāt, it was first necessary for him to mortify his carnal soul with fasting, practicing the *ṣawm al-wiṣāl*, and keeping nightly vigils of prayer. When the aspirant was finally allowed to attend Abū Madyan's *majlis adh-dhikr*, he had to adhere to other rules of behavior as well: 'We were with the leaders of our Sufi companions and when we wanted to hold an ecstatic session the door was locked. None of us would come to the session until he had passed ten days calming his carnal soul, subsiding his fires, and purifying his thoughts. Then every one of us would come [to the session] wrapped in his cloak.'[83]

The way of Abū Madyan was thus similar to other 'sober,' or *sharʿī* Sufi spiritual methods employed throughout the Muslim world in that it accorded full importance to the value of exoteric as well as esoteric teachings and attempted to dissuade those who followed the shaykh's doctrines from falling into the error of mixing their passions with their devotions. Although its doctrines were firmly grounded in religious orthopraxy, participation in Abū Madyan's *ṭarīqa* was not closed to any group—neither to those who had an interest in higher questions of metaphysics nor to those who desired the 'taste' of gnostic illumination. The shaykh's poems, reproduced below, give ample evidence of his ability to transmit highly sophisticated esoteric teachings both clearly and eloquently. The full enjoyment of such insights and experience was not accessible to every disciple, however, but was instead reserved for those adepts who had adequately prepared themselves, in terms of doctrinal learning and ascetic practice, to assimilate them without being spiritually damaged or harming the Way itself. For those who succeeded in reaching this goal, the wider community of orthodox mystics in the western Maghrib was to become, under the guidance of Abū Madyan and his successors, a broadly-based fellowship which extended its influence far beyond the strict confines of doctrine and methodology. Through the influence of the shaykh's lectures, as well as his poems, treatises, and aphorisms, the way of Abū Madyan stood for centuries as a model for the western Islamic *ṣāliḥ* and *qudwa*—the paradigmatic Sufi proponent of ethical righteousness and social reform, who sought to improve the spiritual orientation of society by exercising his responsibility to 'command the good and forbid evil' (Qur'ān, III [*Āl ʿImrān*], 104). As such, Abū Madyan's message and others like it were to resurface, time and again throughout the history of the western Maghrib, whenever the Islamic community appeared threatened by decay or corruption from within.

82. Ibid, p. 82 below. 83. Ibid, p. 88 below.

THE TEXTS AND THEIR TRANSLATION

Extant manuscript copies of Abū Madyan's writings can be found, mostly in fragmentary form, in numerous collections on four continents—from North America in the west to Asia in the east. Needless to say, such widely scattered materials present particularly difficult problems for the editor and translator, not only because they are often incomplete and disparate, but also because, due to the largely oral nature of their transmission, the more lengthy of these manuscripts are seldom identically worded or even of equal length. To this may be added the equally serious problem of authenticity, for one can find many poems and sayings attributed to Abū Madyan that belong instead to other, earlier Sufis, or employ vocabulary and elements of style that are inconsistent with the literary traditions of the western Maghrib. Further exacerbating these difficulties is the fact that the present author has been unable to find any example of Abū Madyan's writings that was written down in manuscript form less than two hundred years after the death of the shaykh himself.

Consequently, it is difficult to imagine any modern version of the shaykh's writings that could realistically be represented as a final, definitive edition of Abū Madyan's literary output. This is not meant to imply, however, that the task of editing such works is completely hopeless or that the problems of verification are entirely insurmountable. One advantage of the oral tradition of Sufi instruction, especially in the Maghrib, is that a number of shorter works, such as poems and aphorisms, have been transmitted from generation to generation until they have attained the status of popular folklore. This has been the case, for example, with a number of Abū Madyan's more famous poems, such as *al-Qaṣīda an-nūniyya*, as well as a significant minority of his *ḥikam*, which can be found on the tongues of many thousands of Muslims from Morocco to as far away as Egypt without their being fully aware of the identity of the person ultimately responsible for composing them. Whenever oral traditions of this kind exist, it becomes possible for the researcher to rely on present-day informants in order to practice a sort of 'literary archaeology', which allows one to determine the accuracy or inaccuracy of otherwise unverifiable manuscript versions of poetry or popular sayings.

Recognizing the difficulties of analysis that exist in such a genre, but also being cognizant of the need for more of the seminal works of Maghribi orthodox mysticism to appear before a wider audience, it was decided to include in the present volume a representative sample of the most clearly verifiable works of Abū Madyan that are currently available. Practically speaking, this meant that most of the following texts were taken from major manuscript collections in Western Europe and North Africa, including the

British Library in London, the Bibliothèque Nationale in Paris, the Biblioteca Nacional in Madrid, and the Bibliothèque Générale (*al-Khizāna al-ʿĀmma*) in Rabat. Additional collections of Abū Madyan's writings, such as those found in Algeria or Turkey, that could not be utilized at the present time for political, bureaucratic or other reasons, will have to wait for the appearance of a second edition of this work or until another scholar attempts to take up the challenge of collecting and editing their contents.

Whenever possible, the texts translated and edited below were cross-checked with at least one other manuscript copy. This was the case, for example, with *Bidāyat al-murīd*, which was edited with the help of a relatively recent manuscript belonging to a private collector from Rabat, Morocco, and *Uns al-waḥīd wa nuzhat al-murīd*, which was compiled with the help of manuscripts in both London and Paris, as well as a printed partial collection of aphorisms from an edited Algerian work originally written in the eighth/fourteenth century. Whenever possible, the available manuscript copies were reconciled with each other and the orthography of each text was rendered into Modern Standard Arabic. When differing manuscript texts could not be reconciled, a problem that occurred with several of the aphorisms, alternate readings were provided as footnotes to the English text. Since there is at present no way to create a truly 'definitive' Arabic copy of the disputed versions of Abū Madyan's output, it was considered less confusing for the prospective reader to leave such notations out of the published Arabic text and to present the latter only as an approximate, 'standardized' version.

In the case of Abū Madyan's *ʿAqīda* and some of his poems, no known alternative existed that could aid in editing the available text. In such an event, care was taken to clear up orthographical and syntactical errors in the extant manuscript while remaining as faithful as possible to its original wording. In one case (*al-Qaṣīda an-nūniyya*), the original text was verified orally with the help of members of the Qādirī Sufi zāwiya in Marrakesh, Morocco, who had memorized and transmitted it to their brethren for many generations. Since the Moroccan version of this ode is so universally well known, it is probably safe to assume that it is more faithful to the original than the widely disseminated printed version from Egypt that was published by ʿAbd al-Ḥalīm Maḥmūd in his small volume on the life and works of Abū Madyan.[84] It is also desirable at this point to mention once again the invaluable assistance provided by Dr. Jamil Diab in editing the aphorisms and poems presented in this volume. Considering the poor condition of some of the manuscripts, and the hours of work necessary to undo the effects of water

84. See ʿAbd al-Ḥalīm Maḥmūd, *Shaykh ash-shuyūkh Abū Madyan al-Ghawth: ḥayātuhu wa miʿrājuhu ilā Allāh* (Cairo: Dār al-Maʿārif, 1985), pp. 119–21.

and worm damage to the texts they contained, it is fair to say that what follows could not have been accomplished without him.

In making an English translation of these works, extreme care was taken to present the teachings of Abū Madyan in a form as close to the original as possible. For this reason, it was decided to place all additions to the text made by the translator within brackets, so that the prospective reader could be absolutely sure of the actual words of the shaykh himself. Bracketed passages are most numerous in the translations of certain aphorisms, as well as in the text of *Bidāyat al-murīd*, both of which were found to contain an unusually large number of ambiguous pronouns. This procedure was also followed in consideration of the needs of Western students of Arabic literature, who, in their attempt to match the given translations with their Arabic originals, might be confused by words and phrases that do not appear in the printed text. The edited Arabic texts presented below have also been extensively vocalized as an aid to non-native speakers of the Arabic language.

Finally, it is important to stress to the concerned reader that the use of brackets in the following translations in no way implies a value judgment as to the quality or readability of the original. The present writer is fully aware of the tendency of certain orientalist scholars to overcompensate for supposed 'shortcomings' in the Arabic works that they have edited by adding commentaries within the body of their translations. This is most emphatically not the case here. The final version of the works rendered into English below, like any translation from one language to another, constitutes a compromise between what can be rendered literally and what must be understood by the prospective reader. As such, certain arbitrary decisions had to be made that necessarily affected the outcome of the final product. At all times the overriding consideration in translating these passages was accuracy of presentation, even when this meant the abandonment of a certain amount of poetic license and elegant style in the English language. The optimal outcome desired by the editor/translator of this volume is that the reader will feel confident that the words and concepts presented in English are close approximations to those of Abū Madyan himself. It is earnestly hoped that this goal has been adequately realized.

Texts and Translations

I

THE SUPPLICATION FOR FORGIVENESS

(*AL-ISTIGHFĀR*)[1]

IN THE Name of God I begin, with all my respect,
And all praise belongs to God, for my strength and maturity.

I seek the forgiveness of God, our Lord and Creator,
For all mankind and for the evils of my [soul's] turmoil.

I seek the forgiveness of God, motivator of the heavenly spheres in
the darkness,
For our failure to thank Him enough for His bounty.

I seek the forgiveness of God, the Savior of one who seeks His aid,
Whenever he suffers misfortune or calamity.

I seek the forgiveness of God, Forgiver of the sins of one
Who comes to Him broken, humiliated, and full of remorse.

I seek the forgiveness of God, Concealer of the faults of
The morally deficient, and their Savior from adversity.

I seek the forgiveness of God for my secret thoughts and overt acts,
For the fickleness of my heart and for the smile upon my lips.

I seek the forgiveness of God for my speech and my behavior,
For my evil character, type, and nature.

1. The text of this poetic supplication in *mīm* has been taken from MS Add. 7596 (folios 34–35) of the British Library, London. A second copy can be found in the Biblioteca de El Escorial, Spain, MS 1702 (folio 260r). Other copies of this work can be found in the Süleymaniye Library, Istanbul: Tirnovali No. 1376/9, folios 27–33 (1137/1724–25); Shehid Ali No. 2736/12, folios 48–54; Halet Effendi No. 800/20. A lithographed copy of this work was also published in Istanbul in the year 1265/1849. Another English translation of most of this text can be found in R. W. Austin, 'I Seek God's Pardon', *Studies in Comparative Religion*, vol. 7 (2), Spring 1973.

الاستغفارُ

بِسْمِ اللهِ ابْتِدائي في كُلِّ مُحْتَرَمِي	وَالحَمْدُ للهِ في أَيْدي ومُحْتَلَمِي
أَسْتَغْفِرُ اللهَ مَوْلانا وخالِقَنا	عَنِ العِبادِ [و] مِن سَوْآتِ مُلْتَطَمِي
أَسْتَغْفِرُ اللهَ مُجْرِي الفَلَكِ في الظُّلَمِ	مِنْ كُلِّ تَقْصِيرِنا بالشُّكْرِ للنِّعَمِ
أَسْتَغْفِرُ اللهَ مُنْجِي المستجيرِ به	إذا أَلَمَّ بهِ ضِيقٌ [أو] في اللَّمَمِ
أَسْتَغْفِرُ اللهَ غَفَّارَ الذُّنُوبِ لِمَنْ	بالانْكِسارِ أَتَى والذُّلِّ والنَّدَمِ
أَسْتَغْفِرُ اللهَ سَتَّارَ العُيُوبِ عَلَى	أَهْلِ العُيُوبِ ومُنَجِّيهِمْ مِنَ النِّقَمِ
أَسْتَغْفِرُ اللهَ مِن سِرِّي ومِن عَلَنِي	ومِن تَقَلُّبِ قَلْبِي وابْتِسامِ فَمِي
أَسْتَغْفِرُ اللهَ مِن نُطْقِي ومِن خُلُقِي	و[مِن] سَيِّآتِ شَأْنِي ومِن شَكْلِي ومِن شِيَمِي

I seek the forgiveness of God for my words and deeds,
For my vain strivings, and the exhaustion of my abilities.

I seek the forgiveness of God for my ignorance and transgressions,
For the greatest of my conscious sins, and the minor ones I have committed.

I seek the forgiveness of God for what my hand has wrought,
For my errors and [the sins] toward which I was inclined.[2]

I seek the forgiveness of God for that which my hand did not earn,
And for that which I earned upon attaining adulthood.

I seek the forgiveness of God for saying 'I' and 'with me',
[For saying] 'belonging to me' and 'mine', and for my suspicions and my
[limited] understanding.

I seek the forgiveness of God for that which I did not know,
For that which I knew, and for that which I wrote by pen.

I seek the forgiveness of God for my sleep, my lethargy,
And my wakefulness, and for that which has maintained me [in life].

I seek the forgiveness of God during the day, its night,
And, its morrow, before it is created from nothingness.

I seek the forgiveness of God for that which occurred during my youth,
And for my disagreements with the aged and mature.

I seek the forgiveness of God, as often as I have feared what He has
bestowed,
And [as often as] the clouds have rained on the plains and hills.

I seek the forgiveness of God, as often as the number of pilgrims, going
Toward lands characterized by purity and sanctity.[3]

I seek the forgiveness of God, as often as the breaking of dawn, and as often
As the doves coo their songs in the branches.

2. The literal translation of the final phrase in this verse is the idiomatic expression, '. . . for what my foot has reached.'

3. This verse refers to the *Ḥajj*, or pilgrimage made by Muslims to the sacred precincts of Mecca and Medina.

أَسْتَغْفِرُ اللهَ مِن قَوْلي ومِن عَمَلي ومِن مُجاهَدَتي جُهْدي ومِن سأَمي

أَسْتَغْفِرُ اللهَ مِن جَهْلي ومِن زَلَلي ومِن كَبائِرِ آثامي ومِن لَمَمي

أَسْتَغْفِرُ اللهَ مِمّا قَدْ جَنَتْهُ يَدي مِنَ الخَطايا ومِمّا قَدَّمَتْ قَدَمي

أَسْتَغْفِرُ اللهَ مِمّا لَمْ تَكُنْ كَسَبَتْ كَفّي وما اكْتَسَبَتْ في مَبْلَغِ الحُلُمِ

أَسْتَغْفِرُ اللهَ مِن قَوْلي «أَنَا» و«مَعي» و«لي» و«عِنْدي» ومِن ظَنّي ومِن فَهْمي

أَسْتَغْفِرُ اللهَ مِمّا لَسْتُ أَعْلَمُهُ وما عَلِمْتُ وما حَرَّفْتُ بالقَلَمِ

أَسْتَغْفِرُ اللهَ مِن نَوْمي ومِن سُباتي ويَقْظَتي وبِهِ ما عِشْتُ مُعْتَصَمي

أَسْتَغْفِرُ اللهَ في يَوْمٍ ولَيْلَتِهِ ومِنْ غَدٍ قَبْلَ أنْ يَبْدو مِنَ العَدَمِ

أَسْتَغْفِرُ اللهَ مِمّا كانَ في صِغَري مِنَ الخِلافِ لِعَصْرِ الشَّيْبِ والهَرَمِ

أَسْتَغْفِرُ اللهَ ما هِبْتُ أَمانِيَهُ وسَحَّتِ السُّحُبُ في السّاحاتِ الأُكُمِ

أَسْتَغْفِرُ اللهَ ما صارَ الحَجيجُ إلى مَعالِمٍ صُرِّفَتْ بالحِلِّ والحَرَمِ

أَسْتَغْفِرُ اللهَ ما لاحَ ضِياءٌ وما تَرَنَّمَ الوُرْقُ في الأَغْصانِ بالنَّغَمِ

I seek the forgiveness of God, as often as the number of letters [in the Qur'ān] and multiplicity of
Qur'anic verses and aphorisms recited during invocation.

I seek the forgiveness of God, as often as the number of riding animals,
Worlds beyond the horizons, and landmarks in the earth.

I seek the forgiveness of God, as often as the number of plants and
Sheep on the land and [the amount of] bounty in the sea.

I seek the forgiveness of God, as often as the number of heavenly bodies
Encompassed by knowledge, and for everything that is apparent and hidden.

I seek the forgiveness of God, as often as the number of [grains of] sand,
And the [amount of] rain that falls continuously on the earth.

I seek the forgiveness of God, as often as the number of created things—
Of human beings and *jinn*, of Arabs and non-Arabs.

I seek the forgiveness of God, as often as the number of thoughts in
The breasts of those endowed with trust, authority, and wisdom.

I seek the forgiveness of God—all majesty be to God, our Creator,
Creator of mankind and the One who brought us forth from nothingness.

I seek the forgiveness of God—all majesty be to God, Who provided for us
Prior to physical existence, and Who apportions all the shares [of worldly destiny].

I seek the forgiveness of God, Whose bounties are without number,
The All-Encompassing, the Most Excellent, [the One] noted for generosity.

I seek the forgiveness of God—all majesty be to God, Who gathers us in [at death],
The annihilator of centuries, and annihilator of all nations.

I seek the forgiveness of God—all majesty be to God, Who resurrects us
After death, and Who gives life to decaying bones.

أَسْتَغْفِرُ اللهَ تَعْدادَ الحُرُوفِ وما ... فِي الذِّكْرِ مِنْ آيِهِ تُتْلَى وِمِنْ حِكَمِ
أَسْتَغْفِرُ اللهَ تَعْدادَ الهَوامِّ وما ... فِي الأُفُقِ مِنْ عَالَمٍ والأَرْضِ مِنْ عَلَمِ
أَسْتَغْفِرُ اللهَ تَعْدادَ النَّباتِ وما ... فِي البَرِّ مِنْ غَنَمٍ والبَحْرِ مِنْ نَعَمِ
أَسْتَغْفِرُ اللهَ تَعْدادَ في ... صُدُورِ عِلْمٍ [و] مِنْ بادٍ ومُكْتَتِمِ
أَسْتَغْفِرُ اللهَ تَعْدادَ الرِّمالِ وما ... يَنْهَلُّ فِي عَالَمِ الدُّنْيا مِنَ الدِّيَمِ
أَسْتَغْفِرُ اللهَ تَعْدادَ الخَلائِقِ مِنْ ... إِنْسٍ وجِنٍّ ومِنْ عُرْبٍ ومِنْ عَجَمِ
أَسْتَغْفِرُ اللهَ تَعْدادَ الخَواطِرِ في ... صُدُورِ أَهْلِ التُّقَى والحُكْمِ والحِكَمِ
أَسْتَغْفِرُ اللهَ جَلَّ اللهُ خَالِقُنا ... بَارِي البَرَايَا ومُنْشِؤُنا مِنَ العَدَمِ
أَسْتَغْفِرُ اللهَ جَلَّ اللهُ رازِقُنا ... قَبْلَ المَوْجُودِ وقَدَّرَ سائِرَ القِسَمِ
أَسْتَغْفِرُ اللهَ لا تُحْصَى لَهُ نِعَمٌ ... المُجْمِلُ المُفَضِّلُ المَوْصُوفُ بالكَرَمِ
أَسْتَغْفِرُ اللهَ جَلَّ اللهُ قابِضُنا ... مُفْنِي القُرُونِ ومُفْنِي سائِرِ الأُمَمِ
أَسْتَغْفِرُ اللهَ جَلَّ اللهُ باعِثُنا ... بَعْدَ المَماتِ ومُحْيِي الأَعْظُمِ الرِّمَمِ

I seek the forgiveness of God, innumerable times,
As often as the number of known species and breaths of life.

I seek the forgiveness of God—on Him be praises without number,
[For] He causes Himself to be praised pre-eternally.

I seek the forgiveness of God, the Forgiver of sins Who, whenever
The slave disobeys, forgives him with indulgence and generosity.

So forgive me the greatest of my transgressions, and
[On] the Day of Judgment, when my feet are about to stumble.

Then may blessings be on the Chosen One from Muḍar,
The Best of Mankind, among those who weep or smile.[4]

And may his family and companions be preserved
By our Lord, along with all of [their] followers.

4. Abū Madyan's purpose in writing this verse is to invoke blessings on the Prophet Muḥammad as the best of all human creation, inclusive of every possibility.

أَسْتَغْفِرُ اللهَ أَضْعافاً مُضاعَفَةً   مِمَّا ذُكِرَتْ مِنَ الأَجْناسِ والنَّسَمِ

أَسْتَغْفِرُ اللهَ لا أُحْصِي عَلَيْهِ ثَنَى   أَثْنَى عَلَى نَفْسِهِ مِنْ قَبْلُ القِدَمِ

أَسْتَغْفِرُ اللهَ غَفَّارَ الذُّنُوبِ إِذَا   مَا العَبْدُ يَعْصَى عَفَا بِالحِلْمِ والكَرَمِ

وَاغْفِرْ لِي كَبائِرَ زَلَّاتِي وَ   يَوْمَ الحِسابِ إِذا ما زَلَّتْ قَدَمِي

ثُمَّ الصَّلاةُ عَلَى المُخْتارِ مِنْ مُضَرَ   خَيرِ البَرِيَّةِ مِنْ بادٍ وَمُبْتَسِمِ

والآلِ والصَّحْبِ والتَّسْلِيمُ   مِنْ رَبِّنا وَعَلَى الأَتْباعِ كُلِّهِمِ

II

THE BLESSED CREED

(*AL-ʿAQĪDA AL-MUBĀRAKA*)[1]

This is a blessed creed by the Perfect Shaykh Sīdī Abū Madyan, may God be pleased with him and make him a benefit to us:

ALL PRAISE belongs to God, who is free from limitation, from 'where' and 'how', and from time and place. [He is] the Speaker who speaks with eternal, never-ending speech—[speech that is] an attribute from among [the totality of] His attributes, coexistent with His essence, inseparable from Him [but] not dependent upon Him, and not incarnated in created things. He does not resemble created beings in form, nor can He be described by letters or sounds. The attributes of our Lord are independent from [anything on] earth or [in] the heavens.

Oh God, verily we affirm Your oneness but do not limit You, we believe in You but do not conceive of You in a specific form, we worship You but do not conceive of You as resembling anything. Furthermore, we believe that one who conceives of You as resembling what You have created will never know the difference between the Creator and creation.

'Say: "He is God the One; God the Incomparable; He begets not, nor is He begotten, and there is none like unto him".'[2]

Thus has God spoken truly—Whose essence has been sanctified from all evidence of contingency, Whose attributes have been freed from all resemblance to the attributes of corporeal bodies, and Whose signs testify to His oneness. He is the First for Whose firstness there is no beginning, the Last for Whose everlastingness there is no end, the Apparent in Whom there is no doubt, and the Hidden for Whom there is no likeness. He is the Living who never dies or is annihilated; the All-Potent who is neither unable nor anxious; the Possessor of Will who both leads astray and guides, who impoverishes and enriches; the All-Hearing who hears one's innermost secrets and what is hidden; the All-Seeing who perceives an ant crawling below [the surface of the soil]; the All-Knowing who is not misguided and never forgets.

1. The Arabic text of this creed was taken from an undated manuscript, number 21,553 (folios 50v–51r), of the Biblioteca Nacional, Madrid. Works such as these are found quite commonly in manuscript collections throughout the western Maghrib. They were often written by prominent Sufis, who used them as public statements of doctrinal orthodoxy whenever their teachings were opposed by the state or condemned by exoteric religious scholars.

2. Qur'ān, CXII (*Ikhlāṣ*).

العَقيدَةُ المُبارَكَة

هذه عَقيــدَةٌ مُباركَةٌ للشَّيْخ الكامِل سَيّدي أبي مَدْيَن رَضيَ اللهُ تعالى عنهُ ونَفَعَنا به:

الحَمْد للهِ الذي تنزَّه عن الحدّ والأين والكَيْف والزّمان والمكان. المُتَكلِّم بكلامٍ قَديمٍ أزَلِيّ. صِفَةٌ مِن صِفاتِه قائمٌ بذاتِه لا مُنْفَصِلٌ عنه ولا عائدٌ إليه [و] لا يحلُّ في المحدَثاتِ ولا يجُانسُ المَخْلوقاتِ ولا يوصَفُ بالحُروفِ والأَصْواتِ. تنزَّهَتْ صفاتُ ربّنا عن الأَرْض والسَّموات.

اللّهُمَّ إنّا نوحّدُكَ ولا نحُدُّكَ ونؤمِنُ بكَ ولا نُكَيِّفُكَ ونَعْبُدُكَ ولا نشَبّهُكَ. ونَعْتَقِدُ أنَّ مَن شبَّهكَ بخَلْقكَ لَمْ يعْرفْ الخالِقَ مِن المَخْلوقِ.

﴿ قُلْ هو اللهُ أَحَدٌ اللهُ الصَّمَدُ لَمْ يَلِدْ ولَمْ يولَدْ ولَمْ يكُنْ لَهُ كفُواً أحد ﴾.

صدَقَ اللهُ الذي تقدَّسَتْ عَن سمَةِ الحُدُوثِ ذاتُهُ وتنزَّهَتْ عن التَّشْبيهِ بصِفَةِ الجُثَثِ صِفاتُهُ وشَهِدَتْ بوحْدانِيّتِهِ آياتُهُ. الأوَّلُ الذي لا بدايَةَ لأوَّليّتِه الآخِرُ الذي لا نِهايَةَ لأبديّتِهِ، الظّاهِرُ الذي لا شَكَّ فيهِ، الباطِنُ الذي لَيسَ لَهُ شَبيهٌ. الحَيُّ الذي لا يموتُ ولا يفْنى، القادِرُ الذي لا يَعْجز ولا يعْنى، المُريدُ الذي أضَلَّ وهَدَى وأفْقَرَ وأَغْنَى، السَّميعُ الذي يَسْمَعُ السِّرَّ والأخفى، البَصيرُ الذي يُدْرِكُ دَبيبَ النَّمْلِ على السُّفْلَى، العالِمُ الذي لا يَضِلُّ ولا يَنْسَى.

He is the Speaker whose speech does not resemble that of Moses, [yet] He spoke to Moses with His eternal speech. He is far removed from [the limitations of] posteriority and anteriority. He does not call attention to Himself by means of a voice, He is not heard by means of a call, and He is not comprehended by means of letters, [for] all letters, voices, and calls are created with an end and a beginning.

May our Lord be the Exalted and Magnified, the Blessed and Glorified! To Him belong all grandeur and majesty, all power and high rank—His are the most beautiful names and the most exalted attributes.

His life has no beginning, for the beginning of a thing is preceded by nothingness. His power has no end, for the end of a thing is affected by particularity. His will is not created, for created things are beset by contradiction. His hearing is not by means of a physical extremity, for a physical extremity can be torn off. His sight is not by means of the pupil of the eye, for the pupil of the eye can be split open. His knowledge is not by means of acquisition, for acquired knowledge is known by investigation and proof. Nor is [His knowledge] necessary, for that which is necessary is necessitated by [pre-existent] will and inclination. His speech is without a voice, for voices come into and go out of existence; nor is it by means of a letter, for letters are followed and preceded [by prior and subsequent letters].

Exalted is our Lord over any likeness to His creation, [and exalted is He over] all His creatures [and] beyond physical existence by virtue of His essential Truth. Indeed, He is the Eternal, the Everlasting, the Unceasing, the Never-Ending—Who has no form to His essence, no physical arm to His hand, no defect in His countenance, and for Whom there is neither posterity nor anteriority.

He is without physical substance, for a substance is known by [its] partiality. He is without width, for width is characterized by the impossibility of endlessness. He is without body, for a body is enclosed within sides. He is the Creator of bodies and souls;

[هو] المتَكَلّمُ الذي لا يُشْبِهُ كلامُهُ كلامَ مُوسَى [عليه السَّلام] . كَلَّمَ مُوسَى بكلامِهِ القَديم . [هو] المنزّهُ عن التّأْخِيرِ والتّقْديم . لا بصَوْتٍ يُقْرِعُ ولا بنداء يُسْمَعُ ولا بِحرُوفٍ تُرْجَعُ . كلُّ الحُرُوفِ والأَصْواتِ والنّداء مُحْدَثَةٌ بالنّهايَةِ والابتِداء .

جَلَّ رَبُّنا وعلا وتَبارَكَ وتعالى . لهُ العَظَمَةُ والكِبرياءُ والقُدْرَةُ والسَّناءُ ولهُ الأَسماءُ الحُسْنى والصِّفاتُ العُلْيا .

حَياتُهُ لَيْسَتْ لها بِدايَةٌ فالبدايَةُ بالعَدَمِ مَسْبُوقَةٌ . قُدْرَتُهُ ليستْ لها نِهايةٌ فالنّهايَةُ بالتّخْصِيصِ مَلْحُوقَةٌ . إرادَتُهُ ليستْ بحادِثَةٍ فالحوادِثُ بالأَضْدادِ مَطْرُوقَةٌ . سَمْعُهُ ليسَ بِجارِحَةٍ فالجارِحَةُ مَخْرُوقَةٌ . بَصَرُهُ ليسَ بِحَدَقَةٍ فالحَدَقَةُ مَشْقُوقَةٌ . عِلْمُهُ ليسَ بكَسْبِيٍّ فالكَسْبِيُّ بالتّأَمُّلِ والاسْتِدْلالِ يُعْلَمُ ولا بضَرُورِيٍّ فالضَّرُورِيُّ على الإرادةِ والانْحِرافِ يُلْزَمُ . كلامُهُ لَيْسَ بصَوْتٍ فالأَصْواتُ تُوجَدُ وتُعْدَمُ ولا بحَرْفٍ فالحُرُوفُ تُؤَخَّرُ وتُقَدَّمُ .

جَلَّ رَبُّنا عن التَّشْبيهِ بخَلْقِهِ و[عن] كُلِّ خَلْقِهِ [و] عن القيامِ بكُنْهِ حَقِّهِ . بَلْ هو القَدِيمُ الأَزَلِي الدّائِمُ الأَبَدِيُّ الذي ليس لِذاتِهِ قَدٌّ ولا لِيَدِهِ زَنْدٌ ولا لِوَجْهِهِ خَلَلٌ ولا له قَبْلُ ولا بَعْدُ .

ليسَ بِجَوْهَرٍ فالجَوْهَرُ بالتَّحَيُّزِ مَعْرُوفٌ ولا بعَرَضٍ فالعرضُ باسْتِحالَةِ البَقَاءِ مَوْصُوفٌ ولا بجِسْمٍ فالجِسْمُ بالجِهَةِ مَحْفُوفٌ . فهو خالِقُ الأَجْسامِ والنّفُوسِ

the Provider for the prosperous and the wretched; the Apportioner of happiness and misfortune; the Designer of the spheres and suns [in the heavens].

He is God; there is no deity but Him—the King, the Most Holy, firmly established on the Throne—without fixedness or physical sitting. Before Him the Throne had no permanence, no stability or constancy in physical space. The Throne possesses limitation and physical measure, but the Lord is far removed from the perception of sight. The Throne can be specified by mental images and can be characterized by width and length, yet [God] is beyond all of this. He it is who never changes and is never removed. The Throne, in itself, implies 'place' and possesses sides and supports. [Yet] it belonged to Him and was without place—now He presides over that which formerly was. It has no bottom that might diminish Him, no top that might shade Him, no sides that might confine Him, no back that might support Him, no front that might limit him. [God] is Exalted beyond [the limitations of] abstraction, fixedness, specification, form, resemblance, or likeness.

'Nothing is like unto Him, and He is the All-Hearing, the All-Seeing.'[3]

3. Ibid., XLII (*ash-Shūrā*), 11.

وَرازِقُ أَهْلِ الجُودِ والبُؤْسِ ومُقَدِّرُ السُّعُودِ والنُّحُوسِ ومُدَبِّرُ الأَفْلاكِ والشُّمُوسِ .

هو اللهُ لا إلَهَ هو المَلِكُ القُدُّوسُ على العَرْشِ اسْتَوى مِن غيرِ تَمَكُّنٍ ولا جُلُوسٍ .

لا العَرْشُ له مِن قَبْلِهِ القَرارُ ولا التَّمَكُّنُ له مِن جِهَةٍ ولا الاسْتِقْرارُ . العَرْشُ له حَدٌّ ومِقْدارٌ

والرَّبُّ لا تُدْرِكُهُ الأَبْصارُ . العَرْشُ تُكَيِّفُهُ خَواطِرُ العُقُولِ وتَصِفُهُ بالعَرْضِ والطُّولِ وهو

مع ذلكَ مَحْمُولٌ . و [هو] الذي لا يَحُولُ ولا يَزُولُ . العَرْشُ بنفسِهِ هو المَكانُ وله

جَوانِبُ وأَرْكانٌ . وكانَ إليهِ ولا مَكانَ وهو الآنَ على ما عليهِ كانَ . ليس له تَحْتَ

فيُقِلَّهُ ولا فَوْقُ فيُظِلَّهُ ولا جَوانِبُ فتَعْدِلَهُ ولا خَلْفٌ فيُسْنِدَهُ ولا أَمامٌ فيَحُدَّهُ . جَلَّ

عن التَّجْرِيدِ والتَّقْرِيرِ والتَّكْيِيفِ والتَّصْوِيرِ والتَّشْبِيهِ والنَّظِيرِ .

﴿ لَيْسَ كَمِثْلِهِ شَيْءٌ وهو السَّمِيعُ البَصِيرُ ﴾ .

III

BIDĀYAT AL-MURĪD[1]

(Basic Principles of the Sufi Path)

HE SAID (may God be pleased with him): The primary requirement for the aspirant is companionship with a practicing spiritual master who is knowledgeable, fears God, is conversant with both the exoteric and the esoteric sciences, and is aware of the Transcendent Truth and Reality. [This shaykh] must be one who follows [the Sunna], is not heterodox in his religious practices, is patient with his student, who takes personal charge of [his student's] spiritual upbringing, is indulgent with his mistakes, and does not charge him with the responsibility of making invocations unless he knows that [his student] will be constant in their recitation. [The aspirant to the Sufi way] finds a sweetness in his heart because of [his shaykh] and takes pleasure in him through his words, for [the shaykh] makes his [student's] heart his vocation and behaves with him according to the words of the Messenger of God (may God bless and preserve him): 'The work most loved by God is that done regularly, even if it be infrequently.'[2]

It is necessary for the shaykh to teach his student the requirements of prayer and the ways of performing them as well as what [variations] are allowed and forbidden while performing them.

1. This edited translation was made primarily from MS 731Q (folios 328–335) of the Bibliothèque Générale, Rabat, Morocco. Cross-checking of the text was done with the aid of a partially complete private manuscript, dated 1269/1852–53, provided by Mr. Muṣṭafā an-Nājī of Rabat, Morocco. Bracketed passages and phrases in the Arabic text represent additions found in the an-Nājī copy. These correspond to added passages in parentheses in the English translation. Bracketed words and phrases in the English translation represent additions made by the editor/translator. The Moroccan historian Mohamed B. A. Benchekroun (*La Vie intellectuelle marocaine sous les Mérinides et les Wattāsides* [Rabat: 1974], p. 440) attributes this work, based on a copy he examined at Zāwiya al-Ḥamzawiyya (MS 278), to Abū Madyan's Moroccan 'successor,' Abū Muḥammad Ṣāliḥ ibn Yanṣāren al-Māgirī (d. 631/1234). Although Abū Mūḥammad Ṣāliḥ's name also appears at the head of the Rabat MS of *Bidāyat al-murīd* (whereas Abū Madyan's name appears on the an-Nājī copy), the style of this manuscript is considerably different from that of *Risāla fi't-taṣawwuf* (Bibliothèque Générale MS 305Q)—another, undisputed work by Abū Muḥammad Ṣālih, in which the name of Abū Madyan is not mentioned. Barring further categorical evidence as to the authorship of the present work, one must continue to assume that it constitutes a faithful representation of the teachings of Abū Madyan.

2. al-Bukhārī, *Kitāb ar-riqāq* (18). The hadith quotations in this text were verified by using A. J. Wensinck, *Concordance et indices de la tradition musulmane* (Istanbul: Cagri Yayinlari, 1986), an authorized reprint of the E. J. Brill edition of 1936. Further references will list author of hadith collection, book, and section number, according to the usage in Wensinck.

بِدَايَةُ الْمُرِيد

قال رضي الله عنه : أوَّلُ مَا يَجِبُ عَلَى المُرِيدِ صُحْبَةُ شَيْخٍ عالِمٍ عامِلٍ تقيِّ عالِمٍ بعِلْمِ الظَّاهِرِ والباطِنِ وعالِمٍ بالحَقِّ والحَقِيقَةِ. ويَكُونُ مُتَّبِعاً غيرَ مُبْتَدِعٍ صَبُوراً على تِلْمِيذِهِ مُرَبِّياً لهُ ومُتَغافِلاً عَن زَلاّتِهِ ولا يُكَلِّفُهُ مِن الأَوْرَادِ إلاّ ما يَعْلَمُ أَنَّهُ يَدُومُ عليهِ ويَجِدُ بهِ حَلاوةً في قلْبِهِ ويَتَلَذَّذ بهِ لِقولِهِ ويَحَرّف قلْبَهُ ويَسْلُكُ بهِ لِقولِ رَسُولِ اللهِ ﷺ : «أحَبُّ الأَعْمالِ إلى اللهِ أدْوَمُها وإنْ قلّتْ».

ويَجِبُ على الشّيخِ أنْ يُعَلِّمَ تِلْمِيذَهُ فَرائِضَ الصَّلاةِ وسُنَنَها وما يُجَزّء مِنها وما لا يُجَزَّء

55

Next [the shaykh] must teach him to recite the opening chapter of the Qur'ān if he is unfamiliar with it. He must then teach [his student] what is allowed and what is forbidden, what is agreed upon and what is a matter of doubt. He must command him to take precautions against falling into error by abolishing hypocrisy, by requiring retreat from human society, by purifying the lower soul, by the avoidance of gazing at what is forbidden, by keeping oneself chaste, by the maintenance of constant invocation and reflection, by acting only when aroused by necessity, by asceticism in the severing of worldly attachments, and by the total rejection of the material world.

Among the praiseworthy acts and [signs of] obedience toward God that the shaykh teaches his student are his injunction to fast the months of Rajab and Shaᶜbān, the day of ᶜAshūrā', and three days out of every month. He also commands [his student] to observe the fast of [the Prophet] David (may peace be upon him), who used to fast one day and eat the next.[3] This is the most preferable of fasts for one who adheres to it. After that [the shaykh] commands him to [seek] 'intimate union' (*wiṣāl*) with God, for intimate union with God is the fruit of piety.[4]

Verily the way of the People of Reality is hunger and then hunger. Al-Junayd[5] (may God have mercy upon him) was asked the meaning of piety and replied, 'Hunger.' [This is because] one who passes the night hungry and obedient toward God passes the night upright [as if in prayer], even if he were asleep, for hunger comes from fear.

Shaykh Abū Madyan (may God be pleased with him) said: 'Oh People of Will,[6] practice hunger, the fast of intimate union, solitude, and remembrance, for by [the practice of hunger] you will attain what you desire, you will see how the gushing springs of wisdom will issue forth from your hearts and your tongues, and by means of it you will arrive at your Lord.'

3. On the fasts mentioned in this passage, including the 'Fast of David,' see al-Bukhārī, *Kitāb aṣ-ṣawm* (56).

4. The reference here is to the fast of intimate union (*ṣawm al-wiṣāl*) mentioned in the Introduction (pp. 31–32), above.

5. Abu'l-Qāsim al-Junayd ibn Muḥammad al-Khazzāz of Baghdad (d. 298/910) is known to posterity as one of the greatest Sufis of all time and is widely regarded in the Maghrib as the founder of the 'sober', *sharᶜī* school of mysticism with which Abū Madyan identified himself. The best account of al-Junayd's life and works in English can be found in Ali Hassan Abdel-Kader, *The Life, Personality and Writings of Al-Junayd* (London: Luzac & Company, Ltd., 1976).

6. The use of the term, 'People of Will' (*ahl al-irāda*) in this passage indicates that Abū Madyan may have assimilated the teachings of the Almerían Sufi Abu'l-ᶜAbbās ibn al-ᶜArīf from his instructor of hadith, Abu'l-Ḥasan ᶜAlī ibn Ghālib al-Qurashī. Ibn al-ᶜArīf used the term, 'Way of the Will' (*ṭarīq al-irāda*), as a name for his spiritual method. See Ibn al-ᶜArīf, *Miftāḥ as-saᶜāda wa taḥqīq ṭarīq al-irāda*, cited in the Introduction (n. 45, and pp. 5, 22) above.

ويجُوّدَهُ أُمَّ القرآنِ إِنْ كَانَ غَيرَ عَارِفٍ بِهَا . ويُعَلِّمَهُ الحَلالَ والحَرامَ والارْتِفَاعَ عَنِ الشُّبُهات ويأْمُرَهُ بِالاحْتِيَاطِ عَنِ إدْلالِه بِسُقُوطِ الرّياءِ ولزُومِ الخَلْوةِ وطُهرِ النَّفسِ وغضِّ البَصَرِ عَنِ المَحارمِ وحفْظِ الفَرْجِ والدَّوامِ على الذِّكرِ والاعْتِبارِ والاقْتِضاءِ والزُّهْدِ وقطْعِ العَلائِقِ ورفْضِ الدُّنْيا . ومِمَّا يُعَلِّمُ الشيخُ لِتِلميذِه مِنَ الأعْمالِ المَحمودةِ والطَّاعاتِ لله أنْ يأْمُرَهُ بِصيامِ رَجَبَ وشعْبانَ ويوْمِ عاشُوراءَ وثَلاثةِ أيامٍ مِن كُلِّ شَهرٍ ويأْمُرَهُ بِصيامِ داوُودَ عليه السَّلامُ وكانَ داوُودُ عليه السلامُ يصُومُ يوماً ويَفطِرُ يوماً وهو أفْضَلُ الصّيامِ لِمن دَامَ عليه . ويأْمُرَهُ بَعْدَ ذلكَ بالوصالِ فإنَّ الوصالَ ثمرَةُ العبادةِ .

فإنَّ الطَّريقَ عِندَ أهلِ الحقيقةِ الجُوعُ ثُمَّ الجُوعُ . وسُئِلَ الجُنيْدُ رحمَهُ اللهُ عنِ العبادةِ فقال : «الجُوعُ» . ومَن باتَ جائِعًا مُطِيعًا للهِ باتَ قائِمًا ولوْ كَانَ نائِمًا لأنَّ الجُوعَ لِسَبَبِ الخَوفِ .

قال الشَّيخُ أبو مَدينَ رضي الله عنه : «يا أهْلَ الإرادَةِ عَلَيكُمْ بالجُوعِ والوصالِ والخَلْوةِ والذِّكرِ وبه تصِلُونَ إلى مطْلُوبِكُمْ وتُبصِرُونَ كيْفَ تَخرُجُ ماينابيعُ الحِكْمةِ مِن قلُوبِكُمْ وألْسِنتِكُمْ وبه تصِلُونَ إلى ربِّكُمْ» .

He who is hungry arrives and he who is satiated is cut off. He who remembers God [is moved] to meditate, while he who forgets is himself forgotten. This is because hunger comprises ten qualities: the purification of the lower soul from lusts and doubts; remembrance; meditation; the shedding of blameworthy attributes and the acquisition of those that are praiseworthy; the emulation of spiritual masters who have gone before, as well as of the Companions of the Prophet and those who succeeded them among the first generations of the pious; preoccupation with suppressing the lower soul; and preventing [the lower soul] from following its lusts.

Have you not observed [the case of] Adam (may peace be upon him)? Iblīs could not prevail over him except by means of his lust.

Thus, hunger is the vehicle of the worshippers, the way of the pious, the method of the gnostics, the key of those who are guided, and the goal of those who have arrived at the highest [level] of *ᶜIlliyyīn*.[7] Said Shaykh Abū Madyan (may God have mercy upon him): 'I have examined the writings of the Prophets, the pious, the Companions [of the Prophet and their] Successors, and the scholars of past generations; yet I have not found anything that causes attainment to God Most High without [the addition of] hunger. [This is because] one who is hungry becomes humble, one who is humble begs, and the one who begs attains. So hold fast to hunger, my brother, and practice it constantly, for by means of it you will attain what you desire and will arrive at that for which you hope.'

Ibrāhīm ibn Adham[8] (may God be pleased with him) was asked about union with God Most High, and said: 'Hunger and asceticism are one. He who is hungry abstains and he who abstains arrives; he who arrives attains (and he who attains remains).'

7. Qur'ān, LXXXIII (*al-Muṭafifīn*), 18–21. *ᶜIlliyyīn* literally means 'the High Places', but here it is used as a contrasting term for *Sijjīn* (ibid., verses 8–9). Inasmuch as this latter term is defined in the Qur'ān as being a register in which evil deeds are inscribed until the Day of Judgment, *ᶜIlliyyīn* can be understood as referring to a similar register, in which are inscribed the deeds of the righteous.

8. Abū Isḥāq Ibrāhīm ibn Adham (d. 165/782) was reputed to be a prince of the northeastern Iranian city of Balkh who renounced his kingdom for a life of complete asceticism. He is considered to be one of the earliest and most influential Sufis and stood for later generations of ascetics as a paradigm for the practice of worldly renunciation. See, A. J. Arberry, *Muslim Saints and Mystics* (London: Routledge and Kegan Paul, 1979), pp. 62–79.

مَنْ جاعَ وصلَ ومَن شبِعَ انقطَعَ ومَن ذكَرَ تفكَّرَ ومَن غفَلَ غُفِلَ عَنْهُ. لأنَّ في الجوعِ عَشرةَ خِصالٍ: طهارةُ النَّفْسِ عن الشَّهَواتِ والشُّبُهاتِ والذِّكْرُ والتَّفكُّرُ والانفِصالُ عن الصِّفاتِ المَذْمومَةِ إلى الصِّفاتِ المحْمُودةِ والاقْتِداءُ بالمَشايِخِ المُتَقَدِّمينَ والصَّحابَةِ والتَّابعِينَ مِن أَهْلِ السَّلَفِ الصَّالِحِ والاشْتِغالُ بمُجاهَدَةِ النَّفْسِ وامْتِناعِها عَنِ الشَّهَواتِ. أَلا تَنْظُرُ إلى آدمَ عليه السَّلام، ما انْتَصرَ عليه إبْليسُ إلاَّ بسَبَبِ شَهْوَتِه.

والجوعُ مَطِيَّةُ العابدينَ وطريقُ الصَّالِحينَ ومِنْهاجُ العارِفينَ ومِفْتاحُ المُهْتَدِينَ ونِهايَةُ الواصِلينَ إلى أَعْلَى العِلِّيِّينَ.

قالَ الشَّيخ أَبو مَدْيَنْ رحمه الله: «نظَرْتُ في كُتُبِ الأَنْبِياءِ والصَّالحينَ والصَّحابَةِ والتَّابعينَ والعُلماءِ الماضِيِّينَ مِنَ المُتقدِّمينَ فما وَجدْتُ شيْئاً يُتوصَّلُ به إلى اللهِ تعالى إلاَّ بالجوعِ. فمَنْ جاعَ تواضَعَ ومَن تواضَعَ تضرَّعَ ومَن تضرَّعَ بلَغ. فعليكَ يا أَخِي بالجوعِ والدوامِ عليه فبِهِ تنالُ ما تريدُ وبه تصِلُ إلى ما تتأَمَّلُ».

وقد سُئِلَ إبْراهِيمُ بْنُ أَدْهَم رضي الله عنه عن الوُصُولِ إلى اللهِ تعالى فقال: «الجوعُ والزُّهْدُ واحِدٌ. فمَنْ جاعَ زهَدَ ومَن زهَدَ وَصلَ ومَن وَصلَ بلَغ [ومَن بلَغ سكَنَ]».

Someone said to Rābiᶜa al-ᶜAdawiyya[9] (may God be pleased with her): 'By what is the Intimate united to God Most High?' 'By hunger,' she replied. So she was asked, 'Then what is hunger?' She replied: 'Hunger is the act of keeping the lower soul away from [sensual] delights. He who keeps his lower soul away from worldly delights attains his goal in the Hereafter.'

God Most High said to Moses the son of ᶜImrān: 'Fasting is for My sake and I bestow rewards for it'.[10]

The Messenger of God (may God bless and preserve him) said: 'The supplication of one who fasts is answered'.[11] This [tradition] is evidence of the excellence of hunger, so accustom your carnal souls to it, for it is the root of piety as well as its foundation, method, and guiding light. By hunger he who arrives arrives, he who obtains obtains, and he who attains attains.

Someone said to Bahlūl al-Majnūn (the Possessed): 'Inform us, by what means does one who arrives arrive?' 'By hunger,' he replied. So he was asked: 'By what means did you arrive at this station? For we have seen you flying through the air, walking upon the water, eating from whatever is at hand, and taking gold and silver from the air. [We have seen] lions wag their tails [in greeting] for you, [we have seen you] speak subtleties of wisdom and openly tell the secrets of men.' [Bahlūl] said: 'All of that is due to hunger, asceticism, and irrevocably divorcing oneself from the material world.'[12]

Someone said to al-Fuḍayl ibn ᶜIyāḍ (may God be pleased with him): 'By what means did you arrive at this noble station?' 'By hunger,' he said, 'and asceticism, humility, abandonment of the vain hopes of the lower soul, the [maintenance of] constant union with God, the obligation of spiritual retreat, and by fearing God Most High.'[13]

9. Rābiᶜa bint Ismāᶜīl al-ᶜAdawiyya (d. 135/752 or 185/801) was one of the most revered saints of the city of Basra in Iraq. Sold into slavery as a child, she eventually became a noted ascetic and is popularly credited with being the first to conceptualize the Sufi path of love. Ibid., pp. 39–51. See also, Margaret Smith, *Rabi'a the Mystic* (San Francisco: The Rainbow Bridge, 1977).

10. al-Bukhārī, *Kitāb aṣ-ṣawm* (2). This *ḥadīth qudsī* (non-Qur'anic Divine inspiration) comes directly from the Prophet Muḥammad and was not transmitted via Moses, as is claimed in the text.

11. On the supplication of one who fasts see Ibn Ḥanbal (2), 477 and Ibn Mājja, *Kitāb aṣ-ṣiyām* (48). The exact wording of this hadith could not be found in Wensinck.

12. This phrase, which can be translated literally as 'thrice divorcing oneself from the world', refers to the stricture in Islamic law that prevents a couple from remarrying if they have been divorced from each other a total of three times. The intended meaning of this passage, of course, is that one must cut himself off from all attachments to the material world in such a way that he never feels the urge to return to it. The phrase appears to have been used first by ᶜUtba al-Ghulām. See Farīḍ ad-Dīn ᶜAṭṭār, *Tadhkirat al-awliyā'* (Tehran: Intishārāt Ravār, 1364/1945), p. 70.

13. Al-Fuḍayl ibn ᶜIyāḍ b. Masᶜūd b. Bishr at-Tamīmī (d. 187/803) is said to have been born in the city of Samarqand in the present Republic of Uzbekistan. Originally a thief, he turned to asceticism and the practice of altruism and became known as a famous transmitter of Sufi hadith. See Arberry, *Muslim Saints and Mystics*, pp. 52–61. For an account of his sayings and teachings see Abū ᶜAbd ar-Raḥmān as-Sulamī (d. 412/1021-22), *Kitāb ṭabaqāt aṣ-ṣūfiyya* (Cairo: Dār al-Kitāb al ᶜArabī, 1372/1953), pp. 8–14.

وقيلَ لرابعةَ العَدَويَّةِ رضيَ اللهُ عنها : «بأيِّ شيءٍ يَصِلُ الواصِلُ إلى اللهِ تعالى»؟ فقالت : «بالجوعِ» . فقيلَ لها : «وما الجوعُ»؟ فقالت : «الجوعُ تنزيهُ النفسِ عن اللذّاتِ . فمَنْ نزَّهَ نفسَهُ عن اللذّاتِ في الدُّنيا نال مَقْصودَهُ في الآخِرَةِ» .

قال اللهُ تعالى لِموسى بْنِ عِمْرانَ : (الصَّوْمُ لي وأنا أجْزي به) . وقال رسول اللهِ ﷺ : «دَعْوَةُ الصّائِمِ مُسْتَجابَةٌ» .

فهذا دَليلٌ على فضْلِ الجوعِ فعوِّدُوا أنْفُسَكُم به فإنَّهُ أصْلُ العِبادَةِ وأَساسُها ومِنْهاجُها ومَنارُها . وبالجوعِ وصَلَ مَن وصَلَ ونالَ مَن نالَ وبلغَ مَن بلَغَ .

وقيلَ لِبَهْلُولَ المجنون : «أخْبِرْنا بماذا وَصَلَ مَن وصَلَ» . فقال «بالجوعِ» . فقيل له «بماذا وَصَلْتَ إلى هذا المَقام؟ رأيناكَ تطيرُ في الهواءِ وتَمْشِي على الماءِ وتأْكُلُ مِن الكَوْنِ وتَخطَفُ مِن الهواءِ الذَّهَبَ والفِضَّةَ وتُبَصْبِصُ لكَ السِّباعُ بأَذْنابها وتَنْطِقُ بالحِكْمَةِ وتَتَكَلَّمُ بأَسْرارِ الخَلْقِ» . قال : «ذلك بالجوعِ والزُّهدِ وتَطْليقِ الدُّنيا ثلاثًا» .

وقيل للفضَيْلِ بْنِ عِياضٍ رضي الله عنه : «بماذا وَصَلْتَ إلى هذا المقامِ الكَريم»؟ فقال : «بالجوعِ والزُّهدِ والتَّواضُعِ وتَرْكِ حُظُوظِ النَّفسِ والدَّوامِ على الوِصالِ ولُزُومِ الخَلْوةِ والخَوْفِ مِن اللهِ تعالى» .

Someone said to ᶜUtba al-Ghulām (the Slave)[14]: 'What is the nature of the hunger that unites [man] to God Most High?' 'Fasting,' he replied, 'and its constant practice.'

Said Shaykh Abū Madyan: 'True spiritual inclination is only made correct for the aspirant by lowering the gaze [out of modesty]; preserving one's chastity; avoiding that which is forbidden; abandoning vanity, concern with one's reputation, and lusts; constantly maintaining prayer in the mosque; leaving aside that which does not concern you; obliging retreat from mankind; and practicing asceticism in regard to the material world.'

He also said: 'He who goes to bed with a full stomach will spend his nights ranting and raving [with nightmares and hallucinations]. This is an act of heresy in the Way and is something created [by man], not actualized [through God].'

The first stage of spiritual aspiration consists of asceticism, hunger, the practice of invocation, constant obedience [toward God], and the companionship of a practicing shaykh who is ascetic, a follower [of the Sunna], not heterodox in practice, intelligent, conversant with the exoteric and esoteric sciences, knowledgeable of Transcendent Reality and the Way, and who opposes the lusts of the lower soul.

The eminent scholar of his age, the Imam Abū Ḥāmid al-Ghazālī (may God be pleased with him) forbade companionship with a spiritual master who is desirous of the material world, saying, 'His heart is veiled by heedlessness from its natural vocation.'

The Messenger of God (may God bless and preserve him) said: 'Love for the material world is the source of every error and affliction; for he who loves it forgets the way of the Hereafter.'[15]

God the Almighty has said: 'God did not create two hearts in a man's body.'[16]

14. ᶜUtba ibn Abān al-Ghulām was a repentant ascetic who was supposedly converted to the Sufi way by al-Ḥasan al-Baṣrī (d. 110/728). He died young and was martyred on the field of battle fighting against the Byzantines. On his life and sayings see ᶜAṭṭār, *Tadhkirat al-awliyā'*, pp. 69–71. See also, Abū Nuᶜaym Aḥmad ibn ᶜAbdallāh al-Iṣfahānī (d. 430/1038–39), *Ḥilyat al-awliyā' wa ṭabaqāt al-aṣfiyā'* (Cairo: Maktabat al-Khanānjī, 1932) (6), pp. 226–38.

15. This hadith cannot be identified in Wensinck as coming from the major collections of Prophetic tradition. It can, however, be found in Jalāl ad-Dīn as-Suyūṭī (d. 911/1505), *Jāmiᶜ al-aḥādīth*, ᶜAbbās Aḥmad Ṣaqr and Aḥmad ᶜAbd al-Jawād eds. (Damascus: Muḥammad Hāshim al-Kutbī, n.d.) (3), p. 747. Although the authenticity of this hadith is thus open to question, it was also transmitted via al-Bayhaqī [*Shuᶜab al-īmān*] and ad-Daylamī [*Firdaws al-akbar*].

16. Qur'ān, XXXIII (*al-Aḥzāb*), 4.

وقيل لعُتْبَةَ الغُلامِ: «ما صِفةُ الجوعِ الذي يُتَوَصَّلُ به إلى الله تعالى»؟

قال: «الصّيامُ والدّوامُ عليه».

وقال الشَّيخ أبو مَدْيَن: ولا تصِحُّ للمُريدِ حقيقةُ الإرادةِ إلا ببغضّ البَصرِ وحِفْظِ الفَرَجِ وتَرْكِ الحَرامِ والخُروجِ مِن الرّياءِ والسُّمْعَةِ والشَّهواتِ والدَّوامِ على الصَّلواتِ في الجماعَةِ وتركِ ما لا يَعْنِي ولزومِ الخلوةِ عن النّاسِ والزُّهدِ في الدُّنيا.

وقال أيضًا رحمه الله تعالى: ومَن باتَ شَبْعانًا فذلك تَهْدِيرٌ وهَذَيانٌ وزَنْدَقَةٌ في الطَّريقِ. وهي مَخلُوقَةٌ غيرُ مُحَقَّقَةٍ.

فأوَّلُ الإرادةِ زُهْدٌ وجوعٌ وأَوْرادٌ والدَّوامُ على الطَّاعَةِ وصُحْبَةُ شَيخٍ عامِلٍ زاهِدٍ مُتَّبِعٍ غيرِ مُبْتَدِعٍ عاقلٍ عارفٍ عالِمٍ بعِلمِ الظّاهِرِ والباطِنِ والحَقيقَةِ والطَّريقةِ مُخالِفٍ لهوى النفسِ. وقد نهى الإمامُ عالِمُ زَمَنِهِ أبو حامِدٍ الغزالي [رضي الله عنه] عن صُحْبَةِ شَيخٍ راغِبٍ في الدُّنيا فقال: «يُحجبُ قَلْبُهُ عن الفِطْرَةِ بالغفلةِ».

وقال رسول الله ﷺ: «حُبُّ الدُّنيا رأْسُ كُلِّ خطيئةٍ وبَلِيَّةٍ. فمَنْ أَحَبَّها غفَلَ عن طريقِ الآخِرَةِ».

قالَ اللهُ العَظيمُ: ﴿ما جَعَلَ اللهُ لِرَجُلٍ مِن قَلْبَيْنِ في جَوْفِهِ﴾.

[The Prophet] said as well: 'The material world and the Hereafter are two opposites. He who loves one of them abandons the other.'[17]

Someone said to Bahlūl al-Majnūn: 'What is the sign of the shaykh?' 'Asceticism and truthfulness,' he replied, 'as well as total abandonment of the material world.'

It was asked of him as well: 'To whom belongs the material world in its entirety?' 'To the heretic,' he said. '[Then] for whom is it forbidden?' he was asked. 'The pious saint,' he answered, 'according to the words of the Prophet (may God bless and preserve him): "The trustworthy believer is deprived, but the liar prospers".'[18]

Rābiᶜa al-ᶜAdawiyya said: 'One who is satisfied with the acceptance of others and seeks to amass [the goods of] the material world is nearest to heresy and farthest from Reality.' [This is because] the sign of inner truthfulness is asceticism in the material world and the sign of heresy is desire for [the material world].

From the book *Qawāᶜid aṣ-ṣūfiyya* [Rules of the Sufi Way]: Ibrāhīm al-Khawwāṣ[19] said: 'It is not part of Sufi conduct to have [financial] means upon which to rely in case of need, nor something that can be accepted by another [in payment], nor sight nor tongue with which to beg if one is hungry, nor a word by which to beseech mankind in case of misfortune.'

Among the rules stated by Abū ᶜAbdallāh aṣ-Ṣubḥī [one finds]: 'The poverty of the ascetic is not made complete until he gives up all of his possessions. After giving up his possessions he must work to transform his reputation until he has no reputation. When he has expended his reputation, there remains for him [only] the power of his ego. So he expends that as well on his companions by serving them and working for his sustenance. Only then is poverty perfected for him.'

17. The exact wording of this hadith cannot be found in Wensinck. For a tradition containing a similar meaning, see at-Tirmidhī, *al-Qiyāma* (24). In Ismāᶜīl ibn Muḥammad al-ᶜAjlūnī (d. 1162/1748) [*Kashf al-khafā' wa muzīl al-albās*, Aḥmad al-Qalāṣ ed. (Beirut: Mu'assasat ar-Risāla, 1399/1979) (1), p. 491] the text reads: 'The material world and the Hereafter are two wives (*darratān*) . . ..'

18. This hadith cannot be found in Wensinck. Similar meanings, however, can be found in Muslim, *Kitāb al-munāfiqīn* (58) and an-Nasā'ī, *Kitāb aṭ-ṭalāq* (42).

19. Abū Isḥāq Ibrāhīm al-Khawwāṣ (d. 291/904) of Samarrā, a companion of al-Junayd and disciple of the celebrated ascetic Abū ᶜAbdallāh al-Maghribī (d. 299/911–12), is considered to be one of the early masters of *tawakkul*—the complete trust and reliance upon the will of God and Divine determination in all affairs. As such, his teachings strongly influenced the later doctrine of Abū Madyan, who was himself considered a master of *tawakkul* by the Sufis of the Maghrib. See Arberry, *Muslim Saints and Mystics*, pp. 272–76. See also, al-Iṣfahānī, *Ḥilyat al-awliyā'* (10), pp. 325–26. The book quoted in this passage, *Qawāᶜid aṣ-ṣūfiyya* ('Rules of Sufism'), apparently written by Abū ᶜAbdallāh aṣ-Ṣubḥī, cannot as yet be identified.

و[كان] يقول: «الدُّنيا والآخرة ضِدَّان. فَمَنْ أَحَبَّ أَحَدَهُما تَرَكَ الآخر».

قيل لِبَهْلُول المجْنُون: «ما عَلامَةُ الشَّيخ»؟ قال: «زهدٌ وصِدْقٌ وتَرْكُ الدُّنيا بالكُلِّيَّةِ». فقيل له: «لِمَنْ تَقْبَلُ الدُّنيا بالكُلِّيَةِ؟» قال: «لِلزِّنْدِيقِ».

فَقيل: «مَنْ يحْرُمُ مِنْها»؟ قال: «الوَلِيُّ الصَّالِح لِقول النبي ﷺ: المؤْمِنُ الصَّادِقُ مَحْرُومٌ والفاجِرُ مَرْزُوقٌ».

وقالت رابعةُ العَدَوِيَّة: «مَن رَضِيَ بِتَقْبِيلِ يَدَيْهِ وجَمعَ الدُّنيا فَهو إلى الزَّنْدَقَةِ أَقْرَبُ ومِن الحَقِيقَةِ أَبْعَدُ».

وعَلامَةُ الصِّدْقِ زُهدٌ في الدُّنيا وعلامةُ الزندقةِ رَغْبَةٌ فيها.

ومِنْ كِتاب قواعِدِ الصُّوفِيَّةِ»: قال إبراهيمُ الخَوَّاص: «لَيس مِنْ آدابِ الصُّوفي أَنْ يَكُونَ له سَبَبٌ يَرْجِعُ إليه حِينَ يحتاجُ أو شَيءٌ يُقْبَلُ مِنْهُ أو رَأْيٌ أو لسانٌ يُطْلَبُ به إذا جاعَ أو كَلِمَةٌ يَنْطِقُ بها عِنْدَ الشَّدائِدِ إلى النَّاس».

ومِن أَحْكامِ ما قالَهُ أبو عَبْدِ اللهِ الصُّبْحِي: «لا يصِحُّ لِلفَقِيرِ الفَقْرُ حَتَّى يخْرُجَ عن الأَمْلاكِ كُلِّها. فإذا خرَجَ عن الأملاكِ يَنبَغِي أَنْ يُبَدِّلَ جاهَهُ حتَّى لا يَبْقى له جاهٌ. فإذا بَدَّلَ جاهَهُ بَقِيَ عليه قوةُ نفسه. فَيُبَدِّلُها أَيضًا لأَصْحابِه بالخِدْمَةِ والحَرَكَةِ في أَسْبابِه. فعند ذلك يَصِحُّ له الفَقْرُ».

Confirmation of [the above attitude] can be found in what Ibn Shāh [al-Kirmānī] related about [Shāh] ibn Shujāᶜ al-Kirmānī.[20] Despite his age and vocation, he used to serve his companions and said 'I have looked into all types of spiritual discipline, but I have not found among them anything more meritorious than [the act] of serving a Muslim man.'

Al-Junayd (may God have mercy upon him) said: 'Beware of [wastefully] expending your spiritual abilities by dispersing and diluting them in association with those not of your type, for you will be characterized by [their] knowledge. In this way [your insight] will be lost to you, your inspiration will be stolen from you, and the suppression of innate spirituality and rejection of the Truth will lead you astray. This is my counsel to you.'

Abū Manṣūr ibn al-Ḥallāj [al-Ḥusayn ibn Manṣūr al-Ḥallāj][21] said: 'He who wishes to attain [to God] practices hunger and scrupulousness and renounces the material world. He makes himself the companion of an ascetic and scrupulous shaykh, [who is] desirous of God and who has not the slightest trace of the material world upon him. This [alone] is the beneficial spiritual master, who exemplifies [the Way of] God the Almighty.'

It was asked of Qaḍīb al-Bān: 'How does the aspirant attain his desire?' 'When he makes his stomach hungry,' he replied, 'and makes his heart sincere, affirms his intention, and makes himself accord with Divine pleasure and total submission.'

Shaykh [Abū Madyan] said: 'It is obligatory for one who is aware to fear God [both] in sickness and in health.'

20. Abu'l-Fawāris Shāh ibn Shujāᶜ al-Kirmānī (d. before 300/912–13) was the descendant of a royal family from Merv in northeastern Iran. After moving to Nishapur, he became one of the most knowledgeable and respected practitioners of the doctrine of *futuwwa*, or Islamic chivalry. During Abū Madyan's lifetime the letters of Shāh ibn Shujāᶜ and a work of his entitled *Mir'āt al-ḥukamā'* ('Mirrors of the Sages') were widely circulated in the Muslim East. See as-Sulamī, *Ṭabaqāt aṣ-ṣūfiyya*, pp. 192–94.

21. Abu'l-Mughīth al-Ḥusayn ibn Manṣūr al-Ḥallāj (244-309/858–913) is the paradigm for the intoxicated lover of God in Islamic mysticism. Although al-Ḥallāj remained a controversial figure throughout his life and was accused of the Islamic heresy of incarnationism, the circumstances of his death by execution allowed his memory to be preserved as one of the first Sufi martyrs in the way of the Truth. He is the author of a number of works of both prose and poetry, of which the most famous is *Kitāb at-ṭawāsīn*. For an English translation of this work see, Aisha Abd ar-Rahman at-Tarjumana, trans., *The Tawasin of Mansur al-Hallaj*, (Berkeley and London: Diwan Press, 1974).

وتَصْحِيحُ ذلك حَكاه إبْنُ شاهِ [الكِرماني] عن (شاهِ) ابْن شُجاع الكِرمانِي مع كِبَر سِنِهِ وعَمَلهُ كان يَقوم بِخدْمةِ أصْحابه ويقول: «نظَرْتُ في جَمِيعِ الأَعْمال ولَمْ أَجِدْ فيها شيئًا آجَرَ مِن خدمةِ امْرءٍ مُسْلِمٍ».

وقال الجُنيدُ رحمه الله: «إيّاكُمْ أَنْ تبيعُوا أنوارَكُمْ، تفرّقوا وتَمْزجوا بمُخالطةِ غير أبْناء الجِنس فتعُودُوا إلى وَسْمٍ مُتَوَسّمٍ بعلم. لإنْ غابَ عَنكُمْ فيَسْلُبكُم الخواطِرَ أو ظُلمةَ الأسْرارِ أو طرْدَ الحق. هذه وَصِيَّتِي لكم».

وقال أبو منصُورٍ بْنُ الحَلّاج [حُسَين بن منصور الحلّاج]: «مَن أرادَ الوُصُول جاعَ في الدُّنيا وزهَدَ فيها وتورّعَ ويُصاحِبُ شَيخًا زاهِدًا ورعًا ليس عليه مِن الدُّنيا شيءٌ ولو كان وَزْنَ ذرّةٍ وتكونُ له رَغْبَةٌ في اللهِ. فهذا هو الشّيخُ المفيدُ إلى قدْوَةِ اللهِ تعالى».

وقيل لِقضِيب البَان: «بماذا يَصِلُ المرِيد إلى ما يُرِيدُه»؟ وقال: «إذا جاعَ بَطْنُه وأخلص قلبُهُ وحقق نِيّتهُ ووُفق مع الرّضى والتّسْليم».

وقال الشّيخ [أبو مدْيَن]: يجِبُ على العاقِلِ أنْ يخافَ مِن اللهِ في مَرَضِهِ وصِحّتِهِ.

The Messenger of God (may God bless and preserve him) said: 'The Muslim possesses five things before five others: youth before old age, health before weakness, idleness before work, wealth before poverty, and life before death.'[22]

Said the Shaykh [Abū Madyan] (may God have mercy upon him): 'Devote yourself, my brother, to visiting spiritual masters, because in visits to spiritual masters [one can attain] praiseworthy qualities. The first of them is an increase in faith, certainty, knowledge, the inner life, character, and support on the Way. [The second of them is] the acquisition of pleasing characteristics and praiseworthy qualities. [The third is] attainment to the Master of Glory and Honor. [The fourth is] knowledge of the Way and of Transcendent Reality, [and the fifth is the acquisition of] recompense and merit.'

Indeed, eighty shaykhs have agreed upon [the merits of] visits to spiritual masters and the acquisition of praiseworthy states from them. These shaykhs have also agreed that no one prevents an aspirant from making his visit except the heretic, whose goal in his perversity is the garden of the material world, for questions of immorality and piety are not of concern to the aspirant.[23] [The Caliph] Abū Bakr visited [the Caliph] ʿUmar, while [the Caliph] ʿAlī visited ʿĀ'isha (may God be pleased with them);[24] ash-Shāfiʿī and Abū Ḥanīfa visited Mālik [ibn Anas]; Aḥmad ibn Ḥanbal visited Dhū'n-Nūn [al-Miṣrī] and al-Junayd; and al-Fuḍayl [ibn ʿIyāḍ] visited Abū Yazīd [al-Bisṭāmi].[25] Thus, one who forbids the practice of visiting [spiritual masters] has gone against [the practice of] the Companions of the Prophet (may God be pleased with them). He who visits a saint derives benefit from his majesty and is not excluded from his blessings. Thus no one forbids visits to spiritual masters other than a heretic [and] a lying hypocrite.

22. This hadith cannot be found in Wensinck.

23. By making this somewhat surprising assertion, Shaykh Abū Madyan perhaps means that the goal of the aspirant is knowledge of God, not merely the way of blamelessness in one's outward observance of the *Sharīʿa*.

24. This point is significant because ʿĀ'isha, the daughter of Abū Bakr and favorite spouse of the Prophet Muḥammad after the death of his first wife, Khadīja, opposed the claim of ʿAlī (cousin and son-in-law of the Prophet) to the caliphate. Shaykh Abū Madyan is thus attempting to stress that in spite of the political opposition between these two most beloved companions of the Prophet, neither ʿAlī nor ʿĀ'isha failed to give the other the respect that was due.

25. The point made above is repeated here, for Imam Aḥmad ibn Ḥanbal was known for his strong opposition to the doctrines of Sufism. According to Abū Madyan, he none the less maintained a personal respect for the piety of those whose doctrines he opposed. It is probably safe to assume that the present comment was directed at the exoteric Mālikī scholars of sixth/twelfth-century al-Andalus, who appear to have been more strongly prejudiced against Sufism than were their counterparts in North Africa.

وقال رسول الله ﷺ : «لِلمُسْلِمِ خمسٌ قَبْلَ خمْس : شَبابُكَ قبلَ هَرَمِكَ وصِحّتُكَ قبلَ سَقمِكَ وفراغُكَ قبلَ شُغْلِكَ وغِناؤُكَ قبلَ فَقْرِكَ وحياتُكَ قبلَ مَوْتِكَ» .

قال الشّيخ [أبو مَدْيَن] : فعليكَ يا أخِي بزيارةِ المشايخِ لأنّ في زيارةِ المشايخِ خِصالاً محمُودَةً. أوّلُها زيادَةٌ في الإيمانِ واليَقِينِ والعلمِ والباطِنِ والطّباعِ وإدامُ الطّريقِ و[ثانيُها] اكْتِسابُ الخُلقِ المَرضيّةِ والصّفاتِ المحْمودَةِ و[ثالِثُها] الإصالُ إلى ذِي الجَلالِ والإكْرامِ و[رابعُها] مَعْرِفَةُ الطّريقِ والحقيقَةِ و[خامِسُها] الأَجْرُ والثّوابُ.

وإنّ ثمانِينَ شيخاً اتّفقُوا على زيارةِ المشايخ واكْتِسابِ الأحْوالِ المحمودةِ مِنهُم.

وقد اتّفقَ المشايخ على أنّهُ لا يَرُدُّ المريدَ عن الزّيارةِ إلاّ زنديقٌ له غَرَضٌ في الفَسادِ إلى رَوْضَةِ الدُّنيا لأنّ المريدَ لا يَعْنى له عَينُ الفسادِ والصّلاحِ.

وقد زارَ أبو بكرٍ عُمَرَ وزار عليٌّ عائشةَ رضي اللهُ عنهم وزار الشّافِعِي مالِكاً وأبو حَنيفَةَ زار مالِكاً وأحمدُ بنُ حنبلَ زارَ ذا النّونِ والجُنيد وزار الفُضَيلُ [بن عياض] أبا يَزيد [البِسْطامِي] . فمَنْ منعَ الزّيارةَ فقدْ خالفَ الصّحابةَ رضيَ اللهُ عنهم.

ومَن زارَ وليّاً اكْتَسَبَ مِن جَلالِهِ ولم يخلُ مِن برَكاتِهِ. ولا يَنهى عن زيارةِ المشايخِ إلاّ زِنْديقٌ مُرائِيٌّ مُحتالٌ.

Ibn ᶜUmar al-Mahdī ar-Ruṣāfī said, addressing [people who forbade visits to spiritual masters] in *Qawāᶜid aṣ-ṣūfiyya*: 'A faction [of Sufis] behaved excessively while on their travels and wanderings and made themselves objects of reproof in [many] lands by visiting their inhabitants. When [the people] became accustomed [to them], they ate from every good thing. Even more, they would boastfully say, "I have seen So-and-So." Although [this story] continues to be told, [the practice] is incorrect. Indeed, travel requires a guide, wherever [the destination] may be. Its goal is a total change of state and the [acquisition of] guidance that leads toward the Way of God the Almighty.'

Said the Shaykh (may God have mercy upon him): 'It is obligatory for the aspirant to choose a shaykh who is learned, scrupulous, knowledgeable about [formal] religion, fearful [of God], learned in the exoteric and esoteric sciences, and who is a master of the state of repentance in the material world. If [the skaykh] deviates from his path, then the compact between the two of them is removed because of the alteration in [his] states.'

It is desirable for the aspirant to be ascetic, satisfied [with what God provides], pleasant in nature, obedient toward God, tearful and sad because of his past disobedience toward his Lord, generous [toward others], and firm in [his acquisition of] praiseworthy attributes and in avoiding blameworthy attributes. He passes his days fasting and his nights standing in prayer. If he sees something he reflects upon it and if he is silent he meditates, feels remorse, and calls himself to account. When he eats, he eats only [what is necessary] for his own sustenance and extols the praise of his Lord. He repents and asks forgiveness for blameworthy thoughts and mortifies himself by starving his carnal soul, feeding the poor, showing mercy to the indigent and the orphan, being compassionate toward his neighbor, visiting the graves [of the pious and saintly], giving his relatives their due, advocating good and forbidding evil, going regularly to the mosque for prayer, being mindful of the time [for prayer and personal appointments], keeping his food, drink, clothing, dwelling, and mount pure from what is forbidden, avoiding the swearing of false oaths, distancing himself from oppression and those who practice it as well as people of evil morals, busying himself with the purification of his carnal soul [and protecting himself from] the sins of mankind, seeking forgiveness from the

قال لهم ابن عُمر المَهْدِي الرُّصافي في «قواعِدِ الصُّوفِيَّة» : إنَّ طائفةً غَلَّطُوا في سياحَتِهِم وأَسْفارهم فجَعَلوا لأنفسهم مِن التَّوبِيخِ في البُلْدان ورُؤْيةِ أَهْلِها . ولَمَّا أَلِفَتْهُم النُّفوسُ أَكَلوا مِن كُلِّ طَيِّبَةٍ وزيادةً على ذلك يقولون «رأَيتُ فلانًا وفلانًا» ويَفْتَخِرُونَ بذلك . رُوِيَ ويُرْوَى وهذا غَلَطٌ . وإنَّما السَّفَرُ يطلُبُ المُرْشِدَ حَيْثُ ما كان . يَنوي في ذلك الهِجْرَةَ والرَّشادَ إلى طريقِ اللهِ تعالى .

قال الشَّيخ رحمه الله تعالى : يجبُ على المريد اتِّخاذُ شيخٍ عالمٍ صادقٍ ورعٍ عارفٍ بالدِّين خائفٍ يَعْلَمُ عِلْمَ الظَّاهر والباطن ويكون على حالِ النَّدَمِ والزُّهدِ في الدُّنيا . فإذا انحرَفَ عن طريقتِه انسلَخَتِ البَيْعَةُ بَيْنَهُما بتَقْلِيبِ الأَحْوال . ويَنبَغِي أَنْ يكونَ المريدُ زاهِدًا مَرْضِيًا بشُوشًا طائِعًا باكِيًا حزينًا على ما فاتَ مِن طاعةِ رَبِّهِ حَلِيمًا باقِيًا مع الصِّفاتِ المحمودةِ مُنحرفًا عن الصِّفاتِ المذمومةِ . سائِرٌ نهارَه صائِمٌ ولَيْلَه قائِمٌ . إنْ نَظَرَ اعْتَبَرَ وإنْ سَكَتَ تفَكَّرَ وتأَسَّفَ ويُحاسِبُ نَفْسَهُ وإنْ أَكَلَ أَكَلَ قوتَهُ وأَثْنى بحَمْدِ رَبِّه . ويَسْتَغْفِرُ ويَتوبُ مِن الخَواطِرِ المذمومةِ ويكونُ مُجْتَهِدًا يُجَوِّعُ نَفْسَهُ ويُطْعِمُ الفقيرَ ويَرْحَمُ المِسْكِينَ واليَتِيمَ ويَعْطِفُ على الجار ويَزُورُ القُبورَ ويَصِلُ الرَّحِمَ ويأْمُرُ بالمَعْرُوفِ ويَنْهى عن المُنكَر ويَمْشِي إلى المَساجِدِ ويَتَحَفَّظُ على الأَوْقاتِ ويُنظِّفُ المطعَمَ والمَشْرَبَ والمَلْبَس والمَسْكَنَ والمركَبَ مِن الحَرام ويجْتَنِبُ الأَيمانَ الكاذِبَةَ ويَبْعُدُ عن الظُّلْمِ وأَهْلِهِ وخُلُقِ السُّوء ويَشْتَغِلُ بطِيبِ نفسِه عن عُيوبِ النَّاسِ ويَسْتَغْفِر

whisperings of Satan, showing sincere repentance, making the required pilgrimage [to Mecca] and loving the expenditure of self in defense of the faith. These are the attributes of the true *faqīr*.

From the book, *Qawāʿid aṣ-ṣūfiyya*: It was related that Anas ibn Mālik (may God have mercy upon him) mentioned that the Messenger of God (may God bless and preserve him) said, 'Oh God, bring me to life as one of the poor, make me die as one of the poor, and raise me up in the ranks of the poor.' Anas ibn Mālik said, 'Oh Messenger of God, verily you make this supplication often.' Then [the Prophet] said to Anas ibn Mālik, 'Do not separate yourself from [the poor] for a single moment, for nothing in the material world will harm you or will be taken from you after you have possessed good fortune.'[26]

Said Abū Sulaymān [ad-Dārānī][27]: 'We have learned that the poverty of a poor man who has no desire [for the material world] equals one thousand years of a rich man's piety.' One of the early Muslims [also] said: 'Worship combined with the search for material things is a garden atop a garbage heap.' Thus, the worship of a poor man is like a jeweled necklace in its great value.

As for poverty, it is [both] ordinary and extraordinary. Ordinary poverty is the need for God. This is the attribute of every creature, whether one is a believer or an unbeliever. It is the meaning of the words of God Most High: 'Oh people, you are utterly in need of God.'[28] Extraordinary poverty is the attribute of saints and those who are beloved of God. This entails emptying one's hands of the material world and emptying one's heart of attachment to it, busying oneself with God alone, being desirous of God, and making one's time conform to [the practice of] seclusion for the sake of God.

26. The exact wording of this hadith cannot be found in Wensinck. Its closest approximation can be found in Ibn Ḥanbal (2), 168. See also, Ibn Ḥanbal (2), 424. The wording given here can be found in as-Suyūṭī [*Jāmiʿ al-aḥādīth* (2), p. 31] after at-Tabarānī.

27. Abū Sulaymān ʿAbd ar-Raḥmān ibn ʿAṭīya ad-Dārānī (d. 215/830), originally from the village of Dārayyā near Damascus, was a famous transmitter of hadith. He was also an early ascetic and master of the pietistic mystical tradition, which specialized in advocating the mortification of carnal urges. See as-Sulamī, *Ṭabaqāt aṣ-ṣūfiyya*, p. 75.

28. Qur'ān, XXXV (*Fāṭir*), 15.

مِن وَسْوَسَةِ الشَّيْطانِ ويَتوبُ بتَوْبَةٍ صادِقَةٍ ويَحُجُّ الفَريضَةَ ويُحِبُّ الجِهادَ . فهذه صِفاتُ الفقيرِ الصَّادِقِ .

ومِن كتابِ «قَواعِد الصُّوفِيَّةِ» : رُوِيَ عن أَنَس بْن مالِكٍ رضي الله عنه قال : قال رسول الله صلى الله عليه وسلم : «اللهُمَّ أَحْيِني مِسْكِيناً وأَمِتْني مِسْكِيناً واحْشُرْني في زُمْرَةِ المساكِينِ» . فقال أَنسُ بْنُ مالك «يا رَسُولَ اللهِ إنكَ لتَدْعُو بهذا الدُّعَاءِ كَثِيراً» . فقال لأَنَس بْن مالِكٍ «لا تُفَارِقْهُمْ طَرْفَةَ عَينٍ ما ضَرَّكُمْ ما فاتَكُمْ مِن الدُّنيا بَعْدَ أَنْ كانَتْ لَكُمْ حَظّاً» .

وقال أَبو سُلَيْمانَ (الدَّارانِي) : «بَلغنا أَنَّ تَفَقُّرَ الفَقِيرِ دُونَ شَهْوَةٍ يَعْدِلُ عِبادَةَ الغَنِيِّ أَلْفَ عامٍ» . وقال بَعْضُ السَّلَفِ : «العِبادةُ مع طَلَبِ الدُّنيا رَوْضَةٌ على مَزْبَلَةٍ» . والعِبادةُ لِلفقيرِ كعِقْدِ جَوْهَرٍ في جِيدِ حَسْناءَ .

والفقرُ عامٌّ وخاصٌّ . فالعامُّ الحَاجَةُ إلى اللهِ وهذا وَصْفُ كلِّ مخلوقٍ مُؤْمِن وكافِرٍ . وهو مَعْنى قوله تعالى : (يا أَيُّها النَّاسُ أَنتُمُ الفُقَراءُ إلى اللهِ) . والخَّاصُ وَصْفُ أَوْلياءِ اللهِ وأَحْبابِهِ وهو خُلوُّ اليَدِ مِن الدُّنيا وخُلوُّ القلبِ مِن التَّعَلُّقِ بها اشْتِغالاً باللهِ وشَوْقاً إلى اللهِ وأُنساً بالفراغِهِ والخلوة مع اللهِ .

God Most High said to [the Prophet] David (peace be upon him): 'Oh David! Proclaim to the people of the Earth that I am the Beloved of one who loves Me, the Choice of one who chooses Me, and the Master of one who obeys Me. No slave loves Me with certainty in his heart but that I know of it and take him to Myself. He who searches for Me by means of the truth will find Me, but he who searches by means of anything else will never find Me. So reject, oh people of the Earth, its abundance, and draw near to My generosity, friendship, companionship, and intimacy. Be intimate with Me, so that I may be intimate with you, and that I may hasten toward loving you.'

God said to one of His saints: 'Verily some among My worshippers love Me and I love them, are desirous of Me and I desire them, remember Me and I remember them, gaze at Me and I gaze at them.' Said [the saint], 'Oh Lord, what is their sign?' And [God] said: 'They call for darkness during the day, just as the compassionate shepherd calls his flock, and they yearn for sunset, just as a bird yearns for its nest at sunset. When night falls, when darkness overcomes [the light], when the bedcovers are spread out, when the family is at rest, and when every lover is left [alone] with his beloved—then they arise, pointing their feet toward Me, turning their faces to Me, and speak intimate words, adoring Me by virtue of My grace. They [find themselves witless], between crying and weeping, between moaning and complaining, between standing and sitting, and between bowing and prostrating themselves in My sight. [All of this] they bear for My sake and reveal what they suffer for the sake of My love. The first thing I give them is that I kindle My light in their hearts so that they may know of Me. The second is that were the heavens and the Earth and all that is between them on their balance [against them at the Day of Judgment], I would make it light for them. The third is that I turn My face toward them, redeeming the one toward whom I have turned My face, so that one may know what I want to give him.'

أَوْحى اللهُ تعالى إلى داوُودَ عليه السَّلام: «يا داوُودُ بَلِّغْ أَهْلَ الأَرضِ أَنِّي حَبيبٌ لِمَنْ أَحَبَّني ومختارٌ لِمَنْ اختارَني ومُطِيعٌ لِمَنْ أَطاعَني. ما أَحَبَّني عَبْدٌ أَعْلَمُ ذلك يَقِينا مِن قلبه إلاَّ قَبِلْتُهُ لنفسي. مَن طَلَبَني بالحقِّ وَجَدَني فمَنْ طلبَ غيرَهُ لَمْ يجِدْني. فارْفضُوا يا أَهلَ الأَرض غَرَرَها وهَلُمُّوا إلى كَرامَتي ومُصاحَبَتي ومجالَسَتي ومُسْتَأْنَسِي. وآنسُوا بي أُؤْنِسْكُمْ وأُسارِعْ إلى محبَّتِكم».

وأَوْحَى اللهُ إلى بعضِ الأولياء: «إنَّ لي عِباداً مِن عِبادي يحبُّونني وأُحِبُّهُمْ ويَشْتاقُونَ إليَّ وأَشْتاقُ إليهم ويذكُرُونني وأَذْكرُهُم ويَنْظُرُونَ إليَّ وأَنْظُرُ إليهم».

قال: «يا ربِّ ما علامَتُهُم»؟ قال: «يَدْعُونَ الظَّلامَ بالنَّهار كما يَدْعُو الرَّاعِي الشَّفِيقُ غنمَهُ ويحِنُّونَ إلى غُرُوبِ الشَّمْس كما تحِنُّ الطَّيرُ إلى أَوْكارها عندَ الغُرُوب. فإذا أَجْنحَ الليلُ واختلط الظَّلامُ وفُرِشَتْ الفُرُوشُ وتنفست الأُسْرَةُ وخلا كلُّ حَبيبٍ بِمَحْبُوبِهِ نصَبُوا إليَّ أَقْدامَهُم وافْتَرَشُوا إليَّ وُجُوهَهُم وناجُوني بكلامٍ وتملَّقُوا إليَّ بأَنْعُمِي. فهُمْ بَيْنَ صارخٍ وباكٍ ومُتأَوِّهٍ وشاكٍ وبين قائمٍ وقاعدٍ وبين راكعٍ وساجدٍ بعَيْني وما يَتَحمَّلُونَ مِن أَجْلي وبِمَا بِهِم مِن حُبِّي. أوّلُ ما أُعْطِيهم أَقْذِفُ في قلُوبِهم نُورِي ويخبرُونَ عنّي والثَّانِيَةُ لو كانت السَّمواتُ والأَرضُ وما بينَهُما في موازينِهِمْ لاسْتَقلَلْتُها لهم. والثَّالثة أُقْبِلُ بوجْهي عَلَيهِمْ افتدي مَن أَقْبلتُ بوجْهِي عليه يَعْلَمُ أَحدٌ ما أُريدُ أَنْ أُعْطِيهُ».

It is related that David (peace be upon him) said, 'Oh Lord, show me the people whom You love.' And God Most High said to him: 'Oh David, go to Mount Lebanon, for upon it are fourteen men—some who are young, some who are mature, and some who are old. When you go to them, send them greetings from Me and say to them: "Verily your Lord sends you greetings and asks you why you do not ask Him to fulfill your needs. For you are His loved ones, His pure ones, and His friends".'

So David (peace be upon him) went to them and found them at a spring of water, humble and busy with the glorification of God the Almighty, may He be Exalted and Glorified. When they saw David (peace be upon him), they jumped up to flee from him. 'I am a Messenger of God unto you,' he said. 'He sends you greetings and says to you, "Why do you not ask Me to fulfill your needs and call upon Me, for I hear your voices and your words? Verily you are My loved ones, My pure ones, and My friends".'

Then David (peace be upon him) said: 'I saw tears on their cheeks and the eldest of them said, "Glory be to You! We are Your slaves and the sons of Your slaves, so forgive us for that which has passed in our lives, causing our hearts to be cut off from the remembrance of You." Then another said, "Glory be to You! We are Your slaves and the sons of Your slaves, so be gracious toward us by looking kindly upon what [stands] between us and You." Another said, "Oh God, I ask of You the most exalted way for us." Said another, "We are intent upon seeking Your good pleasure, so be satisfied with us through Your generosity." Another said, "Oh God, forgive us our shortcomings on Your Way." Said another,

رُوِيَ أَنَّ داوُودَ عليه السَّلام قال: «يا رَبِّ أَرِنِي أَهلَ محبَّتِكَ». فأَوْحى اللهُ تعالى إليه: «يا داوُودُ آتِ جَبَلَ لُبنانَ فإنَّ فيها أَرْبَعَةَ عَشَرَ رَجُلاً فيهم شَبابٌ وفيهم كُهُولٌ وفيهم مشايخُ. فإذا أَتَيْتَهُم فاقرَأْهُمْ منِّي السَّلامَ فقُلْ لهم: إنَّ ربَّكُمْ يُقرِئُكُمُ السَّلامَ ويقولُ لكم أَلا تَسْأَلُونِي حاجَةً؟ فإنَّكُم أَحْبابُهُ وأَصْفِياؤُهُ وأَوْلِياؤُهُ». فأَتاهُم داوودُ عليه السَّلام فوَجَدَهُم عندَ عَينِ ماءٍ مُتَضَرِّعِينَ مُشْتَغِلِينَ بتَعْظِيمِ اللهِ تعالى عَزَّ وجَلَّ. فلمّا نَظَرُوا إلى داوودَ عليه السَّلام نَهَضُوا لِيَفْتَرِقُوا عنهُ. فقال: «إنِّي رسولُ اللهِ إليكُمْ [إنَّهُ] يُقْرِئُكُمُ السَّلامَ ويقولُ لكم أَلا تَسْأَلُونِي حاجةً ولا تُنادُونِي أَسْمَعُ صَوتَكم؟ فإنَّكم أَحبابي وأَصفيائِي وأَولِيائِي». فقال [داوود عليه السلام]: فرَأَيتُ الدُّمُوعَ على خُدُودِهِمْ فقال شَيخُهم: «سُبْحانَكَ نحنُ عَبِيدُكَ وبَنُو عَبِيدِكَ فاغْفِرْ لنا ما قَطَعَ قلُوبَنا عَن فيما مَضَى مِن أَعْمارِنا». وقال آخَرُ: «سبحانك نحن عبيدك وبنو عبيدك فامْنُنْ علينا بحُسْنِ الظَّنِّ فيما بَيْننا وبَيْنَكَ». وقال آخر: «اللهم اسْلُكْ بنا أَرْفَعَ طريقٍ إليكَ». وقال آخر: «نحن مَقْصُورُونَ في طَلَبِ رِضاكَ فارضَ علينا بِجُودِكَ». وقال آخر: «اللهم اغفِرْ لنا تقصِيرَنا في شَرْعِكَ». وقال آخر:

"Oh God, verily You know that no need have we other than to behold Your countenance." Another said, "Oh God, grant us a light with which we may be guided toward You." Said another, "We ask You to accept us and make [Your acceptance] eternal for us." Another said, "We ask for the completeness of Your grace in that which you have granted us." Said another, "Oh God, I ask You to blind my eye from sight of the material world and its folk, and [to blind] my heart from being preoccupied with other than You." Another said, "We know that You love Your friends, so bestow on us the preoccupation of our hearts [in avoidance of] everything other than You." Said another, "Our tongues have become moist from calling on You, so that we may magnify Your praise and Your nearness to Your friends—for Your favors have increased toward those who love You".'

Then God Most High said to David (peace be upon him): 'Verily I have heard your words, and have loved you for That which you have loved. So let everyone separate from his companion and keep My affair secretly to himself, for verily I am the Concealer of whatever is between Me and you.'

David (peace be upon him) asked, 'How have they obtained this from You?' And God Most High said: 'By [maintaining] a favorable opinion [toward creation] and by abstaining from the material world.'

It is [also] related that God Most High said to David (peace be upon him): 'Tell my worshippers, "Turn toward My love. You will not be harmed if I veil you from My creatures or if I raise the veil between Me and you so that you see the light of your hearts. That from which I have hidden you in the material world will not harm you when it is revealed to you, and the enmity of creatures will not harm you when you have been touched by My good pleasure." Oh David! Do you [not] imagine that if you love Me and continue to love Me I will remove love for the material world from your heart? Verily in My love are two aspects which do not mingle in the heart. Oh David! The fellowship of My loved ones is one mixture and the fellowship of the folk of the material world is another. Oh David! Be close to Me by being an enemy of your carnal soul and forbid it from [attaining] its desires. Look into yourself and see the veil between Me and you lifted!'

Said Shaykh Abū Madyan: 'Oh God, allow us to taste the sweetness of intimate converse with You, take us along the path of Your pleasure, cut off from us everything that distances us from Your presence, ease for us that which you have eased for those whom You love, and forgive us, along with our parents and all Muslims.'

«اللهم إنَّكَ تَعْلَمُ لا حاجَةَ لنا إلاَّ النظَرَ إلى وَجْهِكَ» . وقال آخر : «اللهم هَبْ لنا نوراً نَهْتَدِي به إليكَ» . وقالَ آخرُ : «نَسْأَلُكَ أَنْ تقْبَلَ عَلَيْنا وتَدِيمَ ذلِكَ لنا» . وقال آخر : نَسْأَلُكَ تمامَ نعْمَتِكَ فيما وَهَبْتَ لنا» . وقال آخر : «اللهم إنّي أَسْأَلُكَ تُعْمِ عَيْني عَن النَّظرِ إلى الدُّنيا وأَهلِها وقَلْبي مِن الاِشْتِغالِ بغيرِكَ» . وقال آخر : «عَلِمْنا أنَّكَ تُحِبُّ أَوْلِياءَكَ فامْنُنْ علينا بإشْتِغالِ القلبِ عن كلّ شيءٍ دُونَكَ» . وقال آخر : «بَلَتْ أَلْسِنَتُنا عن دُعائِكَ لِتَعْظِيمِ ثنائِكَ وقُربكَ مِن أَوليائِكَ وكَثُرَتْ مِنَّتُكَ على أَهلِ مَحَبَّتِكَ» . فأَوحَى اللهُ تعالى إلى داوود عليه السَّلام : «إنّي قدْ سَمِعْتُ كلامَكُم فلْيُفارِقْ كُلُّ واحِدٍ صاحِبَهُ وليَتَّخِذْ أَمْري لِنفْسِهِ سِرّياً فإنّي كاشِفٌ فيما بَيْني وبَيْنكم» . وقال داوود عليه السَّلام : «بِماذا نالوُا هذا مِنكَ» ؟ قال اللهُ تعالى : «بحُسْنِ الظَّنِّ والكفِّ عن الدُّنيا» . ويُرْوى أنَّ اللهَ تعالى أَوحى إلى داوودَ عليه السَّلام : «قُلْ لِعبادي يَتوجَّهُونَ إلى مَحبتي ما ضرَّكم إذا احْتَجَبْتُم مِن خَلْقِي ورَفَعْتُ الحِجابَ بَيني وبَينكُم حتى تنْظُرُوا إلى نورٍ . وما ضرَكُم ما زَويتُهُ مِن الدُّنيا إذا انْبَسَطَتْ لكُم . وما ضَرَكُم سَخَطُ الخَلْقِ إذا الْتَمَسْتُم رِضائِي . يا داوودُ (هَلْ) تزْعُمُ أَنَّكَ تُحِبُّني وإنْ كُنتَ تُحِبُّني فاخرِجْ حُبَّ الدُّنيا مِن قلبكَ؟ إنَّ حُبّي وحُبَّها لا يجْتمعانِ القلبِ . يا داوودُ خلاطُ أَحْبابي مُخالطةٌ وخلاطُ أَهلِ الدُّنيا مخالطةٌ . يا داوودُ تحَبَّبْ إليَّ بمُعاداةِ نَفْسِكَ وامْنَعْها [مِن] الشَّهواتِ . أَنظُرُ إليكَ وترَى الحِجابَ ما بيني وبينكَ مرْفوعٌ» !

(قال الشيخ أبو مدْيَن) : اللهم أذِقْنا حلاوةَ مُناجاتِكَ واسْلُكْ بنا سبيلَ مَرْضاتِكَ واقْطَعْ عنّا كُلَّ ما يُبْعِدُنا عن حَضْرَتِكَ ويَسّرْ علينا ما يَسَّرْتَهُ لأَهلِ مَحَبَّتِكَ واغْفِرْ لنا ولِوالِدِينا ولِجميعِ المُسْلِمِينَ .

SECTION EXPLAINING THE SESSION OF AUDITION AND ITS NATURE[29]

As for the session of audition, it constitutes correct behavior—[a point which] no one doubts except the ignorant. It is the method of the saints and the pious. In a well-substantiated hadith from the Prophet (may God bless and preserve him) it has been transmitted that Ḥassān ibn Thābit (may God be pleased with him) composed some verses of poetry, in which he said:

> The fever of desire flared up in my heart,[30]
> But there is no doctor for it, nor any healer,
>
> Except the One for whose love I have yearned,
> With Him [alone] is my recuperation and my antidote.

At this the Messenger of God (may God bless and preserve him) became so moved that his cloak fell from his shoulders. This [tradition] is evidence of the permissibility of ecstatic sessions.

Audition has its 'Folk', its 'Men', its 'Group', and its 'League'. The 'Folk of Audition' are a group of people who moan, do penance, and blame themselves. They spend their days fasting and their nights standing [in prayer]. Then they break into weeping, wailing, (crying out), imploring, and sobbing. They completely renounce the material world and devote their hearts to their Beloved, irrevocably divorcing the material world. When they perceive [God] they are alone [with Him], considering and meditating [upon Him], and when they speak, their tongues are eloquent with wisdom and they are truthful. Their states are praiseworthy and their behavior corresponds to [the dictates of] the Sunna.[31] When they hear a teaching, the lights of love are kindled in their hearts, which clothe their external bodies with the onset of ecstasy. In their ecstasy they occupy the station of the possessed—they become agitated and lose their senses, but they bear no blame. [In this way] ecstatic sessions become permissible for them (and their ecstasy becomes a right, an act of truthfulness, a spiritual method, and a reality).

29. The 'session of audition', or *samāᶜ*, is usually taken in Eastern Sufism to mean a session of invocation, or *dhikr*, in which either songs or instrumental music are performed. Although Shaykh Abū Madyan mentions the use of a flute in the following pages, Sufi practice in the Maghrib has tended to preclude any use of musical instruments in group invocations, except those that are deemed absolutely necessary for maintaining rhythm. The Classical Arabic term, *samāᶜ*, as used here, must thus be understood in its Maghribi cultural context as referring not specifically to a 'session of musical audition,' but rather to an 'ecstatic session' in a general sense, and can be taken as a synonym for the popular Dialectical Arabic term, *ḥaḍra*, or 'state of Divine presence'.

30. The word, *kabidī*, translated here as 'my heart,' literally means 'my liver.' Arabic folk belief, contrary to European usage, assigns the seat of the emotions to the liver rather than to the heart, which instead is regarded as the seat of intuitive perceptions and spirituality. The verses quoted above cannot be found in the lithographed Tunis edition (1281/1864–65) of the *Diwān Ḥassān ibn Thābit*.

31. In the an-Nājī copy: '. . . their behavior is faultless and their Way is correct.'

بابٌ في بيانِ السَّماعِ وحَقيقَتِهِ

فأمَّا السَّماعُ فهو الصَّحيحُ لا يَشُكُّ فيه إلاَّ جاهِلٌ. وهو طريقُ الأولياء والصَّالِحِينَ. وقد وَرَدَ في الحَديثِ الصَّحيحِ عن النَّبي ﷺ: اسْتَشْهَدَ حسَّانُ بْنُ ثابت رضي الله عنه شِعْرًا قال فيه:

«لَقَدْ سَعَّرَتْ حُمَّى الهوَى كَبدِي | فَلا طَبِيبَ لَها ولا راقِي
إلاَّ الذي شَقَيْتُ بحُبِّهِ | فَعِنْدَهُ راحَتي وتِرْياقِي»

فَتَواجَدَ رسولُ اللهِ ﷺ حَتَّى سَقَطَ رداؤُهُ عن مَنْكِبَيْهِ. فهذا دَليلٌ على إباحَةِ السَّماعِ.

ولِلسَّماعِ أَهْلٌ ورِجالٌ وجَماعَةٌ وعُصْبَةٌ. وأَهْلُ السَّماعِ قَوْمٌ تأَوَّهُوا وتابُوا وأنابُوا. صامُوا نهارَهُم وقامُوا لَيْلهم وقطعُوا بالبُكاء والنَحيبِ [والصِّياحِ] والتَّضرُّعِ والشَّهيق. وزَهَدُوا في الدُّنيا بأَسْرِها وتَعلَّقتْ قُلوبُهُم بمَحْبُوبِهم (و) طَلَّقُوا الدُّنيا ثَلاثًا. إنْ نَظَرُوا إنْفَرَدُوا [اعْتَبَرُوا وتفَكَّرُوا] وإنْ تكلَّمُوا فصَحَتْ أَلْسِنَتُهم بالحِكْمَة فصَدَقُوا. أَحْوالُهُمْ محْمُودَةٌ وآدابُهم سُنِّيَّةٌ [سَلِيمَةٌ وطريقُهم صحيحةٌ]. إذا سَمِعُوا عِلْمًا [العلم] هاجَتْ نِيرانُ المحبةِ في قلوبهم وكَسَتْ عند الوَجْدِ ظَواهِرَهم. فقامُوا في الوجدِ مَقامَ المجانينِ فتواجَدُوا وغابُوا في وَجْدِهم فلا جُناحَ عليهم. فهؤُلاءِ يُباحُ لهمُ السَّماعُ [فصارَ وَجْدُهُم حقًا وصِدْقًا وحَقِيقَةً]

The 'Men of Audition' differ in their states, attributes, and actions. Among them are those for whom the ecstatic state comes upon them while they are sitting; they make no movement, as in the words of God Most High: 'You see the mountains and think them firmly fixed, but they shall pass away as clouds pass away.'[32] Among them are those who begin to laugh and cry, those who act remorseful, and those who sob and tremble.

Ecstatic states differ according to one's spiritual state, rank, station, and degree. Ecstasy is like lightning—it flashes and disappears. Audition is both truth and a lie; one who 'hears' with his heart is confirmed [in his state], while one who 'hears' with his carnal soul becomes a heretic. There is no doubt about this, except on the part of one who is ignorant of it, according to the words of the Prophet (may God bless and preserve him): 'He who is ignorant of a thing disapproves of it.'[33] The Philosopher said, 'No one knows yearning except he who has felt it, and no one knows ardent love except he who is affected by it.'[34]

The Shaykh [Abū Madyan] (may God be pleased with him) said: 'Audition is a private thing—no one but its folk should know of it. When [Sufis] are present for ecstatic sessions they should lock the doors of their homes and when the food is brought they should open them again.'

He also said: 'The most serious impediment [to *samā*ᶜ] is the Sufi who is selfish. Holding ecstatic sessions with those who are not suited for them is also forbidden. Being present and taking part in them is permissible only for those who are their folk.[35] This has been mentioned by many shaykhs.

The beginner should not be present at ecstatic sessions until he has mortified his carnal soul with fasting, performing the fast of intimate union, and standing [in prayer]. Only then is it allowable for him to be present and is [participation] permissible for him. The Shaykhs, the Exemplars, and the Folk of Guidance have [all] agreed [on this point].

32. Qur'ān, XXVII (*an-Naml*), 88.

33. This hadith cannot be found in Wensinck. Al-ᶜAjlūnī [*Kashf al-khafā'*(2), p. 320] reproduces it, but states that there is some question as to whether or not it can be counted as actual hadith.

34. The 'Group' and 'League' of audition, mentioned above, are not discussed in either available copy of this text.

35. In the an-Nājī copy: 'One of the evils of the Sufis is beginning an ecstatic session with those who are not its folk.'

والرّجالُ في السَّماعِ يَختَلِفُونَ في الأحوالِ والصّفاتِ والحَركات . فمنهم مَن يأخذُهُ الحالُ قاعداً ولا يَتَحَرَّكُ كما قال (اللهُ) تعالى : ﴿ وتَرَى الجبالَ تَحسبُها جامدةً وهي تَمُرُّ مَرَّ السَّحابِ ﴾ . ومنهم مَن يأخذُهُ بالضَّحِكِ والبُكاءِ والنَّدَمِ والشَّهيقِ والرَّعْدَةِ .

والأحوالُ مختَلِفةٌ على حسبِ الأحوالِ والتَّرتيبِ والمقاماتِ والدَّرَجاتِ .

والسَّماعُ كالبرقِ ـ يَلوحُ ويَروحُ . والسَّماعُ حَقٌّ وخُلِقَ فمَن سمعَ بقلبهِ تحقَّقَ ومَن سمعَ بنفسهِ تَزَندَقَ . ولا يَشكُّ فيه إلا جاهلٌ به لقولِ النبيِّ ﷺ : «مَن جَهِلَ شيئاً عاداهُ» . وقال : «لا يَعرِفُ الشَّوْقَ إلا مَن يُكابدُهُ ولا الصَّبابةَ إلا مَن يُعانيها» .

وقالَ الشَّيخُ (أبو مَدْيَن) رحمه اللهُ : السَّماعُ عَورةٌ لا يطَّلِعُ عليهِ إلا أهلُهُ . فإذا حضَرُوا السَّماعَ أغلَقُوا بُيوتَهم وإذا حضَرُوا الطَّعامَ فَتَحُوها . وقال أيضاً : أقْبَحُ كلِّ هَيْجٍ الصُّوفيِّ الشَّحيحِ . والسَّماعُ مع غيرِ أهلهِ حَرامٌ لا يَحِلُّ حُضورُهُ ولا استماعُهُ إلا مع أهلِهِ . وقدْ ذَكَرَ ذلك عِدَّةُ مَشايخَ .

وليس للمُبْتَدِئِ حُضورُ السَّماعِ حتى يُجاهدَ نفْسَهُ بالصِّيامِ والوصالِ والقيامِ وحينَئذٍ يَحِلُّ له حُضورُهُ ويُباحُ له . على هذا اتَّفقَ المشايخُ وأهلُ الاقتداءِ والاهتداءِ .

They take their example from the learned and are guided by the gnostics. He who opposes them is destroyed, has become lost, and has left the Way of the Folk of Realization.'[36]

He also said: 'One who takes part in an ecstatic session without truly participating [in its spirituality] has stripped the necklace of Islam from his throat; one must therefore fear him, according to the words of God Most High: "He who sees you when you stand [in prayer] and your movements among those who prostrate themselves . . .".'[37]

Said the Shaykh (may God have mercy on him): 'In our time there has come to us a faction who call themselves Sufis; they beautify their outward appearances and sully their inner natures by turning toward amusements.[38] They are habitually in *samāᶜ*, fantasizing, and deviating from the way without any *sunna* to believe in and without any other means by which to attain it. They characterize themselves by mortification and avoid the practice of invocation. When they eat, they eat what is forbidden and when they sleep, they sleep until morning. They are not known for their mortification, and they do not act upon their knowledge. [Instead], they wander freely among men and women. They strip away the taste for modesty and rend the garment of desire. They claim arrival [at the Essence] by attributing paranormal knowledge and clairvoyance [to themselves] and say: "The best result has already been ordained for us by God, for we desire the best outcome from God".

'Among them is [another] faction who imagine that they understand inner realities, saying: "When sins are put aside, when the unseen is made manifest, when all else disappears, when illuminations and inner secrets shine forth, when darkness is stripped away, and when tangible things disappear—at that [moment] clear portents will appear. On that day we shall see with the Eye of Unveiling and will manifest ourselves in the state of forms. We shall eat from the foods of the universe, drinking in and witnessing the hidden affairs of the unseen".'

36. By taking this position Shaykh Abū Madyan stands firmly against the practices of many folkloric Sufi orders in the Maghrib, both in his day and in the present. Today one can see in Morocco such groups as the ᶜIsāwa, Ḥamādsha, and Jilāla, who frequently hold popular sessions of *ḥaḍra*, especially on the Prophet Muḥammad's birthday, in which large numbers of people, both men and women, take part in trance-induced dances and public displays of ecstatic behavior. Such unrestrained expressions of emotionalism by untrained amateurs (*muḥibbīn*) are implicitly criticized by the shaykh in this passage.

37. Qur'ān, XXVI (*ash-Shuᶜarā'*), 218–19.

38. In the an-Nājī copy: ' . . . by turning toward inner secrets.'

فبالعُلماءِ يَقْتَدُونَ وبالعارفينَ يَهْتَدُونَ فمَنْ خالَفَهُمْ فقد هلَكَ وضلَّ وخرَجَ عَنْ طريقةِ المحقِّقِينَ .

وقال : مَنْ كانَ في السَّماعِ مِن غيرِ حقيقةٍ فقد خلَعَ طوْقَ الإسلامِ مِن عُنقِهِ ويخافُ عليه لقوله تعالى : ﴿ الَّذِي يَرَاكَ حِينَ تَقُومُ وَتَقَلُّبَكَ فِي السَّاجِدِينَ ﴾

وقال الشيخُ رحمه اللهُ : تأتِينا في وقتِنا طائفةٌ يُسمُّونَ أنْفسَهُم بالصُّوفيَّةِ يُزيِّنونَ الظَّاهرَ ويُدَنِّسُونَ الباطِنَ مُقبِلينَ على اللهوِ . عادَتُهم السَّماعُ يُخيِّلُونَ ويَبْقَونَ حيَّالاً بالطريقِ مِن غيرِ سنَّةٍ يَعْتقدُونَها ولا وَسيلةٍ يَتوسَّلُونَ بها . يَتوسَّمُونَ بالاجتهادِ ويناؤُونَ عن الأوْرادِ . إنْ أكلُوا أكلُوا سُحْتًا وإنْ ناموا ناموا إلى الصَّباحِ . لا بالمُجاهَدةِ يُعرَفُونَ ولا بالعلمِ يَعْملُونَ سَارِحِينَ بينَ فلانٍ وفلانةٍ . كشَفُوا قِناعَ الحَياءِ ومَزَّقُوا جِلبابَ الشَّوقِ . ادَّعَوا الاتِّصالَ (و) يدَّعُونَ المُكاشَفةَ والفِراسةَ وقالوا «سَبَقَتْ لنا مِن اللهِ الحُسْنى ولنا إرادةٌ» .

فمنهم طائفةٌ زعَمُوا أنَّهم يَعلمُونَ الباطِنَ وقالوا «إذا انجلَتِ الذُّنوبُ وتجلَّتِ الغيوبُ وذهَبَتِ الأغْيارُ وتشَعْشَعَتِ الأنْوارُ والأسْرارُ وانسَلخَتِ الظُّلمَةُ وذهَبَتِ المَحْسوساتُ فتظهَرُ عند ذلك علاماتٌ بيِّناتٌ . فنحْنُ يومَئذٍ نَرى بعينِ الكشفِ وتتجلَّى في حالِ الوصفِ . نأكُلُ مِن طعامِ الكوْنِ شارِبينَ مُشاهِدينَ لما غابَ مِن أُمورِ الغيْبِ» .

Said the Shaykh (may God have mercy on him): 'The signs of the *fuqarā'* are three: they do not eat, except what they need for sustenance; they do not sleep unless sleep overcomes them; and they speak only when necessary.'

He also said: 'The *faqīr* does not attain his goal, except by means of three things: his practice must be based on the Qur'ān, the Sunna, and [his] choice of a teacher.'

He also said: 'One does not occupy the rank of the oath of allegiance[39] unless he possesses twelve attributes: constant sadness and wandering, which he derives from Jesus (peace be upon him); forgiveness and trust, which he derives from Joseph (peace be upon him); yearning and ardent love, which he derives from Job (peace be upon him); sincerity and intimate converse with God, which he derives from Moses (peace be upon him); and knowledge and virtuous morals, which he derives from Muḥammad (may God bless and preserve him). Whenever a shaykh is unable to maintain these attributes, then allegiance to him is clearly forbidden.'

The Shaykh [Abū Madyan] (may God have mercy on him) said: 'The sign of the true *faqīr* is that he opens for himself four things and locks for himself four things: he opens the gate of lowliness and locks the gate of [worldly] glory; he opens the gate of mortification and locks the gate of ease; he opens the gate of poverty and locks the gate of wealth; he opens the gate of nightly vigils and locks the gate of sleep.'

He also said (may God have mercy on him): 'The sign of the true *faqīr* is that he has glory without debasement, wealth without poverty, ease without effort, and sleep without exhaustion.'[40]

39. This refers to the *bayʿa*, or oath of allegiance, which the aspirant makes in order to follow the Way of a spiritual master. One who holds this rank is necessarily regarded as a shaykh.

40. In the an-Nājī copy: '. . . ease without suffering and sleep without excess.'

قال الشيخ (أبو مَدْيَن) رحمه الله : عَلاماتُ الفُقراء ثَلاثَةُ أشْياءَ : لا يَأْكُلُونَ إلاَّ القُوتَ ولا يَنامُونَ إلاَّ مِن غَلَبَةٍ ولا يَتَكَلَّمُونَ إلاَّ مِن الضَّرُورَةِ . وقال أيْضًا : لا يَنالُ الفقيرُ مُرادَهُ إلاَّ بِثَلاثَةِ أشْياءَ : العَمَلُ بالقُرآنِ والسُّنَّةِ واتِّخاذُ الأُسْتاذِ .

وقال أيْضًا : لا يَجْلِسُ على رُتْبَةِ البَيْعَةِ إلاَّ مَنْ تَمَسَّكَ باثْني عَشَرَ وَصْفًا : يَتَمَسَّكُ من عِيسَى (عليه السَّلام) بِإيدامِ الحُزْنِ والسِّياحَةِ ومِن يُوسُفَ (عليه السَّلام) بالعَفْوِ والأَمانةِ ومِن يَعْقُوبَ (عليه السَّلام) بالشَّوْقِ والصَّبابةِ ومِن أيُّوبَ (عليه السَّلام) بالتَّفَكُّرِ والصَّبْرِ ومِن مُوسَى (عليه السَّلام) بالإخْلاصِ والمناجاةِ ومِن مُحَمَّدٍ ﷺ بالعِلْمِ والخُلُقِ الحُسْنَى . فَمَتَى عَجَزَ الشَّيخُ عن هذه الأوصافِ فَبَيْعَتُهُ حَرامٌ مَحْضٌ .

وقال الشيخ رحمه الله : علامةُ الفقيرِ الصَّادقِ أنْ يَفْتَحَ على نَفْسِهِ أرْبَعًا ويُغْلِقَ على نَفْسِهِ أرْبَعًا : أنْ يَفْتَحَ بابَ الذُّلِّ ويُغْلِقَ بابَ العِزِّ ويفتحَ بابَ المجاهَدةِ ويغلِقَ بابَ الرَّاحةِ ويفتحَ بابَ الفقرِ ويغلِقَ بابَ الغِنَى ويفتحَ بابَ السَّهَرِ ويغلِقَ بابَ النَّوْمِ .

وقال أيْضًا رحمه الله : علامةُ الفقيرِ الصَّادقِ عِزٌّ مِن غَيرِ مَذَلَّةٍ وغِنى مِن غَيرِ فَقْرٍ وراحَةٌ مِن غَيرِ جَهْدٍ ونَوْمٌ مِن غَيرِ تَعَبٍ [وراحةٌ مِن غَيرِ تَعَبٍ ونَوْمٌ مِن غَيرِ كَثْرَةٍ] .

The Shaykh also said (May God have mercy on him): 'The rules of Sufism are eight: eating [only] what one earns from the labor of his own hands; possessing only what is lawful; having a peaceful home environment; earning only what is best [from one's own actions]; seclusion for the purpose of worship; taking the companionship of one more knowledgeable than oneself; avoidance of the folk of the material world; (and locking one's door when conducting *samāʿ*).'

The Master Abū Madyan (may God be pleased with him) said: 'We were with the leaders of our Sufi companions and when we wanted to hold an ecstatic session the door was locked. None of us would come to the session until he had passed ten days calming his carnal soul, subsiding his fires, and purifying his thoughts. Then every one of us would come [to the session] wrapped in his cloak. Among them were those who would lose their senses by [reciting] the Qur'ān; among them were those who would lose their senses from the Sunna; among them were those who would lose their senses at hearing the [Divine] Promise and Threat; among them were those for whom the cause [of their trance] would last until the next day; and among them were those who were beset by shivering.'

He also said (may God be pleased with him): 'Among the signs of the true *faqīr* are his love for scholars, his service to the jurisprudents, his companionship with the *fuqarā'*, and his transformation [of self] by fasting and standing [in prayer]. His clothing is ragged and his food is coarse. When he sees [something] he reflects on it, when he speaks he invokes [God], and when he is silent he meditates. He walks like one who is infirm and is immersed [in remembrance] when he sleeps. He resembles a bereaved mother in his ecstatic state, yet no one criticizes him and he criticizes no one; instead, he is the purest of mankind in his actions and his speech. The Qur'ān is on his right, the Sunna is on his left and the [Divine] Threat and Promise is his concern. He hopes for nothing but God, he does not fear the censure of critics, and his heart is attached to [the idea of] being cut off from [the material world]. His similitude is like the Earth, which bears everything that is repugnant.

وقال الشيخ أيضًا رحمه الله: شُرُوطُ التَّصوُّفِ ثمانيةُ أشياء: أَكْلٌ مِن كدِّ يدِهِ ومَسْكٌ مِن الحلال وطيبُ المَسْكَنِ وطيّبٌ مِن الكَسْبِ والخَلْوةُ بالعِبادةِ واتّخاذُ صُحْبَةِ مَنْ هو أَعْلَمُ منكَ والتجنُّبُ عن أبناءِ الدُّنيا [وتَغْليقٌ عِنْدَ السَّماعِ].

وقال السَّيّدُ أبو مَدْيَن رضي الله عنه: كُنَّا مع أئمّةِ أصحابنا الصُّوفِيَّةِ إذا أَرَدْنا السَّماعَ غَلَقت البابُ ولا يأْتِي أَحَدٌ مِنّا إلى السَّماعِ حتّى يواصِلَ عشرةَ أيّامٍ لكي تقرَّ نفسُهُ وتخمدَ نيرانُهُ ويَصْفو خاطِرُهُ. ويأْتِي كلٌّ واحدٍ منّا بكَفَنِهِ في كُمّه. فمنهم مَن تذْهَبُ نَفْسُهُ بالقُرآن ومنهم مَن تذهب نفسُه بالسُّنَّةِ ومنهم مَن تذهب نفسه عند استِماعِ الوَعْدِ والوَعِيدِ ومنهم مَن تكونُ العِلّةُ فيه إلى غدٍ ومنهم مَن تتَمَكّنُ فيه الرِّعْدَةُ.

وقال أيضًا رحمه الله: مِن علاماتِ الفقيرِ الصّادق مَحَبَّتُهُ لِلْعُلَماء وخِدْمَتُهُ لِلْفُقَهاء وصُحْبَتُهُ للفقراء وتقلُّبُهُ في صِيامِهِ وقِيامِهِ. لِباسُهُ ما خرِقَ وطعامُهُ ما خشِنَ. إنْ نظرَ اعْتَبرَ وإنْ تكلّمَ ذكرَ وإنْ سكتَ تفكّرَ. (وهو) مَريضٌ في مَشْيِهِ غريقٌ في نوْمِهِ. يُشْبِهُ الثَّكْلى في وَجْدِهِ ولا يلومُه أحدٌ ولا يلومُ أحدًا وأصغى لِكلِّ النّاس في الأفْعال والأقوال. القرْآنُ عن يمينه والسُّنّة عن شمالِهِ والوَعْدُ والوَعيدُ مسْئلتُهُ. لا يرْجُو غيرَ الله ولا يخافُ لوْمَةَ لائمٍ وقلبُهُ مُتعلّقٌ بانقِطاعٍ عنْهُ. مثلُهُ كمثَلِ الأرْضِ تحمِلُ كلَّ القبيحِ.

(His heart is pure—he is favorably disposed toward the one who envies him.) These are the attributes of the true *faqīr*, whom God ennobles and makes into one of the saints of God Most High. "They are the Party of God. Verily it is the Party of God who have attained felicity".'[41]

Said the Shaykh (may God have mercy on him): 'Sufism is not the [mere] observance of rules, nor does it consist of progressing through stages. Instead, Sufism consists of personal integrity, generosity of spirit, the emulation of what has been revealed, knowledge of the Message, (and following the Way of the Prophets). He who deviates from these sources finds himself grazing in the garden of Satan, submerged in the ocean of lust, and wandering in the darkness of ignorance.'

Said the Shaykh (may God have mercy on him): 'I have examined the "Book of Secrets" (*Kitāb al-asrār*) and have found in it one tradition about the Prophet (may God bless and preserve him), in which he said: "The traces of this poverty will not disappear until there remains nothing but one who is marked by heresy. May the curse of God be upon those who deny [His Word]." [The Caliph] ʿUmar [ibn al-Khaṭṭāb] (may God be pleased with him) said: "Who are the marked ones, oh Messenger of God?" "They are marked by the garments of the pious," he replied.[42]

'A certain faction, who are aware only of the external form of dress, imagine that spiritual aspiration consists [only] in what they display. They eat what is forbidden, they create [competing] parties, they follow the example of those who have no knowledge, and they take the beliefs [of the ignorant] as their own. They spend their mornings and afternoons at the doors of kings and the children of the material world. Their appearance is that of the pious, but their actions are those of the hypocrites. Their external aspect is that of the virtuous, but their inner nature is that of the immoral. They do all that is prohibited and adopt every delusion. Among them is even a faction that has gone so far as to say, "With the sister and the sisters among the women," taking the literal sense of the verse, "For Muslim men and women, for believing men and women,"[43] [thinking that all] the believing women [are lawful for them].

41. Qur'ān, LVIII (*al-Mujādila*), 22.
42. This hadith cannot be found in Wensinck.
43. Qur'ān, XXXIII (*al-Aḥzāb*), 35.

[صَافي القَلْبِ وَدودٌ لِمَنْ حَسَدَهُ] . فهذه صِفَةُ الفقير الصَّادق الذي أَكْرَمَهُ اللهُ وجَعَلَه مِن أَوْلِياء اللهِ تعالى . (قال الله تعالى) : ﴿ أُولَئِكَ حِزْبُ اللهِ أَلا إنَّ حِزْبَ اللهِ هُمُ المُفْلِحُونَ ﴾ .

وقال الشيخ رحمه الله : ليس التَّصوفُ بتَشْهيدِ الأَحْكام ولا بتَدْريجِ الأَقْدام وإنما التَّصوّفُ بسَلامَةِ الصُّدُور وسَخاوَةِ النفُوس والاِقْتِداء بالمنزَّل والعِلم بالمُرْسَل [واتّباعِ الرُّسُل] . ومَن خرجَ مِن هذه الموارِد فقدْ أَصْبَحَ في بُسْتانِ الشَّيْطان راعِيًا وفي بحرِ الهَوى غامِسًا وفي ظُلْمَةِ الجَهْل رائِجًا .

وقال الشيخ رحمه الله : نظَرْتُ في كِتابِ الأَسْرار فأَخَذْتُ مِنه حَدِيثًا واحِدًا عن النَّبي ﷺ أَنَّه قال : «ما يَذْهَبُ أَثَرُ هذا الفقرِ حتّى لا يَبْقَى إلا مُتَوسِّمٌ بالبدَع. أَلا لَعْنةُ اللهِ على الكافِرين» . وقال عُمَرُ (بنُ الخطاب) رضي الله عنه : «مَن المتَوسِّمُونَ يا رَسُولَ الله»؟ قال : المتَوسِّمُونَ بِلِباسِ الصَّالحين» .

والمسْتَشْعِرُونَ بظواهِرِ اللباس طائفَةٌ يزْعُمونَ الإرادَةَ بظواهِرِهِم يأْكُلونَ سُحْتًا ويجتمعُونَ أحْزابًا ويقتَدُونَ بِمَنْ لا عِلْمَ له ويَدِينُونَ دِينَهُ ويُصْبحُونَ ويعيشُونَ على أَبْوابِ المُلوكِ وأَبناء الدُّنيا . سِيماهُم سِيماءُ الصَّالحين وأَفْعالُهم أفعالُ المنافِقِين . ظَواهِرُهُم ظَواهِرُ الأَخْيار وبَواطِنُهم بَواطِنُ الفُجَّار يَصْحَبونَ كلَّ مَحْذُور ويَرْكَبُونَ كُلَّ مَغْرُور . ومِنهم طائِفةٌ ذَهَبُوا إلى أَنْ قالوا «بالأُخْتِ والأَخَوات مِنَ النِّساء» وأَخَذُوا بظَواهِرِ الآيَة : ﴿ إنَّ المُسْلِمِينَ والمُسْلِماتِ والمُؤْمِنِينَ والمؤْمِناتِ ﴾ ، وهُنَّ المُؤْمِناتُ .

Although what they say is supported by the Revelation, nowhere in the Revelation is there any indication of the permissibility of [promiscuous] mixing between men and women. Indeed, within the Revelation is: "Say to the believing men that they should lower their gaze and guard their modesty; that will make for greater purity for them. Verily God is well acquainted with what they do",[44] and: "Say to the believing women that they should lower their gaze and guard their modesty; that they should not display their adornment except for what [must ordinarily] appear thereof; that they should draw their veils over their bosoms and not display their adornments, except to their husbands and their fathers . . .".[45] [The meaning of] this verse includes the two groups—both men and women.'

At-Tirmidhī related a strong tradition about the Prophet (may God bless and preserve him) in which he said: 'He who draws near to women has made fornication pleasurable for himself.'[46]

[Further] evidence for what we have mentioned is the tradition about Maymūna (may God be pleased with her), in which she said: 'Put distance between the souls of men and the souls of women, for verily both Satan and the carnal soul desire a sexual encounter between them.'

Al-Bazzār took a well-substantiated tradition from Abū Hurayra, who related that the Prophet (may God bless and preserve him) said: '[As for] one who makes a habit of sitting with women and maintains companionship with princes, know that he is the enemy of the Merciful and the beloved of Satan. May the curse of God be upon the one who holds fast to that [practice].'[47]

The Shaykh [Abū Madyan] also said: 'The Qur'ān is a light by which one is illuminated; the Sunna is a proof which one takes as his example; and the Prophet (may God bless and preserve him) is an Imam who clarifies them. One who deviates from what we have mentioned finds himself alone and raving, [as if he had] the fever of rabies. May the curse of God be upon him and upon the one who cleaves to other than the Book of God and the Sunna.'

44. Qur'ān, XXIV (*an-Nūr*), 30.

45. Ibid., 31.

46. Although this hadith cannot be found in Wensinck, a similar tradition related by at-Tirmidhī can be found in *Kitāb ar-riḍā'* (16).

47. This hadith cannot be found in Wensinck.

وإذا كان ما قالوا في مُحْكَمِ التَّنزيل فليس في التَّنزيل دَليلٌ على جَوازِ الجمع بين الرّجال والنساء . وإنَّما في التَّنزيل : ﴿ قُلْ لِلْمُؤْمِنِينَ يَغُضُّوا مِنْ أبصارِهِمْ وَيَحْفَظُوا فُرُوجَهُمْ ذلك أزْكَى لهُمْ إنَّ اللهَ خبيرٌ بِما يَصْنَعُونَ ﴾ . و : ﴿ قُلْ لِلْمُؤْمِنات يَغْضُضْنَ مِنْ أبصارِهِنَّ ويَحْفَظْنَ فُرُوجَهُنَّ ولا يُبْدِينَ زِينَتَهُنَّ إلّا ما ظَهَرَ مِنْها ولْيَضْرِبْنَ بِخُمُرِهِنَّ على جُيُوبِهِنَّ ولا يُبْدِينَ زِينَتَهُنَّ إلّا لِبُعُولَتِهِنَّ أوْ آبائِهِنَّ ﴾ . وهذه الآيةُ مُشْتَمِلةٌ على الفريقين مِن الرّجال والنساء . ورَوَى التِّرْمِذي حَديثًا عن النبي ﷺ أنَّه قال : «مَنْ تَقَرَّبَ إلى النسوانِ فقَدْ رَضِيَ لنفسِهِ الزِّنى» . والدَّليلُ على ما ذَكَرْناهُ حَديث مَيمُونةَ رضي الله عنها أنَّها قالت «باعِدوا بين أنْفاسِ الرّجالِ وأنْفاسِ النساءِ فإنَّ الشَّيطانَ يُريدانِ الواقِعةَ بَينهما»! . وحَديثٌ صَحيحٌ أخْرَجَهُ البَزَّارُ عن أبي هُريرَةَ عن النبي ﷺ أنَّهُ قال : «مُجالِسُ النساء عادةٌ والاسْتِمرارُ على صُحْبةِ الأُمَراءِ فاعْلَمْ أنَّهُ عَدُوُّ الرَّحْمانِ وحَبيبُ الشَّيطانِ وألّا لَعْنةُ اللهِ على مَنْ تَمَسَّكَ بذلكَ» .

وقال الشَّيخُ أيضًا : القُرآنُ نورٌ يُسْتَضاءُ به والسُّنَّةُ بُرهانٌ يُقْتَدَى به والنبي ﷺ إمامٌ أوْضَحَهُما . فمن خالَفَ فيما ذَكَرْناه فقَدْ أصْبَحَ في بُرَداءِ الجَهْلِ مُتَوَحِّشًا ألَا لعنةُ اللهِ عليه مَن تَمَسَّك بغير اللهِ والسُّنَّةِ .

From the book, *Qawāʿid aṣ-ṣūfiyya*: A certain faction behaved crudely and imagined that if one of them exercised himself with women and young boys, the one who was given to these practices would thereby attain blessings. [They also believed] that the approach of a pious man to women and young boys was for the sake of 'the life of hearts'. They believed that light would travel from heart to heart, or something that resembled such false adornments. These [false Sufis] are a sect who resemble devils; they make [their sect] appear to the ignorant as if it were [concerned with] matters of Divine love and beautify it with a false form. This [in reality] is the stratagem of immorality, an artifice, an act of deception, and a lie. We seek refuge in God from that.

Said the Shaykh (may God have mercy on him): 'When you see a *murīd* or a *faqīr* who is obedient [only] to himself, who has abandoned his invocations, who goes [to women] without marrying them, and asks for things without any need for them, then whip him as a punishment.'

Abū Ḥāmid al-Ghazālī (may God be pleased with him) said: 'The meaning of the *faqīr* is that he act in a manner consistent with the Book and the Sunna.'

Said the Shaykh: 'He who deviates from matters of the Way and adheres to another [doctrine] has accepted error and misguidance in regard to what has been derived from the Prophet (may God bless and preserve him).'

Said the Shaykh: 'The *faqīr* must never be emptied of four things: purity from the turbidity of worries; satiety from thoughts; sufficiency from questions; and regarding everything as equal, whether it be gold or paper.'

He also said: 'Among the attributes of the *faqīr* are five things: the keeping of secrets; love for the virtuous poor; the avoidance of fools and those who are evil; following the commands of the Subduer; and following the Sunna of the Chosen Prophet.'

ومِن كتابِ قواعِدِ الصُّوفِيَّةِ: أنَّ طائِفةً غَلَّطوُا وزَعَموا أنَّ اجْتِهادَ أحدٍ مِنْهُم مع النّساء والشَّبابِ وتَعاطِي هذه الأُمورِ ممّا تحصُلُ به البَركةُ وإنَّ قُرْبَ المَرْأةِ والشَّبابِ مِن الرَّجُلِ الصّالحِ سَببٌ لحَياةِ القُلوبِ. وزَعَموا أنَّ النورَ يَسْري مِن قلْبٍ إلى قلبٍ وأشْباهَ هذه الزَّخارِفِ الباطِلة. فهؤلاء فِرْقةٌ تشَبَّهُوا بالشَّياطينِ يُصوِّرُونَها للجاهِلِ بأُمورٍ مُحَبَّبةٍ ويُزيِّنونَها بصُورةٍ باطِلةٍ. فهذه حيلةُ فِسقٍ ومَكرٌ وخديعةٌ وكَذِبٌ نعوذُ باللهِ مِن ذلكَ.

قالَ الشَّيخ رحمه الله: إذا رَأيتُم المُريدَ الفَقيرَ مُطيعًا لِنَفْسِه تاركًا لِوِرْدِهِ ماشيًا مِن غير تَزْويجٍ سائِلًا مِن غير حاجةٍ فاجْلِدُوه حَدًّا.

قال أبو حامِدِ الغزالي رضي الله عنه: مَعْنَى الفَقيرِ عِبارةٌ عن والسُّنةِ.

وقال الشَّيخ: فمَنْ خالفَ أُمورَها وأخذَ بغيرِها فقد ذهَبَ إلى المحْظُورِ والضَّلال وممّا ورَدَ عن النبي صلى الله عليه وسلم.

قال الشَّيخ: لا يخلُو الفقيرُ مِن أرْبعةِ أشْياءَ: الصَّفاءُ مِن الكَدَرِ والامْتِلاءُ مِن الفِكْرِ والاكْتِفاءُ عن السُّؤالِ ولسواءٌ عنده الذهَبُ والورَقُ.

وقال أيضًا: مِن خِصالِ الفقيرِ خمْسةُ أشْياءَ: حِفظُ الأَسْرارِ ومحَبّةُ الفقراءِ الأخْيارِ واجْتِنابُ السُّفهاءِ والأشْرارِ وامْتِثالُ أوامِرِ القهّارِ واتّباعُ سُنّةِ النبي المُخْتارِ.

He also said: 'The attributes of the *faqīr* are four: cutting oneself off from worldly attachments; distancing oneself from God's creatures; adhering to the Real; and speaking [only] of fine things.'

He also said: 'Among the attributes of the *faqīr* are seven: that he restrain his lusts; that he glorify God in prayer; that he weep over [the salvation] that has been lost; that he beware of heedlessness; that he distance himself from [venerating] the dead and the scattered bones; and that he seek God's protection from the terrors of the Day of Judgment.'[48]

SECTION ON WEARING THE *Muraqqaᶜa*, THE *Shamriyya*, AND THE *Farajiyya*[49]

Said the Shaykh [Abū Madyan] (may God have mercy on him): 'Oh my brother, verily the wearing of the patched cloak (and the *shamriyya*) is done for the purpose of breaking down and overcoming the ego. You will be rewarded for wearing it because the patched cloak (*muraqqaᶜa*) comprises a soul without an ego—a point about which there is neither doubt nor dispute.'

The true *faqīr* must not be jealous, egotistical, or arrogant with his knowledge and should not be miserly with his money. On the contrary, he must act as a guide—cheerful, merciful of heart, and compassionate with [God's] creatures. To him [all human beings] are like one of his hands. [He is] ascetic; everything is equal to him, whether it be praise or blame, taking or giving, acceptance or rejection, wealth or poverty. He is neither joyful about what comes to him nor sad about what has been lost.

Abū Zayd (may God have mercy on him) said: 'One who possesses these attributes is a *faqīr*: the first is averting one's gaze from that which is forbidden; the second is protecting one's private parts from disobedience toward the Lord of the Worlds; the third is that he preserve his tongue from gossiping about his brothers; the fourth is that he avoid forbidden food or drink; the fifth is that he avoid the taking of usury and ill-gotten possessions; [the sixth is that he avoid] doubts; [the seventh is that] he maintain the requirements of religion, the Sunna, and the consensus of the community; [and the eighth] is that he avoid making false oaths.' At this the wearing of the patched cloak and the *shamriyya* is allowable for him.

48. In the an-Nājī copy: '. . . that he make himself ready for the Appointed Day.'

49. The *shamriyya* (*tshāmir* in Moroccan dialect) is a plain linen or cotton garment similar to the Middle Eastern *qamīṣ*. It has long sleeves, covers the legs, and is usually white in color. It is unadorned, buttons up the front, and has a high collar. The *farajiyya*, on the other hand, is a long outer garment, also made of cotton or linen, that is designed to cover the *shamriyya*.

وقال أيضًا : مِن خِصالِ الفَقيرِ أَربَعَةُ أَشياءَ : قَطعُ العَلائِقِ وهَجرُ عَنِ الخَلائِقِ والأَخذُ
في الحَقائِقِ والكَلامُ في الرَّقائِقِ .

وقال أيضًا : مِن خِصالِ الفَقيرِ سَبعَةُ أَشياءَ : أَن يَجحَدَ الشَّهَواتِ ويُسَبِّحَ في الصَّلَواتِ
ويَبكي على ما فاتَ ويَحذَرَ الغَفَلاتِ ويُبعِدَ نَفسَهُ مِن الأَمواتِ والعِظامِ المُندَرِساتِ
ويَتَجَهَّزَ لِيَومِ المِيقاتِ .

بابُ لِباسِ المُرَقَّعَةِ والشَّمَرِيَّةِ والفَرَجِيَّةِ

قال الشَّيخُ أَبُو مَديَن : يا أَخي إِنَّ لُبسَ المُرَقَّعَةِ [والشَّمَرِيَّةِ] على نِيَّةِ كَسرِ النَّفسِ
وقَهرِها . فأَنتَ في لِباسِها مَأجُورٌ لأَنَّ في المُرَقَّعَةِ رُوحًا بلا نَفسَ لا غَيرَ فيها ولا كَرَرَ .
والفَقيرُ الصَّادِقُ لا يَكونُ حَسُودًا ولا مُتَحَيِّرًا ولا مُتَعَجِّبًا بِعِلمِهِ ولا بَخيلًا بِمالِهِ . بَل
يَكونُ دَليلًا بَشُوشًا رَحيمَ القَلبِ شَفيقًا بالخَلقِ -كُلُّهم عِندَهُ كَإِحدى يَدَيهِ- زاهِدًا
قَد استَوى عِندَهُ المَدحُ والذَّمُّ والأَخذُ والعَطاءُ والقَبُولُ والرَّدُّ والغِنى والفَقرُ لا يَفرَحُ بِما
أُوتِيَ ولا يَحزَنُ بِما فاتَ .

قال أَبُو زَيدَ رَحِمَهُ اللهُ : «مَن كانَت فيهِ هذهِ الخِصالُ فهو فَقيرٌ : أَوَّلُها غَضُّ البَصَرِ
عن المَحارِمِ والثَّانِيَةُ حِفظُ الفَرجِ عن مَعصِيَةِ رَبِّ العالَمينَ والثَّالِثَةُ أَن يَصُونَ لِسانَهُ
عن الوَقعَةِ في الإِخوانِ والرَّابِعَةُ أَن يَجتَنِبَ المَطعَمَ مِن الحَرامِ والخامِسَةُ أَن يَجتَنِبَ مِن الرِّبا
والسُّحتِ والشُّبُهاتِ مُحتَفِظًا على الفَرائِضِ والسُّنَّةِ والجَماعَةِ ويَجتَنِبَ الأَيمانَ » . فهذا
يُباحُ لهُ لُبسُ المُرَقَّعَةِ والشَّمَرِيَّةِ .

As for the *faqīr* who wears them out of vanity or the desire for notoriety, which he affects among the Muslims, I fear that he will die as a Jew, a Christian, or a Magian—making an affectation of the *shamriyya* and remembering God only a little—unless he repents and returns [to a sincere state]. For verily one who repents of his sins is like one who has no sin at all.

The first person to wear the *muraqqaᶜa* was the Messenger of God (may God bless and preserve him), then Abū Bakr, ᶜUmar, ᶜUthmān, and ᶜĀ'isha (may God be pleased with them all). They will be present on the Day of Judgment, and whoever does something in a like manner and with a like meaning will be assembled with them on the Day of Judgment. (But if one wears [the *muraqqaᶜa* and the *shamriyya*] and differs with them in his practice, they will be his adversaries on the Day of Judgment.) Likewise, when one fantasizes, imagining that he is one of the virtuous, and plays the flute,[50] but does not practice the asceticism of Bahlūl al-Majnūn (who was the first to play the flute) and desires the material world, Bahlūl will be his adversary on the Day of Judgment. So look carefully, oh wearer of the *muraqqaᶜa* and *shamriyya* and player of the flute, into which door you will enter and from which door you will come out, and know that you will not be safe from [the curse of] Muḥammad (may God bless and preserve him) or his Companions unless you repent and abandon your blameworthy acts. So beware, oh assembly of sinners,[51] to struggle [against your carnal souls] and receive good tidings. God the Almighty said: 'That Home of the Hereafter We shall give to those who do not intend high-handedness or mischief on Earth; and the outcome is best for the righteous.'[52]

50. Although the literal translation of this phrase in Arabic is 'rides the reed,' the actual reference is to the Persian flute (*al-qaṣab al-Fārisī*). In *Bawāriq al-ilmāᶜ*, his treatise on audition and the ecstatic session, Majd ad-Dīn Aḥmad ibn Muḥammad al-Ghazālī (d. 520/1126), the noted Iranian Sufi and brother of the famed theologian Abū Ḥāmid al-Ghazālī, mentions that playing the flute is permissible because no prohibition of its music appears in hadith literature. The flute is richly symbolic in the Persian mystical tradition and is seen by Aḥmad al-Ghazālī to represent man in microcosm. See James Robson, ed. and trans., *Tracts On Listening to Music* (London: The Royal Asiatic Society, 1938), pp. 96–99. There is presently no way to ascertain the extent to which Shaykh Abū Madyan was influenced by the Sufi methodology of the younger al-Ghazālī. We do know, however, that his teachings had reached the western Maghrib by Abū Madyan's lifetime.

51. In the an-Nājī text: '. . . oh assembly of seekers . . ..'

52. Qur'ān, XXVIII (*al-Qaṣaṣ*), 83.

وأمَّا الفقيرُ الذي يَلْبَسُها رِياءً أو سُمعةً ويَلْبَسُها على المُسْلِمِينَ أخافُ أنْ يَموتَ يَهودِيًّا أو

نَصْرانِيًّا أو مَجوسِيًّا يَراؤُونَ الشَّمَرِيَّة ولا يَذكُرُونَ اللهَ إلَّا قَلِيلاً إلَّا أنْ يَتوبَ ويَرْجِعَ فإنَّ

التَّائِبَ مِنَ الذَّنْبِ كَمَنْ لا ذَنْبَ لَه .

وأوَّلُ مَنْ لَبِسَ المُرَقَّعَة رَسُولُ اللهِ ﷺ ثمَّ أبو بكرٍ وعُمَرُ وعُثْمانُ وعائِشَةُ رضي

اللهُ عنهُم أجمعِينَ . وكانُوا حَضائِرَ يَومِ القِيامَة ومَنْ عَمِلَ مِثْلَهُم و بمَعانِيها حُشِرَ يَوْمَ

القِيامَةِ معهُم [فَمَنْ لَبِسَها وخالَفَهُم في الاتِّباعِ كانُوا لَه خِصْماءَ يَوْمَ القِيامَة] . وكذلك

مَنْ تَخَيَّلَ بتَخَيُّلِ الصَّالِحِينَ ورَكِبَ قَصَبَةً وليسَ يَزْهَدُ في الدُّنْيا مِثْلَ زُهْدِ بُهْلُولٍ المجنونُ

رَحِمَهُ اللهُ لِأنَّهُ أوَّلُ مَنْ رَكِبَها فَمَنْ رَكِبَها وهو راغِبٌ في الدُّنْيا كانَ بُهْلُولاً خصِيمَه

يَوْمَ القِيامَة . فانْظُرْ يا أيُّها المَلبِسُ المُرَقَّعَة والشَّمَرِيَّة ورُكوبُ القَصَبَة مِنْ أيِّ بابٍ تَدْخُلُ

ومِنْ أيِّ بابٍ تَخْرُجُ واعلَمْ أنَّكَ لا يُنجِيكَ مِنْ مُحمَّدٍ ﷺ وأصْحابِه أحَدٌ إلَّا التَّوبَة

والإقلاعُ عَنْ فِعْلِكَ المَذْمُوم . فاحْذَرُوا يا مَعْشَرَ المُذنِبينَ واجْتَهِدُوا وأبْشِرُوا . قالَ اللهُ

العظِيمُ : ﴿ تِلْكَ الدَّارُ الآخِرَةُ نَجعَلُها للذِينَ لا يُرِيدُونَ عُلُوًّا في الأرْضِ ولا فَساداً

والْعاقِبَةُ للمُتَّقِينَ ﴾ .

The Prophet (may God bless and preserve him) said: 'Do not wear woolen garments unless your hearts are clean. For one who wears wool in a state of miserliness or dishonesty will have the curse and anger of God upon him.'[53]

[The Prophet] said (may God bless and preserve him): '[Beware], oh wearers of wool out of desire for the Day of Judgment!' 'Why, oh Messenger of God?' he was asked. 'They have made the Word manifest and have abandoned the work,' [he answered].[54]

Said the Messenger of God (may God bless and preserve him): 'At the end of time will come a people who will be known by their clothing and will claim the tradition of piety. To God, however, they will occupy the station of hypocrites and their hearts will be ruined like an abandoned house. [Even] Iblīs will be amazed at what he sees of their obedience toward him.'[55]

Yūsuf ibn al-Ḥusayn said: 'If you examined the misfortunes of mankind, you would know from whence they came. Thus, I saw the misfortunes of the Sufis to be [caused by] associating with those who are unlike them and by consorting with women.'

Sahl ibn ʿAbdallāh [at-Tustarī][56] said at the beginning of the year 300 (912 A.D.): 'Our doctrine is not revealed [to others] and is not discussed because it has become the study of a group of people who dissimulate for the sake of mankind and beautify themselves with speech. Their source of glory is their clothing, their asceticism is in their speech, and their object of worship is their stomachs.'

53. This hadith cannot be found in Wensinck.
54. This hadith cannot be found in Wensinck.
55. This hadith cannot be found in Wensinck.
56. Abū Muḥammad Sahl ibn ʿAbdallāh at-Tustarī (200–282/815–96) was a famous ascetic from Ahwāz in western Iran who met and possibly studied under Dhū'n-Nūn al-Miṣrī (d. 246/861). He is known to have been a master of the station of repentance (*tawba*) and was famous for a partial commentary on the Qur'ān that was attributed to him. He could not possibly have made the statement quoted above in the year 300/912, for at that time he would have been dead for sixteen years. See Arberry, *Muslim Saints and Mystics*, pp. 153–60.

وقالَ النبيُّ ﷺ: «لا تَلْبَسُوا الصُّوفَ إِلَّا وقُلُوبُكم نَقِيَّةٌ فإِنَّهُ مَنْ لَبِسَ الصُّوفَ عَلَى بُخْلٍ وغِشٍّ لَعَنَهُ اللهُ وغَضِبَ عَلَيْهِ.».

وقالَ ﷺ: «ويا لابِسَ الصُّوفِ مُرِيداً يَوْمَ القِيَامَةِ». قِيلَ «ومَ يا رَسُولَ اللهِ»؟ قالَ: «أَظْهَرُوا القَوْلَ وتَرَكُوا العَمَلَ».

وقال رَسُولُ اللهِ ﷺ: «سَيَأْتِي في آخِرِ الزَّمانِ قَوْمٌ يُعْرَفُونَ بِثِيابِهم يُنْسَبُونَ إِلى العِبادَةِ فهُم عند اللهِ بِمَنْزِلَةِ المُنافِقِينَ وقُلُوبُهُمْ خَرِبَتْ كالبَيْتِ الخَالِي يَتَعَجَّبُ إِبْلِيسُ مِنهم مِمَّا يَرَى مِن طَوْعِهِم لَهُ».

وقال يُوسُفُ بْنُ الحُسَيْنِ: «إِذا نَظَرْتَ في آفاتِ الخَلْقِ تَعْرِفُ مِن أَيْنَ أُتُوا فَرَأَيْتَ آفاتِ الصُّوفِيَّةِ في مَعْشَرِ الأَضْدادِ ومُرافَقَةِ النِّساءِ».

وقال سَهْلُ بْنُ عَبْدِ اللهِ (التُّسْتَري) عند سَنَةِ ثَلاثٍ مائةٍ: «لا يَحِلُّ أَنْ يُتَكَلَّمَ بِعِلْمِنا لأَنَّهُ بَحْثُ قَوْمٍ يَتَصَنَّعُونَ لِلْخَلْقِ ويَتَزَيَّنُونَ بِالكَلامِ تَكُونُ مَا جَدَتُهم لِباسَهُمْ وزُهْدُهم كَلامَهُمْ ومَعْبُودُهم بُطُونَهُمْ».

SECTION ON SERVICE TO SPIRITUAL MASTERS

Shaykh Abū Madyan (may God have mercy on him) said: 'Service is obligatory toward one whose sanctity is manifest. The sanctity of the shaykh, the virtuous saint, is manifested in the answering of his supplications [to God], the scarcity of his possessions, his asceticism toward the material world, and his placing of complete trust in God (and the practice of true and correct trust, the abandonment of means [of livelihood] in the material world, and the cutting off of worldly attachments).[57] If these attributes apply to [a particular individual], then he is the shaykh whom one must serve.'

[Shaykh Abū Madyan] said (may God have mercy on him): '(One who serves a shaykh who is knowledgeable, practices [what he teaches], and trusts in God will be gathered with the virtuous on the Day of Judgment.) But one who serves a shaykh who is not ascetic, knowledgeable, or scrupulous, who lives by material means and amasses [the goods of] the material world, jealously guards them, and loves the service of [the world's] children, will be gathered on the Day of Judgment with Pharaoh, Hāmān, and Qārūn in the deepest level of the Fire.'

The Shaykh also said (may God have mercy on him): 'When one serves a shaykh who is a gnostic and an ascetic, God will not take him from the world until he has seen his abode in Heaven.'

He [also] said: 'When one serves a shaykh who amasses [the goods of] the material world, jealously guards them, and does not spend them for the sake of God, God forbids the scent of Heaven from [reaching] him. For when one jealously guards [material things], his heart dies from the amount of his forgetfulness of God Most High and he wastes his time in idleness, useless ravings, and confusion. Verily we take refuge in God from that!'

The Messenger of God (may God bless and preserve him) said: 'When one serves a man who is knowledgeable and practices [what he teaches], it is as if he has served a prophet.'[58]

57. The phrase in parentheses, from the an-Nājī manuscript, appears to have been a later addition to the text.

58. This hadith cannot be found in Wensinck.

بابٌ في خِدْمَةِ المَشَايخِ

قال الشَّيخُ أبو مَدْيَنَ رحمه الله : مَن ظَهَرَتْ وِلايَتُهُ وَجَبَتْ خِدْمَتُهُ . وتَظْهَرُ وِلايةُ الشَّيخِ الوَليِّ الصَّالِحِ في إجابَةِ دُعائِهِ وقِلَّةِ مَؤُنَتِهِ وزُهْدِهِ في الدُّنيا وتَوَكُّلِهِ على الله [وبالتَّوَكُّلِ الصَّادِقِ الصَّحيحِ وسُقوطِ أسْبابِ الدُّنيا وقَطْعِ العَلائِقِ . فإنْ كان على هذه الصِّفاتِ فهو الشَّيخُ الذي يُخْدَمُ] .

وقال رحمه الله : مَن خَدَمَ شيخًا عالمًا عامِلًا مُتَوَكِّلًا حُشِرَ يومَ القِيامَةِ مع الأبْرارِ . فإنَّ مَن خَدَمَ شيخًا غيرَ زاهِدٍ ولا عالمٍ ولا وارعٍ وهو مُتَسَبِّبٌ جامِعٌ الدُّنيا حَريصٌ عليها مُحِبًّا في خِدْمَةِ أبْنائِها حُشِرَ يومَ القِيامَةِ مع فِرْعَوْنَ وهامانَ وقارونَ في الدَّرَكِ الأسْفَلِ من النارِ .

وقـــالَ الشَّيخُ (أيضًا) رحمه الله : مَن خَدَمَ شيخًا عارِفًا زاهِدًا فلا يُخْرِجُهُ اللهُ من الدُّنيا حَتَّى يَرَى مَنْزِلَهُ في الجنَّةِ .

وقال : مَن خدم شيخًا جامِعًا للدُّنيا حَريصًا عليها ولَمْ يُنْفِقْها في اللهِ حَرَمَهُ اللهُ من رائِحَةِ الجنَّةِ . فإنَّ الحَريصَ عليها يَموتُ قلْبُهُ بكَثْرَةِ الغَفْلَةِ عَن اللهِ تعالى ويَقْطَعُ دَهْرَهُ في البَطالَةِ والهَذَيانِ والحَيرَةِ فنعوذُ باللهِ من ذلك .

وقال رسولُ الله ﷺ : «مَن خَدَمَ رَجُلًا عالمًا عامِلًا فكأنَّما خَدَمَ نَبيًّا» .

He also said (may God bless and preserve him): 'The scholars of my community are like the prophets of the Children of Israel.'[59] He meant by this the truly practicing scholars, who are known for their integrity. This tradition is extremely good if the account is correct, for in a well-substantiated tradition about [the scholars] he said (may God bless and preserve him): 'My companions who are not knowledgeable are better than one over whom the new moon has risen, except for the Prophets and the Messengers.'[60] There is no dispute among the Folk of the Sunna that his Companions (may God be pleased with them all) were more excellent than [the rest of] his community. This [applies] if the account is correct, and God is most knowledgeable about what he intended.

The Prophet (may God bless and preserve him) said: 'He who serves his parents will be gathered with us in Paradise on the Day of Judgment.'[61]

SECTION ON REPENTANCE – ITS REQUIREMENTS, SIGNS, PRESCRIBED PRACTICES, AND PREFERRED OBSERVANCES

The Shaykh (may God have mercy on him) said: 'Repentance is a requirement for every Muslim.' God the Almighty said: 'Those who repent, those who serve, [those who praise, those who wander (in the service of God), those who bow down and prostrate themselves, those who enjoin good and forbid evil, and maintain the limits set by God. So proclaim (good tidings) to the Believers].'[62]

[God] the Glorious and Exalted said: 'Unless he repents, believes, and works righteous deeds—for them God will change their evil into good, and God is Oft-Forgiving, Most Merciful.'[63]

Said God (may He be glorified): 'And repent toward God, oh ye Believers, that you may attain felicity.'[64]

59. This tradition, commonly quoted by Islamic scholars and ideologues, cannot be found in Wensinck. Although hadith specialists generally agree that it has no genuine origin, it has been reproduced by al-ʿAjlūnī [*Kashf al-Khafā*' (2), p. 83]. For substantiated *aḥādīth* on the excellence of the ulama see Ibn Ḥanbal, 'Bāb faḍl al-ʿulamā',' in his *Muqaddima* (17).

60. This hadith cannot be found in Wensinck.

61. This quotation appears to have been a later addition to the text, since its subject does not conform with that of the preceding section. The hadith cannot be found in Wensinck.

62. Qur'ān, IX (*at-Tawba*), 112.

63. Qur'ān, XXV (*al-Furqān*), 70.

64. Qur'ān, XXIV (*an-Nūr*), 31.

وقال ﷺ: «عُلَماءُ أُمّتي كأنبياءِ بني إسرائيل». يعني بذلك العُلَماءَ العامِلينَ الَّذين هُمْ على الاستِقامَةِ. وهذا الحديث في غايَةِ الحُسنِ إنْ صَحَّتِ الرِّوايَةُ لأنَّ في حديثٍ صحيحٍ عنه ﷺ أنَّه قال: «أَصْحابي غيرِ العالمينَ خيرٌ مِمّا طلَعَتْ عليه الشَّمْسُ إلاَّ النَّبيّينَ والمُرسَلينَ». ولا خِلافَ بين أَهْلِ السُّنَّةِ أنَّ أَصْحابَهُ رضيَ اللهُ عَنْهُمْ أجمعين أَفْضَلُ مِن أُمَّتِه. وإنْ صَحَّتْ الرِّوايَةُ فاللهُ أَعْلَمُ بما أراده.

قال النبي (صلى الله عليه وسلّم): «مَن خدمَ أبويهِ حُشِرَ معنا يومَ القِيامَةِ في الجَنَّة».

بابٌ في التَّوْبَةِ وفرائِضِها وعلاماتِها وسُنَنِها وفضائِلِها

قال الشَّيخ رحمه الله: التَّوبَةُ فرْضٌ على كلِّ مُسْلِمٍ. قال اللهُ العظيم: ﴿التّائِبونَ العابِدونَ﴾ . . .

وقال عزَّ وجلَّ: ﴿إلاَّ مَنْ تابَ وآمَنَ وعَمِلَ عَمَلاً صالحًا فأُولئكَ يُبدِّلُ اللهُ سيِّئاتِهم حسناتٍ وكان اللهُ غفورًا رحيمًا﴾.

وقال اللهُ سُبْحانَهُ: ﴿وتوبوا إلى اللهِ جميعًا أيُّها المُؤْمِنونَ لعلَّكم تُفلِحونَ﴾.

The Messenger of God (may God bless and preserve him) said: 'One who repents of a sin is like one who has no sin.'[65] He also said (may God bless and preserve him): 'Hasten toward repentance before the Gate is locked.'[66] [The 'Gate' referred to in this hadith] is a gate in the Far Maghrib, and the evidence for this is in the words of [God] Most High: 'A day on which will come certain of the signs of your Lord; no good will it do for a soul to believe in them then, if it did not believe before, nor earned righteousness through its faith.'[67] Thus, he who dies without repenting is not one of us.

A man from the Banū Umayya complained to ʿUmar ibn al-Khaṭṭāb (may God be pleased with him) and said to him: 'If, when I have committed a sin, then returned [to God] and felt remorse, have I repented?' 'Yes,' he replied. 'The Messenger of God (may God bless and preserve him) said, "Verily in Paradise are eight gates, all of them locked, except the gate of repentance". So repent and trust completely in God, for none but God forgives sins.'

An Abyssinian said, 'Oh Messenger of God, verily I have performed immoral acts and desire to repent. Do I have repentance?' 'Yes,' said [the Prophet].' Then [the Abyssinian] returned and said, 'Oh Messenger of God, did God see me while I was doing [these immoral acts]?' 'Yes,' he replied. At this the Abyssinian let out a cry and his soul departed with it, may God have mercy on him. Said the Messenger of God: 'This one is of the Folk of Paradise and this is true repentance.'[68]

Al-Junayd said to Mālik ibn Dīnār[69] (may God be pleased with the both of them): 'Inform me as to the requirements of repentance, its prescribed practices, its etiquette, and its preferred observances.' [Mālik ibn Dīnār] replied:

65. Ibn Mājja, *Kitāb az-zuhd* (30).

66. On the 'Gate of Repentance and Mercy' see, at-Tirmidhī, *Kitāb ad-daʿwat* (99), in which its location is assumed to be 'in the direction of the Maghrib' (*min qibal al-maghrib*). See also, Ibn Hanbal (1), 242, 345.

67. Qur'an, VI (*al-Anʿam*), 158. Shaykh Abū Madyan's assertion that the 'Gate of Repentance' is to be found in the Far Maghrib may also be a reflection of a belief among western Muslims that the 'country of the soul' is to be found in the 'beauteous west.' The ancient Egyptians, for example, believed that the heaven for departed souls lay in the western regions beyond the desert—the land of the setting sun. See, Gerardus van der Leeuw, *Religion in Essence and Manifestation* (Princeton, NJ: Princeton University Press, 1968), p. 319.

68. This hadith cannot be found in Wensinck. For other traditions on the same subject, see Ibn Ḥanbal (2), 14.

69. Mālik ibn Dīnār as-Sāmī (d. 130/748) was a former slave from Sijistān, who, like ʿUtba al-Ghulām, was a disciple of al-Ḥasan al-Baṣrī. He was a noted early traditionist and calligrapher of the Qur'ān. There is no way in which he could have met al-Junayd, since he died nearly two centuries before the latter. See Arberry, *Muslim Saints and Mystics*, pp. 26–31.

وقال رسولُ الله ﷺ : «التَّائبُ مِن الذَّنبِ كَمَنْ لا ذَنبَ لَه» . وقال أيضًا ﷺ : «بادِرُوا بالتَّوْبَةِ قبل أَنْ يُغْلَقَ البابُ» . وهو بابٌ بالمَغْربِ الأَقْصَى والدَّلِيلُ على ذلك قوله تعالى : ﴿ يَوْمَ يَأْتِي بَعْضُ آيَاتِ رَبِّكَ لا يَنْفَعُ نَفْسًا إِيمَانُها لَمْ تَكُنْ آمَنَتْ مِن قَبْلُ أَوْ كَسَبَتْ فِي إِيمَانِها خَيْرًا ﴾ . فَمَنْ ماتَ ولَمْ يَتُبْ فَلَيسَ مِنَّا .

وشَكَى رجلٌ مِن بَني أُمَيَّةَ إلى عمرَ بنِ الخطَّابِ ﷺ فقال له : «إِنِّي إذا أَذْنَبْتُ ذَنْبًا ثُمَّ رَجَعْتُ ونَدِمْتُ فُهَل لي من تَوْبَةٍ»؟ فقال : «نعم. إِنَّ رسولَ اللهِ ﷺ قال : إِنَّ للجَنَّة ثَمانيةَ أبوابٍ كلُّها تَغْلَقُ إلاّ بابَ التَّوبة . فتُبْ وتَوَكَّلْ على الله وما يَغْفِرُ الذُّنُوبَ إلاّ اللهُ» .

وقال حَبَشِيٌّ : «يا رسولَ اللهِ إِنِّي كُنْتُ أَعْمَلُ الفواحِشَ وأَرَدْتُ أَنْ أَتُوبَ . فَهَلْ لي من تَوبَةٍ»؟ فقال له : «نعم» . ثم رجع فقال : «يا رسولَ اللهِ كان اللهُ يَرَانِي وأنا أَعْمَلُه»؟ قال : «نعم» . فصاحَ الحبشيُّ صَيْحَةً فخَرَجَتْ رُوحُهُ فيها رحمه الله . فقال رسولُ الله ﷺ : «هذا مِن أَهلِ الجَنةِ فهذه حقيقةُ التَّوبة» .

وقال الجُنَيْدُ لمالكِ بن دينارٍ رضي الله عنهما : «أَخْبِرْنِي عن فَرائضِ التَّوبةِ وسُنَنِها وآدابها وفضائلها» .

'There is no capability and no power except through God, the Most High, the Almighty! As for the requirements of repentance, [they consist of] paying back the injustices [one has committed] to those who have suffered them and making up the prayers, fasts, and alms that have been missed. As for its prescribed practices, [they consist in] avoiding the companions that were befriended during the period of one's disobedience, renouncing [one's past], and weeping for what has gone before. As for its supererogatory acts, [they consist in] continuously reciting invocations and [maintaining] the presence of the heart [with God]. As for its preferred observances, they [consist in] choosing a shaykh who is knowledgeable, God-fearing, scrupulous, and ascetic. As for its etiquette, [it consists of] happiness and excitement in [one's] obedience toward God, the continuous practice [of obedience], visiting other shaykhs, love for the poor and indigent, and the carrying out of [one's] obligations at the first moment that they are due.'

It was asked of al-Junayd: 'What is the reality of repentance?' He said: 'Remorse for what has passed, sincerity, hunger, and asceticism.'

God Most High said: 'He is the one who accepts repentance from His servants and forgives sins; [and He knows all that you do].'[70]

Everyone who makes himself known for [his] repentance and [continues to] commit immoral acts will be gathered in the lowest depths of the Fire on the Day of Judgment.

Said Shaykh Abū Madyan: 'If a repenter repents, it is necessary for him to irrevocably divorce the material world and all disobedience [toward God], while continuing to practice contemplation, work [at perfecting his state], fear [for the wrath of God], weeping [for what he has done], and sadness [for what has gone before].'

Rābiʿa al-ʿAdawiyya said: 'The sign of repentance is remorse, and a heart that is fearful, sincere, and submissive—[one] that is a dwelling place for obedience.' [Thus, the repenter] must be fearful, sorry for what he has neglected that was due to God, loving toward the *fuqarā'*, merciful toward the poor, an intercessor for the poor,[71] [one who is] fond of them, and a visitor to shaykhs.

70. Qur'an, XLII (*ash-Shura*), 25.

71. A strong sense of social responsibility and activism is one of the hallmarks of early Maghribi Sufism. See Vincent J. Cornell, 'The Logic of Analogy and the Role of the Sufi Shaykh in Post-Marinid Morocco', *International Journal of Middle East Studies* (15), 1983, pp. 67–93.

قال: «لا حَوْلَ ولا قُوَّةَ إلاَّ باللهِ العلّي العظيم. أمَا فرائِضُ التَّوبةِ فردُّ المَظالم إلى أهلِها وإعادَةُ الصَّلاةِ التي ضَيَّعَها والصّيامُ والزَّكاة. وأَمَّا سُنَنها فهجْرُ الأَصْحابِ الذّين كانَ بصُحْبَتِهم في أَيَّامِ مَعْصِيَتِهِ والإقْلاعُ والبكاءُ على ما سَلَفَ. وأَمَّا نوافِلُها فدوامُ الأَوْرادِ وحُضورُ القَلْبِ. وأَمَّا فضائِلها فاتخاذُ شَيْخٍ عالمٍ تقيٍّ ورعٍ زاهِدٍ. وأَمَّا آدابُها فالفرحُ بالطَّاعَةِ والنشَّاطُ إليها والدَّوامُ عليها وزيارَةُ المشايخِ وحُبُّ الفُقَراءِ والمساكينِ والتَّحفظُ على الفرائِضِ في أوائِلِ أَوْقاتِها».

قيلَ للجُنَيْدِ: «فما حقيقةُ التَّوْبهِ»؟ قال: «النَّدمُ على ما فاتَ والإخْلاصُ والجوعُ والزُّهْدُ».

قال اللهُ تعالى: (وهو الذي يَقبَلُ التَّوْبَةَ عن عِبادِهِ ويَعْفو عن السَّيِّئاتِ ويَعْلَمُ ما تفْعَلونَ). فكلُّ من أَشْهَرَ نَفْسَهُ بالتَّوبةِ وهو يَعْمَلُ الفواحِشَ حُشِرَ يومَ القيامةِ في الدَّرْكِ الأَسْفَلِ مِنَ النَّار.

قال الشَّيخ أبو مَدْين: إذا تابَ التَّائِبُ يجبُ عليه أَنْ يُطلِّقَ الدُّنيا ثلاثًا والمَعاصيَ كُلَّها ولا يزالُ مُتفكِّرًا عاملاً خائفًا باكِيًا حزينًا. وقالت رابعةُ العدَوِيَّة: «عَلامَةُ التَّوْبَةِ النَّدمُ وقلبٌ خائفٌ خالِصٌ خاشعٌ ويكُونُ موْطِنًا للطاعَةِ». [ويجبُ أَنْ يكون] باكِيًا مُتأَسِّفًا على ما فرطَ في جانبِ اللهِ محُبًّا للفقراءِ رحيمًا بالمساكينِ شَفيعًا للمساكينِ وَدُودًا لهم زائرًا للمشايخ».

Al-Junayd said (may God have mercy on him): 'The repentance of the repenter is not correct until he maintains his prayers, their requirements, their prescribed behaviors, their supererogatory acts, their prostrations, and their appearance.' This is because repentance is an obligation and purity is an obligation. Every obligation must be carried out and maintained. Thus, one who does not carry out that which is obligatory for him has no repentance, because [the maintenance] of obligations comprise the root and foundation of repentance. Furthermore, every person who repents, fails to maintain [even] one of the pillars of repentance, and fails to maintain his obligations has no repentance. Both exoteric and esoteric scholars agree on this [point] and [the principles of repentance] belong to the [true] Folk of the Way.

Thus, the repenter is one who knows what obligations and forms of behavior are required for him. [As for] the shaykh, he speaks with knowledge. One who listens, listens, while one who does not listen is left to himself and his affairs are in the hands of God. This [teaching] they impart, and it is taken as a legacy from others, may God be pleased with them.

Shaykh Abū Madyan also said: 'Place the Sunna firmly in your sight so that your work will be made more pleasing [to God] and will be accepted from you. In this way you will find a sweetness in it and will arrive at what the pious have attained. Oh, my brother! Follow the example of the Messenger of God (may God bless and preserve him), so that you may be gathered with him on the Day of Judgment. And know, my brother, that following the Sunna is the root of piety. So whoever follows the Messenger of God (may God bless and preserve him) follows the Way of Heaven and the Real.[72] But for one who deviates, his work will not be accepted from him. The evidence for this is in the words of God Most High: "So take what the Messenger has given you and deny yourselves that which he has forbidden you".'[73]

That which is given on the subject of repentance in the book, *Sabīl al-khayrāt* (The Way to the Good): God the Almighty has said: 'Oh believers! Repent, all of you, before God so that you may attain felicity.'[74] [And God Most High said]: 'And for one who repents after his transgression and amends his conduct, verily God will forgive him; [for God is Oft-Forgiving, Most Merciful'].[75]

72. In the an-Nājī copy: '. . . attains mastery while he who abandons it is destroyed.'

73. Qur'ān, LIX (*al-Ḥashr*), 7.

74. Qur'ān, XXIV (*an-Nūr*), 31. The book mentioned in this passage, *Sabīl al-khayrāt*, cannot be identified at the present time.

75. Qur'ān, V (*al-Mā'ida*), 39.

وقال الجُنَيْدُ رحمه الله : «لا تصحّ توبةُ التّائبِ حتّى يكونَ محافِظًا على الصّلواتِ وفرائضِها وسُننِها وفضائِلِها وسُجودِها وهَيْئَاتِها» . لأنّ التّوبةَ فَرْضٌ والطّهارةَ فرْضٌ ولا بُدَّ لِكلّ فرْضٍ مِن التّحفُّظِ عليه والقِيام به . ومَن لم يحْفظْ على ما فُرِضَ عليه فلا توْبَةَ لَهُ لأنّ الفرائضَ أصْلُ التّوْبَةِ وأساسُها . وكلُّ مَن تابَ وضَيّعَ رُكْناً مِن أرْكانِ التّوبةِ ويُضيِّعُ الفرائضَ فلا توْبَةَ له . وأجْمعَ على هذا عُلَماءُ الظّاهِرِ والباطِنِ وهذا مِن أَهْلِ الطّريقِ .

فالتّائبُ مَن عرَفَ ما فُرِضَ عليه مِن فرائِضَ وسُنَنٍ . فالشّيْخُ يتكلّمُ بالعِلْمِ فمن سَمِعَ سَمِعَ ومَن لم يسْمعْ فلِنفسِهِ وأمْرُهُ إلى الله . بهذا أوْصوا وتواصَوا رضيَ الله عنهم .

وقال الشّيخ أبو مَدْين أيضًا : إجْعلِ السُّنّة بين عَيْنَيْكَ يطِيبُ العَمَلُ مِنكَ ويُقْبلُ منك وتجدُ له حلاوةً وتصِلُ إلى ما وصَلَ إليه الصّالِحُونَ . يا أخِي إقْتدِ برسُولِ اللهِ ﷺ تُحْشَرْ يومَ القِيامَةِ معه . واعْلمْ يا أخِي أنّ اتباعَ السُّنّةِ أصْلُ العِبادَةِ . فمَن اتبعَ رسُولَ اللهِ ﷺ فقدْ سلكَ طَريقَ الحقِيقَةِ والجنّةِ . ومَن خالفَ لم يُقْبلْ مِنهُ عَمَلُه . والدّلِيلُ على ذلك قوْلُه تعالى : ﴿ وَمَا آتَاكُمُ الرَّسُولُ فَخُذُوهُ وَمَا نَهَاكُمْ عَنْهُ فَانتَهُوا ﴾ .

(ما جاء في التوبة من كتاب سبيل الخيرات) : قال الله العظيم : ﴿ وَتُوبُوا إِلَى اللَّهِ جَمِيعًا أَيُّهَ الْمُؤْمِنُونَ لَعَلَّكُمْ تُفْلِحُونَ ﴾ . [وقال تعالى] : ﴿ فَمَنْ تَابَ مِنْ بَعْدِ ظُلْمِهِ وَأَصْلَحَ فَإِنَّ اللَّهَ يَتُوبُ عَلَيْهِ [إِنَّ اللَّهَ غَفُورٌ رَحِيمٌ] ﴾ .

The Messenger of God (may God bless and preserve him) said: 'Verily God spreads [His hand in] forgiveness for the sinner from night until day and from day until night, until the sun rises in the west.'[76]

And he said (may God bless and preserve him): 'If you committed sins until [their number] reached the sky, and then are remorseful, surely God would still forgive you.'[77]

He said (may God bless and preserve him): 'Verily the slave will commit a sin, through which he will enter Heaven'. 'How is that, oh Messenger of God?' he was asked. He said, 'He concentrates his attention on repentance and the avoidance of sin until he enters Heaven.'[78]

He also said (may God bless and preserve him): 'The expiation of sin is repentance.'[79] Saᶜīd ibn al-Musāyyib (may God be pleased with him) said: 'This verse: "Verily He is Most Forgiving to those who turn to Him again and again", is for the man who sins and repents, and then sins and repents [again].'[80]

Al-Fuḍayl ibn ᶜIyāḍ said: 'God, the Glorious, the Mighty, said: "I shall give sinners the glad tidings that if they repent I will accept [their repentance] from them, provided they follow the example of those who attest to the Truth. If I had exercised My justice upon them I would have made them suffer".'[81] (Ṭalḥa ibn Ḥabīb said: 'The statement of God, Glorious and Mighty, has even more importance if the slave maintains [what is required from it]. Verily, the bounty of God is more than can be conceived, yet [the pious] start their day repenting and end their day repenting.' ᶜAbdallāh ibn ᶜUmar [ibn al-Khaṭṭāb] said: 'When one recalls a mistake, feels guilty about it, and then recognizes what he has done, it will be erased in the *Umm al-Kitāb*.'[82]

It is related that when God, Glorious and Mighty, cursed Iblīs, he asked Him for a postponement, so He postponed [the curse] until the Day of Judgment. Then [Iblīs] said, 'By Your glory and Your might, I will not leave the hearts of the children of Adam as long as they have life.'

76. See Muslim, *Kitāb at-tawba* (31), and Ibn Ḥanbal (4), 395, 404.

77. This hadith cannot be found in Wensinck.

78. Although the hadith as reproduced here is not listed in Wensinck, part of it can be found in aṣ-Ṣuyūṭī [*Jāmiᶜ al-aḥādīth* (2), p. 269] via Ibn al-Mubārak.

79. See Ibn Ḥanbal (1), 289.

80. Qur'ān, XVII (*al-Isrā'-Banī Isrā'īl*), 25.

81. This quotation is a paraphrasis made in the form of an exegesis on one or more Qur'anic verses. It is not part of the Revelation itself.

82. *Umm al-Kitāb*, meaning 'Mother of Books' or 'Sourcebook,' refers here to the *Lawḥ al-Maḥfūẓ* or 'Preserved Tablet' on which are recorded the deeds of all mankind.

وقال رسول الله ﷺ : «إنَّ اللهَ يُبْسِطُ يَدَهُ بالتَّوبَةِ لِمسيءِ اللَّيلِ إلى النَّهارِ ولمسيءِ النَّهارِ إلى الليلِ حَتَّى تطلعَ الشَّمْسُ مِن مَغْربها».

وقال ﷺ : «لوْ عَملتُمُ الخطَايا حتَّى تَبْلغَ السَّماءَ ثُمَّ نَدِمْتُمْ لتابَ اللهُ عَلَيْكُم».

وقال ﷺ : «إنَّ العَبْدَ لَيُذنِبُ الذنبَ فيَدْخلُ به الجَنَّة». قِيلَ: «وكَيْفَ ذلك يا رَسُولَ اللهِ»؟ قال: «يَكُونُ نَصِيبَ عَيْنَيْهِ تائِبًا فارًّا حَتَّى يَدْخلَ الجَنَّة».

وقال ﷺ : «كَفَّارَةُ الذنبِ النَّدامَةُ». وقال سَعِيدُ بْنُ المُسَيّبِ رضي الله عنه : نَزَلَتْ هذه الآيةُ ﴿ فَإِنَّهُ كَانَ لِلأَوَّابِينَ غَفُورًا ﴾ في الرَّجُلِ لَمَّا يُذْنِبُ ثُمَّ يَتوبُ ثُمَّ يُذْنِبُ ثُمَّ يَتوبُ. وقال الفُضَيْلُ بْنُ عِياض: «قالَ اللهُ عَزَّ وجَلَّ: لأُبَشِّرُ المُذْنِبِينَ أنَّهُمْ إنْ تابوا قَبِلْتُ مِنهم وحَذَوْا حَذْوَ الصِّدّيقين. إنْ وَضَعْتُ عَدْلي عليهم عَذَّبْتُهُم. وقال طَلْحَةُ بْنُ حَبيب: «إنَّ قولَ اللهِ عَزَّ وجَلَّ أعْظَمُ أنْ يَقومَ بها العَبْدُ. وإنَّ نِعمَةَ اللهِ أكْثَرُ مِن أنْ تُحصى وَلَكِنْ أصْبِحُوا تائِبينَ وأمْسُوا تائِبينَ». وقال عَبْدُ اللهِ بْنِ عُمَرَ: «مَن ذَكَرَ خطيئَةً أَلَمَّ بها فَوَجَدَ بها مُحيتْ عنه في أُمِّ الكِتابِ».

ويُرْوى أنَّ اللهَ عَزَّ وجَلَّ لَمَّا لَعَنَ إبْليس فَسَأَلَهُ النَّظْرَةَ فَأَنْظَرَهُ إلى يومِ القِيامَةِ. فقال: «وعِزَّتِكَ وجلالِكَ ما أَخْرُجُ مِن قلبِ بَني آدَمَ ما دامَ فيه الرُّوحُ».

It was related that a prophet of the Children of Israel (may God bless them all) committed a sin and God inspired unto him: 'By My Glory and My Might, if you had not returned . . . [lacuna in text] . . . I would certainly have punished you.' Said [the Prophet of Israel]: 'Oh Lord, You are You, and I am I. By Your glory, if You do not absolve me of my sins, I would surely repeat [them].' So God, Glorious and Mighty, absolved him of his sins.

Luqmān [the Sage] used to say to his son: 'Do not delay in seeking repentance, for verily death comes upon one unawares.'

A man asked a question of ʿAbdallāh ibn Masʿūd, and when he turned toward him he saw tears streaming out of the corners of his eyes. Then he said: 'In Heaven are eight gates, each of which are locked and opened except the gate of repentance. There is an angel entrusted with it who will not lock it until the sun rises in the west. So work [for God's acceptance] and do not despair.'

ʿAbd ar-Raḥmān ibn al-Qāsim said: 'ʿAbd ar-Raḥmān and I have attained the repentance of the unbeliever and his Islam.' [Shaykh Abū Madyan?] said: 'Verily I hope that the Muslim will have a better situation with God, for it has been made known to me that the repentance of a Muslim is like [a second conversion to] Islam after Islam.'[83]

ʿUmar ibn al-Khaṭṭāb (may God be pleased with him) said: 'Sit with those who repent, for they avert misfortune.' Said the Messenger of God (may God bless and preserve him): 'One who repents of his sins is like one who has no sin.'[84] This is what has been made known to us from the [body of] hadith.

May Allah bless our Lord Muḥammad and his Family.
The End.
May Allah be praised profusely.

83. It is difficult to ascertain who is addressing whom in this passage.
84. See note 65 above.

ويُروى أنَّ نبيّاً مِن أنبياء بني إسرائيل صَلوات [اللهِ] عليهم أجمعين أصاب ذنْباً فأَوْحى اللهُ إليه: «وعِزَّتي وجَلالي لئِنْ لم تعُدْ - [كذا] - لأُعذِّبَنَّك».

فقال: «يا ربِّ أنت أنتَ وأنا أنا. وعِزّتِك لئِنْ لم تعْصِمْني لأعُودَنَّ».

فعصَمَهُ اللهُ عزَّ وجلَّ.

وكان لُقمانُ [الحكيم] يقولُ لابنه «يا بُنيَّ لا تؤخِر التَّوبة فإنَّ الموتَ يأْتي بغْتَةً».

وسأَل رجلٌ عَبْدَ اللهِ بْنَ مسْعُود ثُمَّ الْتَفَتَ إليه فرأى عَيْنَيْه تدْرِفان دُمُوعاً فقال: «إنَّ للجَنَّة ثمانيةَ أبوابٍ كلّها تُغْلَقُ وتُفْتَحُ إلاّ بابَ التَّوبة. فإنَّ عليه مَلَكاً مُوكَّلاً به لا يُغلِقُهُ حتّى تطْلُعَ الشَّمْسُ من مَغرِبها. فاعْمَلْ ولا تيأَسَنَّ».

وقال عَبْدُ الرَّحمانِ بْنُ القاسِم: «تدارَكْنا مع عَبْدِ الرَّحمانِ توْبَ الكافِرِ وإسْلامه». فقال [الشّيخ أبو مدينَ]: «إنّي لأَرْجُو أنْ يكونَ المُسْلِمُ أحْسَنَ حالاً عند اللهِ ولقَدْ بَلَغني أنَّ توْبَةَ المسلم كإسلام بعد إسلام».

وقال عُمَرُ بْنُ الخطّاب رضي الله عنه: «إجْلِسُوا إلى التوّابين. فإنهم أرْزاءٌ مُقيَّدَةٌ». وقال رَسُولُ اللهِ صلى الله عليه وسلم: «التّائبُ مِن الذنْبِ كمَنْ لا ذنْبَ له». وهذا ما بَلَغنا مِنَ الحديثِ.

وصَلّى اللهُ على سَيِّدِنا مُحمّدٍ وآلِه. إنتهى والحمْدُ للهِ كثيراً.

IV

UNS AL-WAḤĪD WA NUZHAT AL-MURĪD[1]

(The Intimacy of the Recluse and Pastime of the Seeker)

SAID the Spiritual Master and Imam, the Gnostic by the grace of God, the Great Saint, Spiritual Axis of the Gnostics, Guide for followers of the Way to God, [one] for whom evident miracles and dazzling paranormal phenomena are manifest, the Guarantor of the Saints and the Unique among those pure in nature—the Master Abū Madyan Shuʿayb (may God be pleased with him and benefit us with his blessings):

1. The Qur'ān is a Divine inspiration and a revelation, both of which remain until the Day of Judgment.

2. The Truth [God] is independent of physical existence, whereas physical existence is derived. Substantial matter is integral to physical existence. Were [the existence of substantial matter] to be ended, physical existence itself would be destroyed.

3. The learning of this knowledge is appropriate only for one who has acquired four [things]: asceticism, formal doctrine, complete reliance upon God, and certainty.

1. This edited translation is based primarily on two manuscripts: Or. 4273, folios 675–86 (copied at Mecca in 1089/1678), of the British Library, London; and Fonds Arabes 2405/8 (folios 337–44) of the Bibliothèque Nationale, Paris. The contents of these two nearly complete versions were combined and checked against each other for errors. Further cross-checking of the text was undertaken with the aid of a number of partial collections of Shaykh Abū Madyan's aphorisms, the most complete of these being found in Abu'l-ʿAbbās Aḥmad al-Khaṭīb Ibn Qunfudh al-Qusanṭīnī (d. 810/1407–8), *Uns al-faqīr wa ʿizz al-ḥaqīr*, Muḥammad al-Fāsī and Adolphe Faure, eds. (Rabat: al-Markaz al-Jāmiʿī li'l-Baḥth al-ʿIlmī, 1965), pp. 18–19. Numerous partial copies of this text can also be found in the Süleymaniye Library, Istanbul: [under the title *Hikam*] Haci Mahmud Effendi No. 2310/6, folios 53–58; Bagdateli Vehbi Effendi No. 616/1, folios 1–3 (1028/1619); H. Husnu Pasha No. 671/3, folios 78–81 (1197/1783); [Under the title *Uns al-tavhid*] Esad No. 1689/4, folios 90–94; [under the title *Uns al-tavhid ve nuzhat al-murid*] Haci Mahmud Effendi No. 2661/2, folios 8–12 and No. 2634/2, folios 8–11; [under the title *Uns al-vahid*] Laleli No. 3669/8, folios 92–94; [under the title *Uns al-vahid ve nuzhat al-murid fi ʿilm al-tavhid*] Haci Mahmud Effendi No. 2487/4, folios 44–57 and No. 6465/5, folios 8–10. Further copies may also be found in the Princeton University Library: No. 2684, folios 266v–268r, and No. 2685 [under the title, *Min kalām ash-shaykh Abī Madyan*], folios 65v–66r. Bracketed words and phrases in the Arabic text represent items found in the Bibliothèque Nationale copy that are not present in the British Library copy.

«أُنْسُ الوَحِيدِ وَنُزْهَةُ المُرِيدِ»

قال الشَيْخُ الإمامُ العارِفُ باللهِ الوَلِي الكَبيرُ قُطْبُ العارِفين مُرْشِدُ السالِكِينَ ذُو الكَراماتِ الظَّاهِرَةِ والخَوارِق الباهِرَةِ. عُمْدَةُ الأَوْلِياءِ [و] أَوْحَدُ الأَصْفِياءِ سَيِّدِي أَبُو مَدين شُعَيْبُ رَضِيَ اللهُ تعالى عَنْهُ ونَفَعَنا بِبَرَكاتِهِ:

1) القُرْآنُ نُزُولٌ وتَنْزِيلٌ فالنُّزُولُ والتَّنْزِيلُ باقِيانِ إلى يَوْمِ القِيامَةِ.

2) الحَقُّ [تعالى] مُسْتَبِدُّ الوُجُود [والوُجُودُ] مُسْتَمَدٌّ والمادَّةُ مِن عَيْنِ الوُجُودِ فَلَوْ انْقَطَعَتِ [المادَّةُ] لانْهَدَمَ الوُجُودُ.

3) لا يَصْلُحُ لِسَماعِ هذا العِلْمِ إلاّ لِمَنْ حَصَلَتْ لَهُ أَرْبَعَةٌ: الزُّهْدُ والعِلْمُ والتَّوَكُّلُ واليَقِينُ.

4. The Exalted Truth [God] is cognizant of the subtle and apparent aspects [of souls] in every breath and [during] every state. He protects every heart that perceives [Him] and is under His influence from [straying into] the paths of hardship and the errors of temptation.[2]

5. The Exalted Truth is on the tongue of the scholars of every generation, according to the needs of the people of their time.

6. One who is confirmed in the station of servanthood views his acts as hypocrisy, his spiritual states as pretentiousness, and his speech as a lie.

7. When the Truth appears, nothing else remains with it.

8. The duration of your life is but one breath. Take care that you master it and that it does not master you.

9. The heart has no more than one aspect [at a time], such that when it is occupied with [a particular aspect], it is veiled from another. So take care that you are not drawn toward anything but God, lest He deprive you of the delights of intimate converse with Him.

10. Spiritual insight confirms usefulness.

11. The most harmful of things is companionship with a heedless scholar, an ignorant Sufi, or an insincere preacher.[3]

12. Beware of [the preacher] whom you see advocating in the name of God a state that is not outwardly visible in [his behavior].[4]

13. He who goes out among mankind before the existence of a Divine Reality which orders him to do so is a deviant.

14. No one attains true freedom as long as he remains under the influence of the slightest portion of his ego.[5]

2. In *Uns al-faqīr*: 'The Exalted Truth is cognizant of the inner secrets and consciences [of souls] at every moment in time and [during] every state . . .'

3. This aphorism is similar to one attributed by the biographer al-Iṣfahānī to Abū ᶜAbdallāh Muḥammad al-Maghribī (d. 299/911–12). 'The most misguided among mankind is a *faqīr* who flatters a rich man or is subservient toward him. The greatest of creatures is a rich man who lowers himself before a *faqīr* or venerates his sanctity.' See, al-Iṣfahānī, *Ḥilyat al-awliyā'* (10), p. 335.

4. In *Uns al-faqīr*: ' . . . which is not witnessed as outwardly visible in him . . ..' Note the similarity of this aphorism to another attributed to Abu'l-Ḥasan an-Nūrī: 'If you see one advocating in God's name a spiritual state that exceeds the bounds of legal knowledge, then do not approach him.' See Abu'l-Qāsim ᶜAbd al-Karīm ibn Hawāzin al-Qushayrī (fl. 438/1046), *ar-Risāla fī ᶜilm at-taṣawwuf* (Beirut: Dār al-Kitāb al-ᶜArabī, n.d.), p. 20.

5. This aphorism appears to be based on a saying of al-Junayd: 'Verily you will not attain true freedom as long as any trace [of the material world] remains in your worship of [God]' (Ibid., p. 100). In this and many of the following passages, the Arabic word *nafs* is translated as 'ego' whenever shaykh Abū Madyan refers to a sense of self that creates an illusory image of self-sufficiency and ontological independence.

4) الحَقُّ تعالى مُطلّعٌ على السَّرائِرِ والظَّواهِرِ في كلِّ نَفَسٍ وحالٍ. فأَيُّما قلبٌ رآه مُؤْثِراً له حفِظَهُ مِن طوارقِ المحَنِ ومُضلّاتِ الفِتَنِ.

5) الحقُّ تعالى يُجري على ألسنةِ عُلماءِ كلِّ زمانٍ بما يليقُ بأَهْلِهِ.

6) من تحقّقَ بالعُبوديّةِ نظرَ أعمالَهُ بعينِ الرِّياءِ وأحوالَهُ بعينِ الدَّعْوى وأقوالَهُ بعينِ الافْتِراءِ.

7) إذا ظَهرَ الحقُّ لم يَبْقَ معهُ غيرُهُ.

8) عُمْرُكَ نفسٌ واحدٌ فاحْرِصْ أنْ يكونَ لكَ لا عليْكَ.

9) ليسَ للقلْبِ إلاَّ وجْهَةٌ واحِدَةٌ فمَتَى توجَّدَ إليْها حُجبَ عَنْ غيرِها. فإيّاكَ أنْ تَميلَ إلى غيرِ اللهِ فيسلُبَكَ لذّةَ مُناجاتِهِ.

10) البَصيرَةُ تحقّقُ الانْتِفاعِ.

11) أضرُّ الأشْياءِ صُحْبَةُ عالمٍ غافلٍ وصُوفيٍّ جاهلٍ وواعظٍ مُداهِنٍ.

12) مَنْ رأيْتَهُ يدَّعي معَ اللهِ حالاً لا يكونُ على ظاهِرِهِ شيْءٌ مِنهُ فاحْذَرْهُ.

13) مَنْ خرجَ إلى الخَلقِ قبْلَ وُجودِ حقيقةٍ تدْعُوهُ إلى ذلكَ فهُوَ مفْتونٌ.

14) ما وَصَلَ إلى صَريحِ الحُرّيّةِ مَنْ بَقِيَ عليهِ مِن نفْسِهِ بقيّةٌ.

15. One who knows God learns from Him in wakefulness and in sleep.

16. One who is granted the sweetness of intimate converse has sleep taken from him.

17. One who wastes his 'time' is ignorant, while one who is neglectful of it is heedless.[6]

18. Make patience your provision, satisfaction your mount, and the Truth your goal and objective.

19. One who adheres to the Expected Promise does not part company with quiescence. The seeker moves toward it while the gnostic moves within it. Death is a blessing and what has passed is but sorrow and regret.[7]

20. Death is severance from living creatures, but [dependence upon] physical sustenance is severance from the Truth.

21. Surrender is the dispatch of the ego into the realms of divine judgment and the abandonment of pity for its misfortunes and sufferings.

22. Take care that you pass your mornings and evenings as a Muslim and a believer, for perhaps [God] will notice you and be merciful toward you.

23. One who busies himself by seeking the material world is afflicted by disgrace in it.

24. Do not be blinded from the limitations of your passional soul, or you will overstep yourself.

25. One who adorns himself with the ephemeral is misled.

6. On the subject of 'time' (*waqt*) al-Qushayrī wrote:
The reality of 'time' for the Folk of Realization is an imagined event, the actualization of which is associated with a certain event; thus the certain event is the 'time' of the imagined event . . .. I heard the Master Abū ʿAlī ad-Daqqāq say: "Time is what you are in. If you are in the material world, then your "time" is the material world; if you are at the outcome [of a series of acts], then your "time" is the outcome; if you are happy, then your "time" is happiness; if you are sad, then your "time" is sadness' . . .. There is a group of people who say, '*Al-waqt* [time] is between two moments in time,' meaning thereby, the past and the future. [Others] say, 'The Sufi is the son of his time,' meaning that he is concerned with what is most important to him in the [present] state, firmly maintaining what is required from him at the moment . . .. They mean by 'time' the unexpected occurrence of what the Truth has decreed for them without choosing it for themselves. Thus, they say, 'So-and-So is governed by time.' In other words, he has submitted himself to what occurs despite his exercise of choice. (*Risāla*, p. 31)

7. In *Uns al-faqīr*: 'One who adheres to the Expected Call does not part company with quiescence.' The second and third sentences of this aphorism are not given by Ibn Qunfudh.

15) مَنْ عرَفَ اللهَ اسْتَفادَ مِنهُ في اليَقَظَةِ والمَنامِ.

16) مَنْ رُزِقَ حلاوَةَ المُناجاةِ زالَ عَنْهُ النوْمُ.

17) مَنْ ضَيَّعَ حُكمَ وقْتِهِ فهو جاهِلٌ ومَن قَصَّرَ عَنْهُ فهو غافِلٌ.

18) إجْعَل الصَّبرَ زادَكَ والرِّضى مَطِيَّتَكَ والحَقَّ مَقْصَدَكَ ووجْهَتَكَ.

19) مَن تَعَلَّقَ بوعْدِ الأَمانِي لم يُفارِق التَّوانِي. السَّالِكُ ذاهِبٌ إليهِ والعارِفُ ذاهِبٌ فِيهِ. المَوْتُ كرامَةٌ والفوْتُ حَسْرَةٌ ونَدَامَةٌ.

20) المَوْتُ إنْقِطاعٌ عَن الخَلْقِ والفوْتُ إنْقِطاعٌ عَن الحَقِ.

21) التَّسْليمُ إرْسالُ النفْسِ في مَيادِينِ الأَحْكامِ وترْكُ الشَّفقَةِ عَليها مِن الطَّوارِقِ والآلامِ.

22) احْرِصْ أَنْ تُصْبِحَ وتُمسِي مُسْلِمًا أو مُؤْمِنًا لعَلَّهُ يَنظُرُ إليكَ فيرْحَمْكَ.

23) مَن اشْتغَلَ بطَلَبِ الدُّنْيا أبْتُلِيَ بالذُّلِّ فيها.

24) لا تَعْمَ عَن نُقْصانِ نَفْسِكَ فتَطْغَ.

25) مَن تزَيَّنَ بزائِلٍ فهو مغْرُورٌ.

26. Abstinence for the body is the abandonment of that which is inconsistent with [the purpose of] the limbs. Abstinence for the heart is the abandonment of reliance on others. Abstinence for the passional soul means the abandonment of pretentiousness.

27. The most useful knowledge is that which corresponds to the rules of servanthood. The most exalted knowledge is the gnostic perception of Divine unity.

28. God has made the hearts of the worldly a place of heedlessness and delusion, and the hearts of the gnostics an abode for invocation and intimacy.[8]

29. Fear is a whip that urges and restrains; it urges [one] toward obedience and restrains [one] from disobedience.[9]

30. Spiritual work is of no benefit when accompanied by arrogance, and idleness is not harmful when accompanied by humility.

31. If [God] elevates you, you will be firmly established, but if you rely on yourself you will fall.

32. Oh God, allow us to understand You; for verily we do not understand You except through You.

33. One who is beset by the disgrace of impotence is not like one who wears the glory of potency.

34. One who seeks a state or a [mystical] station for himself is far from the ways of [proper] conduct.[10]

35. He who is [truly] happy renounces all joy except that [felt] in the presence of his Master.

8. In *Uns al-faqīr*: '. . . a place for remembrance and intimacy.'

9. On the subject of fear al-Muḥāsibī wrote:

I said, 'By what means does one attain fear and hope?' He said, 'By great knowledge of the great power of the [Divine] Promise and Threat.' I said, 'By what means does one attain the great knowledge of the great power of the Promise and Threat?' He said, 'By fearing the force of the punishment after death and hoping for the Great Recompense.' I said, 'By what means does one attain a fearful attitude (*takhwīf*)?' He said, 'By remembrance of and meditation upon the End. For God, may He be exalted and glorified, has made it known that the slave, once he has lost that which had caused him to be fearful and hopeful, can only return to fear and hope by remembrance and meditation. This is because the unseen cannot be seen by the eye, but can only be perceived by the heart in the realities of certainty. If the slave is veiled from the Hereafter by his heedlessness and preoccupation with the material world, he will never fear, nor will he hope.

See Ḥārith ibn Asad al-Muḥāsibī, *Kitāb ar-riʿāya li ḥuqūq Allāh ʿizza wa jalla*, Margaret Smith, ed. (London: Luzac & Co., 1940), p. 24.

10. In the Bibliothèque Nationale copy: '. . . far from the ways of gnosis.'

26) الحِمْيَةُ في الأَبدَانِ تَرْكُ المُخالَفَةِ بالجَوارِحِ والحِمْيَةُ في القُلُوبِ تَرْكُ الرُّكُونِ إلى الأَغْيَارِ والحِمْيَةُ في النفُوسِ تَرْكُ الدَّعْوَى.

27) أَنفَعُ العُلُومِ العِلْمُ بأَحْكَامِ العُبُودِيَّةِ وأَرْفَعُ العُلُومِ مَعْرِفَةُ التَّوْحِيدِ.

28) جَعَلَ اللهُ قُلُوبَ أَهْلِ الدُّنْيا مَحلاً للغَفْلَةِ والوَسْوَاسِ وقُلُوبَ العَارِفِينَ مَكَاناً للذِّكْرِ والاِسْتِئْنَاسِ.

29) الخَوْفُ سَوْطٌ يَسُوقُ ويَعُوقُ يَسُوقُ إلى الطَّاعَةِ ويَعُوقُ عَنِ المَعْصِيَّةِ.

30) لا يَنفَعُ مَعَ الكِبرِ عَمَلٌ ولا يَضُرُّ مَعَ التَّوَاضُعِ بِطَالَةٌ.

31) إنْ أَقامَكَ ثَبَتَّ وإِنْ قُمْتَ بنفسِكَ سَقَطتَ.

32) اللهُمَّ فَهِّمنا عَنكَ فإننا لا نَفْهَمُ عَنكَ إلا بِكَ.

33) لَيسَ مَنْ أُلبسَ ذُلَّ العَجْزِ كَمَنْ أُلْبِسَ عِزَّ الاقْتِدَارِ.

34) مَن طَلَبَ لِنفسِهِ حَالاً أو مَقامًا فهو بَعِيدٌ عَنْ طُرُقَاتِ المُعَامَلَةِ [المعارِفِ].

35) السَّعِيدُ مَن يَئِسَ مِنَ الفرَحِ إلا مِن عِندِ مَوْلاهُ.

36. That which has passed cannot be rectified because the second [moment of] 'time' is not the first.

37. The most excellent [act of] obedience is spending one's time controlling the self.[11]

38. *Futuwwa* is not to busy yourself with mankind at the expense of the Truth.[12]

39. *Futuwwa* is keeping in sight the virtues of the slaves while staying away from their vices.

40. One who devotes his conduct entirely to God has been freed from false pretenses.

41. The Folk of Truthfulness are rare among the pious.[13]

42. Poverty is an illumination as long as you veil it; but when you reveal it, its light disappears.[14]

43. Fusion (*jamʿ*) is that which abrogates your disunity and effaces your expression of self. Fusion is the total absorption of your attributes and the negation of the qualities [by which you were known].[15]

11. This aphorism appears to have been based on another saying by Abū ʿAbdallāh al-Maghribī: 'The most excellent of all acts is filling one's moments with Divine approval.' (al-Iṣfahānī, *Ḥilyat al-awliyā'* [10], p. 335.)

12. In *Uns al-faqīr*: 'Feebleness consists of busying yourself with mankind instead of the Creator.' In defining Islamic chivalry (*futuwwa*) al-Qushayrī wrote:

> '*Futuwwa* is that you do not see yourself as more preferable than another.' He further expanded upon his definition by claiming: '[*Futuwwa*] is that you do not discriminate in regard to the one with whom you eat, whether he be a saint or an unbeliever.' (al-Qushayrī, *Risāla*, pp. 103–4.)

13. In *Uns al-faqīr*: 'Lust is rare among the Folk of Righteousness.'

14. In the Bibliothèque Nationale copy: ' . . . its light is veiled.'

15. The Arabic term *al-jamʿ* has been renedered as 'fusion' in the above passage because it represents (especially in the 'nuclear' age of the late twentieth century) a uniquely clear expression of the merging of two separate 'identities' into one wholly real, integrated, and transcendent Identity. For a similar use of the concept applied to medieval Christian mysticism see Caroline Walker Bynum, *Holy Feast and Holy Fast* (Berkeley and Los Angeles: University of California Press, 1987), p. 163. On the same subject al-Qushayrī wrote:

> The Master Abū ʿAlī ad-Daqqāq used to say: 'Separation (*farq*) is what pertains to you and fusion (*jamʿ*) is what is taken from you.' This means that what is earned by the slave in the maintenance of his servanthood and what is associated with the states of creaturely existence is separation, while that which belongs to the Truth by way of the manifestation of spiritual insights or the conferral of Divine grace is fusion . . .. One who demonstrates to the Truth 'his' acts of obedience or disobedience toward Him is a slave characterized by separation, but one for whom God shows him what he is authorized to do from [God's] own Actions is a slave who perceives fusion, for the actualization of created beings is derived from separation, while the actualization of the Truth is found in the attribute of fusion. Fusion and separation are necessary for the slave because one who is not in the state of separation has no servanthood and one who is not in the state of fusion has no gnosis. Thus, [God's] words, 'You alone do we worship' (Qur'ān, 1

36) ما فاتَ لا يُسْتَدْرَكُ لأَنَّ الوَقْتَ الثَّانِي غيرُ الأَوَّلِ.

37) أَفْضَلُ الطَّاعاتِ عِمارَةُ الأَوْقاتِ بالمُراقَباتِ.

38) الفُتوَّةُ أَنْ لا تَشْتَغِلَ بالخَلْقِ عَنِ الحقّ.

39) الفُتوَّةُ رُؤْيَةُ مَحاسِنِ العَبيدِ والغَيْبَةُ عَنْ مَساوِئِهِم.

40) مَن أَخْلَصَ للهِ في مُعامَلاتِهِ تَخَلَّصَ مِن الدَّعْوى الكاذِبَةِ.

41) أَهْلُ الصّدْقِ قليلٌ في أَهْلِ الصَّلاحِ.

42) الفَقْرُ نورٌ ما دُمْتَ تَسْتُرُهُ فإذا أَظْهَرْتَهُ ذَهَبَ [حُجبَ] نورُهُ.

43) الجَمْعُ ما أَسْقَطَ تَفْرِقَتَكَ ومَحَى إشارَتَكَ والجَمْعُ إسْتِغْراقُ أَوْصافِكَ وتَلاشِي نعوُتِكَ.

44. One who is pretentious calls attention to himself.

45. Verily [the exoteric scholars] were forbidden attainment [to God] because of their abandonment of the example of [Divine] guidance and their adherence to [the way of] passion.

46. Complete reliance upon God (*tawakkul*) means putting your trust in what is guaranteed and transforming activity into quiescence.[16]

47. Treat people justly in spite of yourself and accept advice from others, so that you will attain the most exalted of stations.

48. If one does not find an impediment in his heart, he is [already] ruined.

49. Put your complete trust in God such that [your concentration upon this attitude] overcomes [even] your invocation. Verily mankind will never avail itself of God at your expense.[17]

50. By self-examination the slave attains the rank of self-dominance.

51. The loss of remorse in the station of personal comportment is one of the signs of failure [on the Way].[18]

52. The heart is pardoned [only] when it is emptied of lusts.

53. God abandons one who does not rely on Him in overcoming his ego.

54. How can one who does not maintain conduct proper for beginners be established in the stations of those who have attained the End?

55. Cast aside the material world in the direction of one who desires it and turn yourself toward your Master.

56. He who frees himself from the activities of the material world is established by the Truth in His service.

[*al-Fātiḥa*], 5) indicate the state of separation, while His words, 'On You alone do we rely' (ibid.) indicate the state of fusion. Whenever the slave addresses the Truth with the language of his intimacy, whether it be by asking, invoking, praising, thanking, in seclusion, or supplicating, he remains in the realm of separation; but when his human nature is attentive to that which his Master confides to him and [when he] listens through Him to His speech when He calls him, whispers to him, makes him understand, or reveals to his heart, after which he sees Him, then he experiences fusion. (*Risāla*, p. 35.)

16. On *tawakkul* al-Muḥāsibī wrote: '*Tawakkul* is the abandonment of reliance upon one's family or children; [it is] embarking on a journey without provisions; [it is] cheerful satisfaction with misfortune when it afflicts the Muslims, [it is] the prohibition of medicines and prayers of supplication; and [it is] the renunciation of hope [in worldly solutions].' (*Riʿāya*, p. 47.)

17. In *Uns al-faqīr*: 'Verily mankind will never avail itself at your expense.'

18. In the British Library copy: 'The loss of remorse and weeping . . ..'

44) المُدَّعِي مَن أَشارَ إلى نَفْسِهِ.

45) إنَّما حُرِمُوا الوُصُولَ لِتَرْكِ الاقْتِداءِ بالدَّلِيلِ وسُلُوكِهِم الهَوَى.

46) التَّوَكُّلُ وُثُوقُكَ بالمَضْمُونِ واسْتِبْدالُ الحَرَكَةِ بالسُّكُونِ.

47) أَنْصِفِ النَّاسَ مِن نَفْسِكَ واقْبَلِ النَّصِيحَةَ مِن دُونِكَ تُدْرِكْ أَشْرَفَ المَنَازِلِ.

48) مَن لم يَجِدْ في قَلْبِهِ زَاجِراً فهو خَرَابٌ.

49) تَوَكَّلْ على اللهِ حَتَّى يَكُونَ الغَالِبُ على ذِكْرِكَ فإنَّ الخَلْقَ لَنْ يُغْنُوا عَنْكَ مِن اللهِ شَيْئاً.

50) بالمُحاسَبَةِ يَصِلُ العَبْدُ إلى دَرَجَةِ المُراقَبَةِ.

51) فَقْدُ الأَسَفِ في مَقَامِ السُّلُوكِ عَلَمٌ مِن أَعْلامِ الخِذْلانِ.

52) إذا خَلا القَلْبُ عَنِ الشَّهَواتِ فهو مُعافى.

53) مَن لم يَسْتَعِنْ باللهِ على نَفْسِهِ مَرَّ [اللهُ] عَنْهُ.

54) مَنْ لم يَقُمْ بآدابِ أَهْلِ البِدايَةِ كَيْفَ تَسْتَقِيمُ لهُ مَقاماتُ أَهْلِ النِّهايَةِ؟

55) إطْرَحِ الدُّنْيا على مَن أَقْبَلَ عَلَيْها واقْبَلْ على مَوْلاكَ.

56) مَن تَفَرَّغَ مِن أَشْغالِ الدُّنْيا أَقامَهُ الحَقُّ في خِدْمَتِهِ.

57. What a difference between one whose concern is with the Houris and palaces [of Heaven] and one whose concern is with lifting the veil and those who partake of the Divine presence!

58. The slave is one who has cut off all his expectations except [those] from his Lord.

59. [Muslims] who live under Divine protection are ranked [in classes]: those who are protected from associating partners with God and infidelity by means of Divine guidance; those protected from great and minor sins by means of Divine care; those protected from vain thoughts and heedlessness by means of Divine patronage.

60. He who avoids argument is the sage who adheres to proper conduct.[19]

61. Love means intimacy with God and desire for Him.

62. Take careful note of how [God] regards you; do not take note of how you regard Him.

63. The veils are not lifted for one who does not abandon restraint.

64. The [true] captive is a captive of the carnal soul, a captive of lust, and a captive of passion.

65. The wealthiest of men is one to whom the Truth has revealed Himself as a manifestation of His transcendence and the poorest of men is one from whom the Truth hides His transcendence.

66. He who is empty of desire is retarded, while he who despairs loses love.

67. Souls are valued trusts and bodies are their protection.

68. If the blast of the bellows does not burn you with its flames, it harms you with [the sparks of] its embers. If the Bearer of Perfume does not grant you His elixir, He favors you with its fragrance.[20]

19. The aphorisms numbered 60 through 78 are not in the Bibliothèque Nationale copy.

20. This aphorism refers to the all-inclusive 'gratuitous love' of God implicit in the Divine name *ar-Raḥmān*. The same concept is also present in Christian theology, where it can be found in terms such as the Greek *agapé* and the Latin *do ut des* ('I give in order that you give'). Abū Madyan's younger contemporary Muḥyī'ad-Dīn Ibn al-ʿArabī (d. 638/1240–41) claimed that God's gratuitous love is motivated by *tashkīr*, or 'mutual constraint', which he saw as a necessary particularization of the all-pervading Divine grace, or *raḥma*. According to this view, God is 'compelled' to act in a certain way because of the structure of the relationship that pertains between the Creator and His creation. Just as a king is constrained, by his role, to defend, protect, preserve, and maintain his subjects, so too is God 'constrained', by His creating and sustaining role, to act mercifully toward the physical universe. A corollary to this belief, that an act of human mercy (*raḥma*) can evoke an even stronger

٥٧) شَتَّانَ بَيْنَ مَنْ هِمَّتُهُ الحُورُ والقُصُورُ وبَيْنَ مَنْ هِمَّتُهُ رَفْعُ السُّتُورِ وذُو الحُضُورِ .

٥٨) العَبْدُ مَنِ انْقَطَعَتْ آمَالُهُ إلاَّ مِن عِندِ مَوْلاهُ .

٥٩) المَحْفُوظُونَ على طَبَقَاتٍ : مَحْفُوظٌ عَنِ الشِّرْكِ والكُفْرِ بالهِدَايَةِ ومَحْفُوظٌ عَن الكَبَائِرِ والصَّغَائِرِ بالعِنَايَةِ ومَحْفُوظٌ عَنِ الخَطَرَاتِ والغَفَلاتِ بالرِّعَايَةِ .

٦٠) مَنْ أَعْرَضَ عَنِ الاعْتِرَاضِ فهو الحَكِيمُ المُتَأَدِّبُ .

٦١) المَحَبَّةُ الأُنْسُ باللهِ والشَّوْقُ إليهِ .

٦٢) شَاهِدْ مُشَاهَدَتَهُ لكَ ولا تشَاهِدْ مُشَاهَدَتَكَ لَهُ .

٦٣) مَن لَمْ يَخْلَعِ العِذَارَ لَمْ تُرْفَعْ لهُ الأَسْتَارُ .

٦٤) الأَسِيرُ أَسِيرُ نَفْسٍ وأَسِيرُ شَهْوَةٍ وأَسِيرُ هَوًى .

٦٥) أَغْنَى الأَغْنِيَاءِ مَنْ أَبْدَى لَهُ الحَقُّ حَقِيقَةً مِن حَقِّهِ وأَفْقَرُ الفُقَرَاءِ مَنْ سَتَرَ الحَقَّ عَنْهُ حَقَّهُ .

٦٦) الخَالِي مِنَ الشَّوْقِ مُؤَخَّرٌ والآيِسُ فاقِدُ المَحَبَّةِ .

٦٧) الأَرْوَاحُ الرِّعَايَةُ والأَشْبَاحُ الوِقَايَةُ .

٦٨) نَافِخُ الكِيرِ إنْ لَمْ يَحْرِقْكَ بِنَارِهِ آذَاكَ بِشَرَرِهِ وحَامِلُ العِطْرِ إنْ لَمْ يَجُدْ بِكَ مِن عِطْرِهِ مَنَحَكَ بِنَشْرِهِ .

69. One who is negligent in maintaining the requirements [of religion] has squandered himself.

70. One who cannot bear companionship with his Lord is dissipated in companionship with slaves.

71. One who knows himself is not affected by people's praise for him.

72. Hypocrisy is due to the prompting of the passional soul and the hypocrite is one who is prevented from [attaining access to] lordship.[21]

73. A disturbance of the heart that is due to [one's] fear of vigilance over the passional soul is more onerous than carrying out the 'Two Burdens' with disciplined activity.[22]

74. The children of the material world are served by slaves, but the slave-girls of the Hereafter are served by the noble and the free.[23]

75. Discipline in personal behavior means ceasing to be [overly] attentive to [one's] actions.

76. By their actions they were veiled from the outcome of their acts; had they not misunderstood the outcome of their acts, they would have been occupied with [the outcome] instead of being concerned about their actions.

77. [Informative] speech is what is implied by the answer; [idle] talk is what prevents you from [meaningful] discourse.

78. Jealousy means that you do not know [anything] and are not known [by God].

79. No one sees the Truth unless he dies; he who does not die does not see the Truth.

80. Love of the mighty among mankind is the cause of relapse [from the Way].

---

response from the Merciful (*ar-Raḥmān*), was expressed by another of Abū Madyan's contemporaries, Abu'l-ᶜAbbās as-Sabtī (d. 601/1205), who coined the phrase, *al-wujūd yanfaᶜilu bi'l-jūd* ('[Divine] Being is affected by [human] generosity'). See Toshihiko Isutzu, *Sufism and Taoism* (Berkeley, Los Angeles, and London: University of California Press, 1983), pp. 182–86. See also, Adolphe Faure, 'Abū-l-ᶜAbbās as-Sabtī (524–601/1130–1204), La Justice et la Charité', *Hespéris* (43), No. 2 (1956), p. 454.

21. In *Uns al-faqīr*: 'Hypocrisy is due to the frivolity of the ego . . .'

22. The 'Two Burdens' (*ath-thaqalayn*) mentioned in this aphorism refer to the Muslim's twin responsibilities of following the Qur'ān and the Sunna.

23. In *Uns al-faqīr*: ' . . . the slave-girls and slaves of the Hereafter are the free and the noble.'

69) مَنْ أَهْمَلَ الفَرائِضَ فقَدْ ضَيَّعَ نَفْسَهُ.

70) مَنْ لم يَصْبِرْ على صُحْبَةِ مَوْلاهُ ابْتَلاهُ بصُحْبَةِ العَبيدِ.

71) مَنْ عَرَفَ نَفْسَهُ لم يُغَيِّرْ بثَناءِ النَّاسِ عَلَيهِ.

72) الدَّعْوى مِنْ دَعْوَةِ النَّفْسِ [و] المُدَّعِي مَنْ مَانَعَ لِلرُّبُوبِيَّةِ.

73) إنْزِعَاجُ القَلْبِ لِرَوْعَةِ الانْتِباهِ أَرْجَحُ مِن أَعْمَالِ الثَّقَلَين بالرِّيَاضَةِ في الأَعْمالِ.

74) أَبناءُ الدُّنْيا تَخْدِمُهُم العَبيدُ وإماءُ الآخِرَةِ تَخْدِمُهُنَّ الأَحْرارُ الكُرَماءُ.

75) الرِّيَاضَةُ في المُعَامَلاتِ قَطْعُ الاِلتِفَاتِ إلى الأَعْمالِ.

76) حُجِبُوا بالأَعْمالِ عَنِ المَعْمُولِ ولَوْ لا أَخْطَؤُا المَعْمُولَ لاشْتَغَلُوا بِهِ عَن رُؤْيَةِ الأَعْمالِ.

77) الحَدِيثُ ما اسْتَدْعَيْتَ مِنَ الجَوابِ والكَلامُ ما صَدَمَكَ مِنَ الخِطَابِ.

78) الغَيرَةُ أَنْ لا تَعْرِفَ ولا تُعْرَفُ.

79) الحَقُّ تَعَالى لا يَراهُ أَحَدٌ إلاَّ مَاتَ. مَنْ لم يُمِتْ لم يَرَ الحَقَّ.

80) حُبُّ العُلُوِ على النَّاسِ سَبَبُ الاِنْتِكَاسِ.

81. The ornaments of the gnostic are shyness and reverential awe.

82. Greed for created things means doubt in the Creator.

83. With the corruption of the masses appears the rule of tyranny; with the corruption of the élite appear false prophets who seduce [the masses] away from religion.

84. Beware of companionship with the heretic out of fear for your religion; beware of companionship with women out of fear for your hearts.[24]

85. One who notices a shortcoming in his shaykh will never benefit from him.

86. Remembrance entails continuous presence and the vision of the One remembered. Do not forget to remember the One who never forgets to remember you and do not forget to thank the One who never forgets your devotion.

87. One who keeps company with the Invokers [of God] becomes mindful of his heedlessness; one who serves the Righteous is exalted by his service.

88. The language of scrupulousness calls one to the idolatry of circumstantiality; the language of piety calls one to continuous mortification; the language of love calls one to rapture and a melted heart; the language of gnosis calls one to self-annihilation and effacement, [as well as] affirmation and sobriety.

89. The manly ideal (*muruwwa*) is the agreement of one's brothers concerning that which formal knowledge does not make known to you.[25]

90. The sustenance of the gnostic is in the Object of his knowledge, while the sustenance of the one enriched [by God] is in the One who enriches him and on Whom he relies.[26]

24. In *Uns al-faqīr*: '. . . beware of companionship with women out of fear for the faith of your hearts.' On Abū Madyan's practice of celibacy and his avoidance of women, see Introduction, p. 14.

25. In *Uns al-faqīr*: '*Muruwwa* is the agreement of one's brethren concerning that from which knowledge does not forbid you.' *Muruwwa* (the idealized notion of manliness) and *futuwwa* (the idealized notion of youthful friendship and brotherhood) are related concepts in both Khurāsānī and western Maghribi Sufism.

26. In *Uns al-faqīr*: 'The strength of the gnostic is in the Object of his knowledge, while the power of another is in his [reliance upon] custom and habit.'

81) حِلْيَةُ العَارِفِ الخَشْيَةُ والهَيْبَةُ.

82) الطَّمَعُ في الخَلْقِ شَكٌّ في الخَالِقِ.

83) بفَسَادِ العَامَّةِ تَظْهَرُ وُلاةُ الجَوْرِ وبفسادِ الخَاصَّةِ تَظْهَرُ الدَّجَاجلَةُ المَيَّالُونَ عَنِ الدِّينِ.

84) إحْذَرْ صُحْبَةَ المُبْتَدِعَةِ اِتقاءً عَلى دِينِكَ واحْذَرْ صُحْبَةَ النِّسَاءِ اِتقَاءً عَلى قَلْبِكَ.

85) مَنْ ظَهَرَ لهُ نَقصٌ في شَيْخِهِ لم يَنتَفِعْ بهِ.

86) الذِّكْرُ شُهودُ المَذْكُورِ ودَوامُ الحُضورِ. مَنْ لم يَغْفَلْ عَنْ ذِكْرِكَ فلا تَغْفَلْ عَن ذِكْرِهِ ومَنْ لم يَغفَلْ عَنْ برِّكَ فلا تَغْفَلْ عَن شُكْرِهِ.

87) مَنْ جَالَسَ الذَّاكِرِينَ إنتبَهَ مِنْ غَفْلَتِهِ. مَنْ خدَمَ الصَّالحِينَ ارْتَفعَ بخِدْمَتِهِ.

88) لِسَانُ الوَرَعِ يَدْعُو إلى شِرْكِ الآفَاتِ ولسانُ التَّعَبُّدِ يَدْعُو لدوامِ الاِجْتِهادِ ولسانُ المحَبَّةِ يَدْعُو إلى الذَوبَانِ والهيمانِ ولسانُ المَعْرفةِ يَدْعُو إلى الفناءِ والمحوِ والثَّباتِ والصَّحْوِ.

89) المَرُوءَةُ مُوافَقَةُ الإخْوَانِ فِيما لا يَحْضُرُهُ العِلْمُ عَلَيْكَ.

90) قُوتُ العَارِفِ بمَعْرُوفِهِ وقُوتُ الغَنيِّ بمَغْنَاهُ ومَأْلُوفِهِ.

91. He was asked (may God have mercy on him) about the prohibition of reliance upon [worldly] phenomena and said: 'It is the initial goal of one who is a beginner on the Way. He has [still] not become experienced and has not [yet] progressed one step, even if he were to be seventy years old. Sahl [at-Tustarī] (may God have mercy on him) said, "Do not inform created beings about secrets until they are firmly established." As for those who are [fixated upon] polluted passional souls and accidental causation, they are the ones for whom the [Divine] command and prohibition are intended. Before understanding created beings as phenomena apart from God, one who is influenced by what he sees and is moved by what he hears is cut off by the fruits of [his] fantasies and does not take notice of causation. He says in his confusion, "How can one find the means to live?"'

92. The ruin of mankind lies in distrustfulness and the ruin of Sufis lies in following the desires.

93. The aspiration of gnostics is not to attain whatever is not the Object of their knowledge.

94. One who seeks to forbid the respect due to saints is afflicted by God with hatred for His creatures.

95. He who desires purity must make loyalty obligatory.

96. One brought near [to God] is joyful in his nearness, while the lover is tormented in his love.

97. This edifice was built on the foundations of effort, self-mortification,[27] the elimination of reliance upon habit, and the practice of worship.

98. Your taste for misfortune is a confirmation of [Divine] satisfaction.

99. Poverty is a characteristic of absolute monotheism, while the sign of uniqueness is that you see nothing but [God].

100. Worship saves you from the tyranny of formal knowledge.

27. In medieval Maghribi Sufism, the Arabic word *ijtihād* (to go beyond the norm in one's efforts) was often used as a synonym for *mujāhada* (the practice of bodily mortification). In *Uns al-faqīr*: 'This matter was founded upon asceticism and self-mortification . . .'

91) سُئِلَ رَحِمَهُ اللهُ عَن نَهْيِهِم عَن صُحْبَةِ الأَحْدَاثِ فَقَالَ: هُوَ المُسْتَقْبِلُ لِلأَمْرِ [مِنْ] المُبْتَدِيءِ فِي الطَّرِيقِ. لم يجرّبِ الأُمورَ ولم يَثْبتْ لَهُ فِيها قَدمٌ وإِنْ كَانَ لَهُ سَبْعِينَ سَنَةً. قَالَ سَهْلُ (التُّسْتَرِي) رَحِمَهُ اللهُ: «لا تُطلِعُوا الأَحْدَاثَ عَلَى الأَسْرَارِ قَبْلَ تمكينِها».

وأَمَّا أَهْلُ العِلَلِ والنُّفوسِ الدَّنِسَةِ فَهُم أَخَصُّ أَنْ يُذْكَرُوا بِأَمْرٍ ونَهْيٍ. وقَبْلَ الإِشَارَةِ بِالأَحْدَاثِ إِلى ما سِوَى اللهِ مِنَ المحدَثَاتِ مَنْ هَمَّهُ أَثَرُ النَّظرِ وأَقلعَهُ سَماعُ الخبرِ. انْقَطَعَ فِي مَفاوِزِ الخطَرَاتِ ولم يَلْتَفِتْ إِلى الآفاتِ. يَقولُ فِي حيرَانِهِ: «كَيْفَ السَّبِيلُ إِلى وَصْلٍ أَعِيشُ بِهِ؟».

92) آفَاتُ الخَلْقِ سُوءُ الظَّنِّ وآفَاتُ الصُّوفِيَّةِ إِتبَاعُ الهَوَى.

93) هِمَّةُ العَارِفِينَ لا تَسْمُو إِلى غَيرِ مَعْرُوفِهِم.

94) مَنْ حَرَّمَ احْتَرامَ الأَوْلِيَاءِ إِبْتَلاهُ اللهُ بِالمَقْتِ بَينَ خَلْقِهِ.

95) مَنْ أَرَادَ الصَّفَاءَ فَلْيَلْتَزِمِ الوَفاءَ.

96) المُقَرَّبُ مَسْرُورٌ فِي قُرْبِهِ والمحِبُّ مُعَذَّبٌ فِي حُبِّهِ.

97) أُسِّسَ هَذا البُنْيَانُ عَلَى الجِدِّ والاِجْتِهادِ وقَطْعِ المَأْلُوفاتِ والاعْتِيَادِ.

98) إِسْتِلْذاذُكَ لِلبَلاءِ تَحقيقٌ بِالرِّضَى.

99) الفَقْرُ أَمَارَةٌ عَلَى التَّوحِيدِ ودَلالَةٌ عَلى التَّفْرِيدِ. لا تَشْهَدُ غَيرَ سِوَاهُ.

100) العِبَادَةُ تُنجِيكَ مِنْ طُغْيَانِ العِلْمِ.

101. The ascetic in the ease of [his] asceticism is [doctrinally] more fundamental than the one who is scrupulous, for being careful consists in the preservation [of a thing] while asceticism means the elimination of everything.

102. Asceticism consists of an obligation, a supererogatory act, and [an act of] nearness. The obligation [lies] in [avoiding] what is forbidden, the supererogatory act [lies] in [avoiding] what is doubtful, and nearness [lies] in [avoiding even] what is lawful.

103. One who acquires knowledge in order to teach mankind is given by God Most High an understanding through which he knows [his fellow man]. One who acquires knowledge in order to learn the Truth is given by God Most High an understanding through which he knows [God].[28]

104. He who cuts the link with his Lord is cut off by [his act].[29]

105. When one is totally occupied in his nearness [to God], the hatred [of others for him] quickly reaches him. Oh ego, this is a warning for you, if you would pay heed![30]

106. When one relies on [contingent beings] other than God in his innermost soul, God strips the [feeling] of mercy for him from their hearts and clothes him in the garments of greed for [their acceptance], while He clothes them in garments of greed for [what they can obtain from] him.[31]

107. The sign of sincerity is that mankind deserts you in [your] contemplation of the Truth.

108. Eternal permanence [with God] is in your annihilation of your self.[32]

28. In the Bibliothèque Nationale copy: '. . . through which the Truth knows him.'

29. In the Bibliothèque Nationale copy: 'When one cuts off the one who attains to his Lord, God cuts him off by means of him.'

30. In *Uns al-faqīr*: 'Oh ego, this is a warning for you, if you would but awaken!' This last sentence is treated as a separate aphorism by the editors of Ibn Qunfudh's text.

31. In *Uns al-faqīr*: 'When one relies on other than God the Exalted, God strips mercy from his heart.'

32. On annihilation (*fanā'*) and permanence (*baqā'*) al-Qushayrī wrote:

By 'annihilation' the Folk mean the elimination of blameworthy characteristics. By 'permanence' they mean the maintenance of praiseworthy characteristics . . . it is understood that when one of these two attributes is not present then the other one is . . .. When one has 'annihilated' his base morals he remains in [the states of] *futuwwa* and veracity (*ṣidq*). When one sees the activity of the Divine capability in the manifestation of the Divine will, it is said that he has been 'annihilated from the anticipation of worldly events'. When he has been 'annihilated' from imagining traces of that which is other than God, he 'remains permanently' in the attributes of the Truth. When one is dominated by the Sultan of Reality so that he perceives neither other, remnant, form, nor

101) الزَّاهِدُ في رَاحَةِ الزُّهْدِ أَعَمُّ مِنَ الوَارِعِ لأَنَّ الوَرَعَ إِبْقَاءٌ والزُّهْدَ قَطْعٌ للكُلِّ .

102) الزُّهْـدُ فَرِيضَةٌ وفَضِيلَةٌ وقُرْبَةٌ . فالفَرْضُ في الحَرَامِ والفَضْلُ في المُشَابَهَةِ والقُرْبَةُ في الحَلالِ .

103) مَنْ سَمِعَ العِلْمَ لِيَعْلَمَ بِهِ النَّاسَ أَعْطَاهُ الله تعالى فَهْمًا يَعْرِفُ بِهِ النَّاسَ . ومَنْ تَعَلَّمَ العِلْمَ لِيَعْلَمَ بِهِ الحَقَّ أَعْطَاهُ الله تعالى فَهْمًا يَعْرِفُهُ بِهِ [يَعْرِفُ بِهِ الحَقَّ] .

104) مَنْ قَطَعَ مَوْصُولاً بِرَبِّهِ قَطَعَ [قَطَعَ الله] بِهِ .

105) مَنِ اشْتَغَلَ مَشْغُولاً بِقُرْبِهِ أَدْرَكَهُ المَقْتُ في الوَقْتِ . يا نَفْسُ هذِهِ مَوْعِظَةٌ لكِ إِنِ اتَّعَظْتِ !

106) مَنْ سَكَنَ إلى غَيْرِ اللهِ بِسِرِّهِ نَزَعَ اللهُ الرَّحْمَةَ مِنْ قُلُوبِهِمْ عَلَيْهِ وأَلْبَسَهُ لِبَاسَ الطَّمَعِ فِيهِمْ وأَلْبَسَهُمْ لِبَاسَ الطَّمَعِ فِيهِ .

107) عَلامَةُ الإِخْلاصِ أَنْ يَغِيبَ عَنْكَ الخَلْقُ في مُشَاهَدَةِ الحَقِّ .

108) بَقَاءُ الأَبَدِ في فَنَائِكَ عَنْكَ .

109. The price of Sufism is the total surrender of your self.[33]

110. One for whom taking is dearer than giving is not a *faqīr*.[34]

111. When fear finds a home in the heart it bequeaths self-control.

112. One who is negligent in [either his] acts or [his] states is not worthy [to stand on] the carpet of Truth.[35]

113. [Spiritual] states are masters for beginners because they determine their behavior, but they are slaves for the advanced because they are under their control.

114. [Having] firm footing on the Way consists of following and adhering to [the teachings of] the Noble Prophets.

115. The slave is perfected only through sincerity and self-control.

116. One who seeks the Truth by way of virtue will attain it.[36]

117. [Personal] glorification consists in filling the heart with the glory of the Lord.

118. The aspirations of the gnostics are dependent upon their Master.[37]

119. Take care to possess something by which you will know everything.

120. He who has not been with the One has not been with anyone. He who knows someone [else] has not known the One.

121. The sign of your impurity is your companionship with the impure. The sign of your worthlessness is your reliance upon the worthless. The sign of your barbarity is your intimacy with the barbaric.

---

trace, it is said that he is 'annihilated from creation and remains permanently in the Truth' . . .. If it is said that he has been 'annihilated from himself and from creation,' his bodily self remains and created things remain, but he has no knowledge of them, nor do they have knowledge of him. He has neither feelings for them nor information about them. Both his individual self and created things continue to exist, but he forgets about them without being aware [even] of his own self or of creation. (*Risāla*, pp. 36–37.)

33. In *Uns al-faqīr*: 'The fruit of Sufism is total surrender.'

34. In the British Library copy: ' . . . dearer than spending . . ..'

35. In *Uns al-faqīr*: 'One who is negligent in [his] states . . ..'

36. This aphorism appears to be a partial reproduction of another attributed to Abū Madyan's shaykh Abū Yaʿzā: 'One who seeks the Truth by way of virtue will attain it; if he does not, he will never arrive.' See al-Kattānī, *Salwat al-anfās* (1), p. 173.

37. In the British Library copy: 'The aspirations of the gnostics act as signs for the one who masters them.'

109) ثَمَنُ التَّصَوُّفِ تَسْلِيمٌ كُلَّكَ .

110) مَنْ كَانَ الأَخْذُ أَحَبَّ إِلَيْهِ مِنَ [الإخْرَاج] الإعْطَاء فَلَيْسَ بِفَقِيرٍ .

111) الخَوْفُ إِذَا سَكَنَ القَلْبَ أَوْرَثَةُ المُرَاقَبَة .

112) المُهْمِلُ فِي الأَعْمَال وَالأَحْوَال لَا يَصْلُحُ لِبِسَاطِ الحَقّ .

113) الأَحْوَالُ مَالِكَةٌ لِأَهْلِ البِدَايَةِ فَهِيَ تَصَرَّفُهُمْ وَمَلُوكَةٌ لِأَهْلِ النِّهَايَةِ فَهُمْ يُصَرِّفُونَها .

114) ثَبَاتُ الأَقْدَامِ فِي سُلُوكِ الاتِّبَاعِ وَالاهْتِمَامِ بِالرُّسُلِ الكِرَام .

115) لَا يُكَمَّلُ العَبْدُ إِلَّا بِالإخْلَاصِ وَالمُرَاقَبَة .

116) مَنْ طَلَبَ الحَقَّ مِنْ جِهَةِ الفَضْل وَصَلَ إِلَيْهِ .

117) التَّعْظِيمُ إِمْتِلَاءُ القَلْبِ بِجَلَالِ الرَّبّ .

118) هِمَمُ العَارِفِينَ [عَلَامَةٌ] عَاكِفَةٌ عَلَى مَوْلَاها .

119) إِحْرِصْ أَنْ يَكُونَ لَكَ شَيْءٌ تَعْرِفُ بِهِ كُلَّ شَيْءٍ .

120) مَنْ لَمْ يَكُنْ بِالأَحَدِ لَمْ يَكُنْ بِأَحَدٍ . مَنْ عَرَفَ أَحَدًا لَمْ يَعْرِفِ الأَحَد .

121) دَلِيلُ تَخْلِيطِكَ صُحْبَتُكَ لِلْمُخَلِّطِينَ . دَلِيلُ بِطَالَتِكَ رُكُونُكَ لِلْبَطَّالِينَ . دَلِيلُ وَحْشَتِكَ أُنْسُكَ لِلْمُسْتَوْحِشِينَ .

122. Asceticism (*zuhd*) means abstaining from the material world, avoiding it because of its vileness, abandoning it because of its pettiness, and perceiving its lowliness.

123. One who squanders the rights of his brothers is afflicted by squandering what is due to God the Exalted.

124. Restrain your passional soul with the shackles of scrupulousness and let that which is other than you loose in the field of knowledge.

125. Your *muruwwa* is in your forbearance toward the shortcomings of others.

126. He who is not influenced by [God] does not know the Truth and he who does not obey Him does not show Him gratitude.

127. He who forsakes [personal] effort and [personal] choice makes his life more pleasant.[38]

128. Sincerity is [a state] which is neither comprehended by the passional soul, nor recorded by the angels, nor seduced by Satan, nor attracted by desire.

129. Halting [on the Way] is the ego's resistance to [self-] extinction.

130. The slave perceives the [Divine] presence, but to his heart the submersion of the heart in remembrance is [the same as] the direct perception of the One remembered.

131. The life of saints in the material world is [similar to] the life of those who dwell in Paradise; their bodies find ease in [Divine] manifestation and their souls are blessed with the perception of [God] and the sight of Him.[39]

132. Poverty is pride, knowledge is wealth, silence is salvation, renunciation is rest, asceticism is well-being, and alienation from the Truth is defeat.

133. Your search for [the Path of] Will before [acquiring] correct repentance is heedlessness.

134. Quiescence is a blessing for the slave; were he to know it, he would be thankful.

38. In the Bibliothèque Nationale copy: '. . . puts his mind at rest.'

39. In the Bibliothèque Nationale copy: '. . . their bodies find ease in [God's] manifestation . . ..'

122) الزُّهْدُ العُزُوفُ عَنِ الدُّنْيَا والإِعْرَاضُ عَنها لِحَقارَتِها وتَرْكُها لاسْتِصْغارِها ورُؤْيَةُ هَوانِها .

123) مَنْ ضَيَّعَ حُقُوقَ إِخْوانِه إِبْتُلِيَ بِتَضْيِيعِ حُقُوقِ اللّٰهِ تَعَالَى .

124) قَيِّدْ نَفْسَكَ بقُيُودِ الوَرَعِ وأَطْلِقْ غيرَكَ في مَيْدانِ العِلْمِ .

125) مُرُوءَتُكَ إِعْفَاؤُكَ عَنْ تَقْصِيرِ غيرِكَ .

126) مَا عَرَفَ الحَقَّ مَنْ لم يُؤْثِرْهُ وما أَطَاعَهُ مَنْ لم يَشْكُرْهُ .

127) مَنْ تَرَكَ التَّدْبيرَ والاخْتِيارَ طَابَ عَيْشُهُ .

128) الإِخْلاصُ ما خَفِيَ عَنِ النَّفْسِ دِرَايَتُهُ وعَلى المَلَكِ كِتَابَتُهُ وعلى الشَّيْطانِ غِوَايَتُهُ وعَلى الهوَى إِمَالَتُهُ .

129) الوُقُوفُ مُجاذَبَةُ النَّفْسِ عَنِ الاصْطِلامِ .

130) العَبْدُ يُشاهِدُ الحُضُورَ واسْتِغْرَاقُ القَلْبِ في الذِّكْرِ لِقَلْبِهِ شُهُودُ المَذْكُورِ .

131) عَيْشُ الأَوْلِيَاءِ في الدُّنْيَا عَيْشُ أَهْلِ الجنةِ . أَبدانُهُمْ تَتَمَتَّعُ [بِأَمْرِهِ] بِنَشْرِهِ وأَرْوَاحُهُمْ تَتَنَعَّمُ بِشُهُودِهِ ونَظَرِهِ .

132) الفَقْرُ فَخْرٌ والعِلْمُ غِنَاءٌ والصَّمْتُ نَجاةٌ واليَأْسُ رَاحَةٌ والزُّهْدُ عَافِيَةٌ والغَيْبَةُ عَنِ الحَقِّ خَيْبَةٌ .

133) طَلَبُكَ الإِرادَةَ قَبْلَ تَصْحِيحِ التَّوْبَةِ غَفْلَةٌ .

134) الخُمُولُ نِعْمَةٌ عَلى العَبْدِ لَوْ عَرَفَهَا لَشَكَرَ .

135. The disappearance of forms and the extinction of formal knowledge is due to the affirmation of what is [intuitively] known.

136. The method [of God], Glorious and Mighty, is to call worshippers to obedience toward Him by giving signs of His bounty and constant forgiveness, so that they may return to Him through His grace. If they do not return to Him, He makes them suffer afflictions and injuries so that they may return; this is because His goal, the Glorious and Mighty, is the return of the slave to Him, whether willingly or unwillingly.

137. One who regards desirable things from the standpoint of possessiveness and desire is veiled from [understanding] their true value and [is prevented] from deriving benefit from them.

138. He was asked (may God have mercy on him) about the words of God the Exalted: 'And if you die, or are slain, it is unto God that you are brought together.'[40] He said: '[This is effected] by means of your actions and your states. The martyr perceives his state and lives by means of it, while one who is [spiritually] dead witnesses [only] his actions, which cause him to be agitated and tormented. The former is granted or rejected through fear, while the latter is through [Divine] mercy and forgiveness, in the form of glad tidings or an honor bestowed.'[41]

139. [God Most High] also said: '. . . and He guides you along the Straight Way.'[42] [Shaykh Abū Madyan] said: '[This entails] hearkening unto Him and transmitting [the Truth] through Him.' He also said: 'It is the way of guidance toward Him and the abandonment of personal effort and strength, except for [that which leads] toward Him.'

140. The most useful words are those which result from a gnostic experience or are based upon a Divine manifestation.[43]

40. Qur'ān, III (*Āl-ᶜImrān*), 158.

41. In the Bibliothèque Nationale copy: '. . . the latter is due to [Divine] mercy, while forgiveness brings glad tidings and bestows honor.'

42. Qur'ān, XLVIII (*al-Fatḥ*), 2.

43. In the Bibliothèque Nationale copy: 'The most useful words are those which allude to a gnostic experience.' This aphorism is similar in form to a saying of Abū Yaᶜzā: 'The most useful words are those which allude to a gnostic experience or give news of a gnostic experience.' See, al-Kattānī, *Salwat al-Anfās* (1), p. 173.

135) إضْمِحْلالُ الرُّسُومِ وفَنَاءُ العُلُومِ لتَحْقيقِ المَعْلُومِ .

136) سُنَّتُهُ عَزَّ وجَلَّ إسْتِدْعَاءُ العِبَادِ لِطَاعَتِهِ بسِيمَةِ الأَرْزَاقِ ودَوَامِ المُعَافَاةِ لِيَرْجعُوا إلَيْهِ بنِعْمَتِهِ . [وإنْ] فإنْ لَمْ يَرْجعُوا ابْتَلاهُم بالبَأْسَاءِ والضَّرَاءِ لَعَلَّهُم يَرْجعُونَ لأنَّ مُرادَهُ عَزَّ وجَلَّ رُجُوعُ العَبْدِ إلَيْهِ طَوْعًا أو كَرْهًا .

137) مَنْ نَظَرَ إلى [المَكُونَاتِ] المَأْلُوفَاتِ نَظَرَ إرادَةٍ وشَهْوَةٍ حُجِبَ عَنِ العِبرَةِ فِيها والانْتِفَاعِ بها .

138) وَسُئِلَ رضي الله عنه عَنْ قَوْلِهِ تَعَالى ﴿ وَلَئِنْ مُتُّمْ أَو قُتِلْتُمْ لإلى اللهِ تُحْشَرُونَ ﴾ . قَالَ : «وأَحْوالِكم» . فالشَّهِيدُ يُشاهِدُ حالَهُ فَيَنْظُرُ بِهِ والمَيِّتُ يُشاهِدُ أَعْمالَهُ فَتُقْلِقُهُ وتُكْرِبُهُ . فَهذا بالقَبُولِ والرَّدِّ بِخَوْفٍ . وَذلِكَ بالرَّحْمَةِ [فالغفرانُ مُسْتَبْشِرٌ ومُشَرَّفٌ] والغُفْرَان يُبَشِّرُ ويُشَرِّفُ .

139) قالَ (تَعَالى) أَيْضًا : ﴿ ويَهْديكَ صِراطًا مُسْتَقِيمًا ﴾ . قالَ (الشيخ أَبو مَدْيَنَ) : الاسْتِمَاعُ مِنهُ والتَّبْليغ عَنهُ . وقالَ أَيضًا : صِراطُ الدَّلالَةِ عَلَيهِ والتَّبَرّي مِنَ الحَوْلِ والقوَّةِ إلاّ إلَيْهِ .

140) أَنْفَعُ ما كانَ [مُشاهَدَةً أَو بناءً] إشارَةً عَنْ مُشاهَدَةٍ [عَنْ حُضُور] .

141. Remembrance (*dhikr*) is that which makes you absent to yourself by virtue of [God's] existence and takes you from yourself through the perception of Him.

142. Remembrance is the direct perception of the Real and the extinction of [apparent] creation.

143. A superfluity of food, sleep, and talking hardens the heart.

144. One who resists the actualization of [spiritual] insight must not engage in the modification of behavior, for he does not fear [God].

145. Concentration upon acts is the business of those who are not worthy of gnosis.

146. No one is separated from [God in reality], yet one cannot join with Him as long as he is 'separated' from Him from the standpoint of the [Divine] Essence.

147. You are not His slave if anything other than Him remains within you.

148. The right to eternal permanence is in your annihilation of self.

149. Bodies are pens, souls are writing-tablets, and spirits are cups.

150. Beware of making judgments [about others] before [adopting] the principles of the Way and [acquiring] control over your spiritual states, for you will be carried away by them.[44]

151. Forsaking the material world is easier than making it an end in itself.

152. 'Finding' the Divine presence (*wajd*) is a thought that inflames, after which it is a perception that deprives.[45]

44. This aphorism cannot be found in the Bibliothèque Nationale manuscript.

45. On *wajd* and its related states al-Qushayrī wrote:

Tawājud is a summons to *wujūd* by virtue of choice, but the possessor of this state is not completely present, for were he to be so he would be enraptured (*wājid*). The state of realization is more characteristic of him than the appearance of a realized attribute . . ..

Wajd occurs in the heart suddenly and comes to you without intent or design. For this reason the shaykhs say: '*Wajd* is an uncontrolled happening and *mawājid* are the [fortuitous] fruits of invocations'. . .. As for 'finding existence in God' (*wujūd*), it comes after one surpasses the state of *wajd*. There is no 'finding' the Truth until after the extinction of human individuality, because some individuality [invariably] remains after the appearance of the Sultan of Reality. This is the meaning of the statement of Abū'l-Ḥusayn (sic.) an-Nūrī: 'For twenty years I have been between [the states of] "finding" (*wajd*) and loss.' In other words, when I find my Lord I lose my heart, and when I find my heart I lose my Lord . . .. So *tawājud* is the beginning and *wujūd* is the end, while *wajd* is the mean between the beginning and the end. I heard the Master Abū ʿAlī ad-Daqqāq say: '*Tawājud* entails the imperfection of the slave, *wajd* entails the drowning of the slave, and *wujūd* entails the annihilation of the slave. [A person in this state] is like one who first sees the ocean, rides upon the ocean, and then drowns in the ocean.' (*Risāla*, pp. 34–35.)

141) الذِّكْرُ مَا غَيَّبَكَ عَنْكَ بِوُجُودِهِ وَأَخَذَكَ مِنْكَ بِشُهُودِهِ .

142) الذِّكْرُ شُهُودُ الحَقِيقَةِ وَخُمُودُ الخَلِيقَةِ .

143) كَثْرَةُ الطَّعَامِ وَالمَنَامِ وَالكَلامِ تُقَسِّي القَلْبَ .

144) مَنْ أَعْرَضَ عَنْ تَحْقِيقِ النَّظَرِ لَمْ يَجِبْ عَلَيْهِ تَغْيِيرُ المُنْكَرِ لِأَنَّهُ لَمْ يَثْبِتْهُ .

145) مَا لَمْ يُصْلِحُوا المَعْرِفَةَ شَغَلَهُمْ بِرُؤْيَةِ الأَعْمَالِ .

146) مَا بَانَ عَنْهُ أَحَدٌ وَلا اتَّصَلَ بِهِ أَحَدٌ مَا بَانَ عَنْهُ مِنْ حَيْثُ الذَّاتِ .

147) لا تَكُونُ لَهُ عَبْدًا وَلِغَيْرِهِ فِيكَ بَقِيَّةٌ .

148) حَقُّ بَقَاءِ الأَبَدِ فِي فَنَائِكَ عَنْكَ .

149) الأَجْسَامُ أَقْلامٌ وَالأَرْوَاحُ أَلْوَاحٌ وَالنُّفُوسُ كُؤُوسٌ .

150) إِيَّاكُمْ وَالمُحَاكَمَاتِ قَبْلَ الطَّرِيقِ الأَحْوَالِ فَإِنَّهَا تَقْطَعُ بِكُمْ .

151) تَرْكُ الدُّنْيَا أَيْسَرُ مِنْ أَخْذِهَا لَهَا .

152) الوَجْدُ خَطْرَةٌ تَلْهَبُ ثُمَّ نَظْرَةٌ تَسْلُبُ .

153. No method leads more directly to the Truth than [that of] following the rules established by the Messenger [of God], may God bless and preserve him.

154. When God desires good for a slave, He draws close to him by means of [the slave's] remembrance of Him and makes him worthy of Him by means of his thankfulness.

155. One who becomes intimate with created things becomes alienated from the Truth.

156. Lust [for the material world] is acquired through heedlessness.

157. Associating with those who alter religion causes the heart to die.

158. Beware of associating with one who possesses even the slightest bit of heresy, for its evil effects may return to haunt you, even after the passage of time.

159. When you see a man displaying evidence of miracles and paranormal abilities, do not be attracted to him; look instead at how he practices commanding [the good] and forbidding [evil].

160. One who is content with the extent of his formal knowledge without being characterized by its inner meaning has strayed from true religion and is cut off; one who is satisfied with his worshipful acts without being able to explain their meaning has deviated and has left the community of believers; one who is content with his legal knowledge without being scrupulous in his behavior is deluded and has been misled; but one who holds fast to the rules he is required to maintain is saved and exalted.

161. The shaykh is one to whom your essence bears witness by entrusting itself [to his care], and [to whom] your innermost self [bears witness] by respecting and magnifying him. The shaykh is one who instructs you with his morals, refines you with his skills, and illuminates your inner being with his radiance. The shaykh is one who makes you whole in his presence [with God] and preserves you when you are far from the effects of his luminosity. With *fuqarā'* the shaykh [behaves with] intimacy and openness; with Sufis [he behaves] with refined conduct and closeness; with [other] shaykhs [he behaves] with service and delight; and with gnostics [he behaves] with humility and self-abasement.

153) لا طَرِيقَ أَوْصَل إلى الحَقّ مِنْ مُتَابَعَةِ الرَّسُول ﷺ في أَحْكَامِه.

154) إذا أَرَادَ اللهُ بعَبْدٍ خيراً آنسَهُ بذِكْرِهِ ووَفَّقَهُ لشُكْرِهِ.

155) مَنْ تأَنَّسَ بالْخَلق اسْتَوْحَشَ مِنَ الحقّ.

156) بالغفلَةِ تُنالُ الشَّهْوَة.

157) مخالطَةُ أَهْلِ البدَعِ تُميتُ القَلْبَ.

158) مَنْ كانَ فِيهِ أَدْنَى بدْعَةٍ فَاحْذَرْ مُجالسَتَه لِئَلاَّ يَعُودَ عَلَيكَ شُؤْمُهَا ولَوْ بَعْدَ حِينٍ.

159) إذا رَأَيتُمُ الرَّجُلَ تَظْهَرُ لَهُ الكرَامَاتُ وتُخْرَقُ لَه العَادَاتُ فلا [تَرْكَنُوا] تَلْتَفِتُوا إليهِ ولَكِنْ انظُرُوا كَيْفَ هُوَ عِنْدَ امْتِثَالِ الأَمْرِ والنَّهي.

160) مَنْ اكْتَفَى بالعِلمِ دُونَ الاتِّصافِ بحَقِيقَتِهِ تزَنْدَقَ وانقطعَ. مَنْ اكْتَفَى بالتَّعَبُّدِ دُونَ فِقْهٍ خرَجَ وَابْتَدَعَ وَمَنْ اكْتَفَى بالفِقْهِ دُونَ وَرَعٍ اغْتَرَّ وانخدَعَ وَمَنْ قَامَ بِمَا يَجِبُ عَلَيهِ مِنَ الأَحْكَامِ تَخَلَّصَ وَارْتَفعَ.

161) الشَّيْخُ مَنْ شَهِدَتْ لَهُ ذَاتُكَ بالتَّقْدِيمِ وَسِرُّكَ بالاحْتِرَامِ وَالتَّعْظِيمِ. الشَّيْخُ مَنْ هَذَّبَكَ بأَخْلَاقِهِ وَأَدَّبَكَ بإطْرَاقِهِ وأَنارَ بَاطِنَكَ بإشْرَاقِهِ. الشَّيْخُ مَنْ جمَعَكَ في حُضُورِهِ وحَفِظَكَ في مُغيبِ آثارِ نورِهِ. الشَّيْخُ مَعَ الفُقَرَاء بالأُنْسِ وَالانبساطِ وَمَعَ الصُّوفِيَّةِ بالأَدَبِ وَالارْتِبَاطِ وَمَعَ المَشَايخِ بالخِدْمَةِ وَالاغْتِبَاطِ وَمَعَ العَارِفينَ بالتَّوَاضُعِ وَالانحِطَاطِ.

162. Virtuous character entails acting in harmony with every individual according to that which brings him close to you and does not alienate him from you. So with religious scholars [practice the virtues of] attentive listening and the appearance of need [for their teachings]; with gnostics [practice the virtues of] stillness and watchfulness; and with the masters of spiritual stations [practice the virtues of] *tawḥīd* and self-abnegation.

163. With the Names of God the Exalted are found an attachment, an unintended consequence, and a certainty. The attachment is awareness of the meaning of a [particular] name; the unintended consequence is that the meaning of the name subsists with you; and the certainty is that you will be annihilated in the meaning of the name.[46]

164. Every 'reality' that does not efface both the trace and the form of the slave is not a [true] Reality.[47]

May Allah bless our lord Muḥammad, Light of Lights, Guide of the Righteous, and Messenger of the All-Forgiving King. May Allah bless him, along with his family and Companions throughout the night and the day, and accord him the fullest salutations. All praise be to Allah, Lord of the Worlds.

46. This aphorism and the one that follows are found only in *Uns al-faqīr* and are in neither the British Library nor the Bibliothèque Nationale manuscripts.

47. This aphorism has also been attributed to Shaykh Abū Yaʿzā. See al-Kattānī, *Salwat al-anfās* (1), p. 173.

162) حُسْنُ الخُلُقِ مُمَالأَتُكَ مَعَ كُلِّ شَخْصٍ بِمَا يُؤْنِسُهُ وَلا يُوحِشُهُ. فَمَعَ العُلَمَاءِ بِحُسْنِ الاِسْتِمَاعِ وَالاِفْتِقَارِ وَمَعَ أَهْلِ المَعْرِفَةِ بِالسُّكُونِ وَالاِنْتِظَارِ وَمَعَ أَهْلِ المَقَامَاتِ بِالتَّوْحِيدِ وَالاِنْكِسَارِ.

163) أَسْمَاءُ اللهِ تَعَالَى بِهَا تَعَلُّقٌ وَتَخَلُّقٌ وَتَحَقُّقٌ. فَالتَّعَلُّقُ الشُّعُورُ بِمَعْنَى الاِسْمِ وَالتَّخَلُّقُ أَنْ يَقُومَ بِكَ مَعْنَى الاِسْمِ وَالتَّحَقُّقُ أَنْ تَفْنَى فِي مَعْنَى الاِسْمِ.

164) كُلُّ حَقِيقَةٍ لا تَمْحُو أَثَرَ العَبْدِ وَرَسْمَهُ فَلَيْسَتْ بِحَقِيقَةٍ.

وَصَلَّى اللهُ عَلَى سَيِّدِنَا مُحَمَّدٍ نُورِ الأَنْوَارِ وَهَادِي الأَبْرَارِ وَرَسُولِ المَلِكِ الغَفَّارِ.

صَلَّى اللهُ عَلَيْهِ وَعَلَى آلِهِ وَأَصْحَابِهِ آنَاءَ اللَّيْلِ وَأَطْرَافَ النَّهَارِ وَسَلَّمَ تَسْلِيمًا كَثِيرًا وَالحَمْدُ للهِ رَبِّ العَالَمِينَ.

V

THE QAṢĪDA IN *RĀ'*[1]

By command of the Almighty His splendor has been magnified,
And with majesty and glory establishes His divine decree.

He—whose judgment inexorably governs creation,
According to what was set down as a record in the Primordial Book.

All praise is Yours! There is no granting what You forbid,
And no forbidding what You abundantly bestow.

Your will is pre-ordained and Your judgment is piercing—
Your knowledge encompasses the seven heavens and the earth.

Your Command subsists between the *Kāf* and the *Nūn*,[2]
[Executed] more swiftly and easily than the blink of an eye.

When You say, 'Be!' what You say has already been,
And Your pronouncement of it is never repeated.

You were, and nothing was before You; You were, and nothing was
Other than You, yet You remain when mortal beings die.

You determined the fate of creatures before creating them,
And that which You determined was a predetermined command.

You loom above the seven heavens as a Conqueror,
And You see what You have created, yet You [Yourself] are not seen.

Lords affirm that You are [their] Lord—
If they denied [You] they would taste the torment of one who disbelieves.

1. The text of this poem can be found in manuscript 774D (folios 68–69r) of the Bibliothèque Générale (*al-Khizāna al-ʿĀmma*), Rabat, Morocco. Although this particular copy is not dated, the names of other Sufi poets included in the collection of which this text is a part indicate that it could not have been transcribed any earlier than the late twelfth/seventeenth century.

2. This verse refers to the two letters contained in the Creative Command, 'Be!' (*kun*) and is based on the following passage from the Qur'ān: 'He it is Who gives life and death; when an affair is decided, He says, "Be!" and it is.' (Qur'ān, XL [*Ghāfir*], 68.) The concept implicit in this passage is similar to that of the Neo-Platonic 'creative word', or *logos spermatikos*.

القَصِيدَةُ الرّائِيَّة

بِأَمْرِ تَعَالَى مَجْدُهُ قَدْ تَكَبَّرَا ... وَجَلَّ جَلالاً قَدْرُهُ أَنْ يُقَرَّرَا

وَمَنْ حُكْمُهُ مَاضٍ عَلَى الخَلْقِ نَافِذٌ ... بِمَا خَطَّ فِي أُمِّ الكِتَابِ مُسَطَّرَا

لَكَ الحَمْدُ لا مُعْطِيَ لِمَا أَنْتَ مَانِعٌ ... وَلا مَانِعَ مَا أَنْتَ تُعْطِي مُوَفَّرَا

قَضَاؤُكَ مَقْضِيٌّ وَحُكْمُكَ نَافِذٌ ... وَعِلْمُكَ فِي السَّبْعِ الطِّبَاقِ وَفِي الثَّرَا

وَأَمْرُكَ بَيْنَ الكَافِ وَالنُّونِ كَائِنٌ ... أَسْرَعَ مِنْ لَحْظِ العُيُونِ وَأَيْسَرَا

إِذَا قُلْتَ كُنْ كَانَ الَّذِي أَنْتَ قَائِلٌ ... وَلَمْ يَكُ مِنْكَ القَوْلُ فِيهِ مُكَرَّرَا

سَبَقْتَ وَلَمْ تُسْبَقْ وَكُنْتَ وَلَمْ يَكُنْ ... سِوَاكَ وَتَبْقَى حِينَ يُهْلَكُ ذَا الوَرَا

وَدَبَّرْتَ أَمْرَ الخَلْقِ مِنْ قَبْلِ خَلْقِهِمْ ... فَكَانَ الَّذِي دَبَّرْتَ أَمْراً مُدَبَّرَا

عَلَوْتَ عَلَى السَّبْعِ السَّمَوَاتِ قَاهِراً ... فَأَنْتَ تَرَى مَا قَدْ خَلَقْتَ وَلا تُرَا

تُقِرُّ لَكَ الأَرْبَابُ أَنَّكَ رَبُّهَا ... وَلَوْ أَنْكَرَتْ ذَاقَتْ عَذَابَ مَنْ

You have put on the cloak of grandeur, and there is not
Anything other than You, Enthroned One, to be exalted.

You it was who named Yourself the Conqueror,
And You are the God of Truth—certainly and beyond doubt.

You raised the firmament to its utmost height,
And then restrained it so it would not engulf the earth.

You fixed the sun and full moon as ornaments
For it, and stars, rising and setting.

You set down the earth, then spread it out,
And made rivers and seas flow upon it.

You created towering mountains and peaks on it,
And caused its waters to pour forth, overflowing.

You it is Who has overwhelming power over [the universe];
You created a fully formed creature out of moist clay,

[Then] endowed him with intellect, hearing, and sight,
And established him as a hearing, seeing individual.

You paired him with a mate from one of his own kind,
And brought forth progeny from them, who multiplied.

Yours is the greatest bounty, by which You guided us,
And made us believers in a pure, primordial religion.

After [our] ignorance You allotted us a [great] responsibility,
And a 'manifest light', as an illumination for hearts.[3]

So glory be to You, oh God, the Grand and Exalted,
Blessed be my Lord, most Majestic and Great!

How much grace have you clothed us with as an honor!
You have covered the naked one with it and continue to shield him.

3. This verse refers to the following passage from the Qur'ān: 'Oh mankind! Verily there has come to you a convincing proof from your Lord; for We have sent unto you a light that is manifest.' (Qur'ān, IV [*an-Nisā'*], 174.)

لَبِسْتَ رِدَاءَ الْكِبرِيَاءِ ولَمْ يَكُنْ … لِغَيرِكَ يَا ذَا الْعَرْشِ أَنْ يَتَكَبَّرَا

وَأَنْتَ الذي سَمَّيْتَ نَفْسَكَ قَاهِرًا … وَأَنْتَ إِلٰهُ الحَقِّ حَقًّا بِلا اجْتِرَا

وَأَنْتَ رَفَعْتَ السَّبْعَ في ذِرْوَةِ العُلا … كَيْ لا تَخِرَّ على الثَّرَا

وَسَخَّرْتَ فِيها الشَّمْسَ وَالبَدْرَ زِينَةً … لَهَا وَنُجُومًا طَالِعَاتٍ وَغُوَّرَا

وَأَنْتَ وَضَعْتَ الأَرْضَ ثُمَّ بَسَطْتَهَا … وَأَجْرَيْتَ أَنْهَارًا عَلَيْهَا وَأَبْحُرَا

وَأَنْشَأْتَ فِيها شَامِخَاتٍ رَوَاسِيا … وَفَجَّرْتَ فِيهَا مَاءَهَا فَتَفَجَّرَا

وَأَنْتَ الذي فِيها بِقُدْرَةِ قَاهِرٍ … خَلَقْتَ مِنَ المَسْنُونِ خَلْقًا مُصَوَّرَا

جَعَلْتَ لَهُ عَقْلاً وَسَمْعًا وَنَاظِرًا … وَسَوَّيْتَهُ شَخْصًا سَمِيعًا وَمُبْصِرَا

وَزَوَّجْتَهُ زَوْجًا مِنْ إِحْدَى نَوْعِهِ … وَنَشَّرْتَ نَشْرًا مِنْهُمُ فَتَنَشَّرَا

لَكَ المِنَّةُ العُظْمَى على ما هَدَيْتَنَا … وَدَيَّنْتَنَا دِينًا حَنِيفًا مُطَهَّرَا

وَأَوْزَعْتَنَا بَعْدَ الجَهَالَةِ حَمَالَةً … وَنُورًا مُبِينًا لِلقُلُوبِ مُنَوَّرَا

فَسُبْحَانَكَ اللَّهُمَّ ذَا المَجْدِ وَالعُلا … تَبَارَكْتَ رَبِّي مَا أَجَلَّ وَأَكْبَرَا

فَكَمْ نِعْمَةً أَلْبَسْتَنَاهَا جَلِيلَةً … سَتَرْتَ بِهَا ذَا عَوْرَةٍ فَتَسَتَّرَا

How many misfortunes and calamities have You eased for us,
Have you warded off from the slave who errs and slackens!

We have erred and sinned often, yet You still
Remain merciful with us, near to us, and watchful.

Were evildoers and sinners not among us,
You would surely create a sinful people in order to pardon them.

Oh Lord, prepare repentance for all of us,
And set aside our errors with preordained forgiveness.

Then bless the Unlettered One and preserve him,
Who came to us as a Messenger, an Apostle, and Bearer of Good Tidings.

And to [his] family and Companions [give] the purest greetings,
Exuding musk and ambergris for all time.

وَكَمْ كُرْبَةٍ فَرَّجْتَهَا وَعَظِيمَةٍ دَفَعْتَ عَنِ العَبْدِ الذي زَلَّ وَأَفْتَرَا

أَسَأْنَا وَأَذْنَبْنَا كَثِيرًا وَلَمْ تَزَلْ رَحِيمًا بِنَا مِنَّا قَرِيبًا وَمُبْصِرَا

فَلَوْ لَمْ يَكُنْ مِنَّا مُسِيءٌ وَمُذْنِبٌ لَجِئْتَ بِقَوْمٍ يُذْنِبُونَ فَتَغْفِرَا

فَيَا رَبِّ هَيِّئْ تَوْبَةً لِجَمِيعِنَا وَحُطَّ خَطَايَانَا بِعَفْوٍ تَقَرَّرَا

وَصَلِّ عَلَى الأُمِّيِّ ثُمَّ سَلِّمْ عَلَى الذي أَتَانَا رَسُولًا دَاعِيًا وَمُبَشِّرَا

مَعَ الآلِ وَالأَصْحَابِ أَزْكَى تَحِيَّةٍ تَفُوحُ مَدَا الأَيَّامِ مِسْكًا وَعَنْبَرَا

VI

THE QAṢĪDA IN *NŪN*[1]

THE world confines us when You are absent from us,
And our souls abandon us because of desire.

Distance from You is death and nearness to You is life,
Were You absent for [but the moment of] a breath we would die.

Far from You we die and in nearness to You we live,
And if good tidings of reunion reach us from You we revive.

We remain alive in remembrance of You when we do not see You,
For only remembrance of the Beloved enlivens us.

Were it not for the quintessence of You that our hearts perceive,
In wakefulness or sleep, when we are absent,

We would surely die from grieving and yearning out of separation
from You;
Yet, in reality, Your essence is within us.

Remembrance motivates us without [need] for word of You;
Were it not because of the desire for You within us [our limbs] would
not move.

So say to one who would forbid ecstasy from those who experience it,
'If you have not tasted the draught of Desire with us, be off!

'When souls tremble, desirous of reunion,
'Even phantoms dance, oh uncomprehending one!'

Do you not see how a caged bird, oh youth,
Breaks into song when it recalls its ancestral home?

1. The text of this poem can be found in two manuscripts: Add. 9514 (folios 95–96) of the British Library, London (dated 1107/1696); and 774D (folios 68–69bis) of the Bibliothèque Générale, Rabat, Morocco.

القَصِيدَةُ النُّونِيَّةُ

تَضِيقُ بنا الدُّنْيا إذا غِبْتُمُ عَنَّا　　وتَذْهَبُ بالأَشْوَاقِ أَرْوَاحُنا مِنَّا
بُعْدُكُمْ مَوْتٌ وقُرْبُكُم حَيَا　　فإنْ غِبْتُمُ عَنَّا ولَو نَفَسًا مِتْنَا
نَمُوتُ بِبُعْدِكُمْ ونَحْيَى بقُرْبِكُمْ　　وإنْ جاءَنا عَنْكُمْ بشْرُ اللِقَا عِشْنَا
ونَحْيَى بذِكْرَاكُمْ إذا لَمْ نَرَكُمُ　　أَلَا إنَّ تَذْكَارَ الأَحِبَّةِ يُنْعِشُنَا
فلو لا مَعَانِيكُمْ تَرَاها قُلُوبُنا　　إذا نَحْنُ أَيْقَاظًا وفي النَّوْمِ إن غِبْنا
لَمِتْنَا أَسًى مِن بُعْدِكُم وصَبَابَةً　　ولَكِنَّ في المَعْنَى مَعَانِيكُم مَعَنا
يُحَرِّكُنا ذِكْرٌ بلا حَدِيثَ عَنْكُم　　ولَو لا هَوَاكُم في الحَشَى ما تَحَرَّكْنَا
فقُلْ لِلَّذِي يَنْهَى عَنِ الوَجْدِ أَهْلَهُ　　إذا لَمْ تَذُقْ مَعَنا شَرَابَ الهَوَى دَعْنَا
إذا اهْتَزَّتِ الأَرْوَاحُ شَوْقًا إلى اللِّقَا　　نَعَمْ تَرْقُصُ الأَشْبَاحُ يا جَاهِلَ المَعْنَا
أَمَا تَنْظُرُ الطَّيْرَ المُقَفَّصَ يا فَتَى　　إذا ذَكَرَ الأَوْطَانَ حَنَّ إلى المَغْنَا

With its chirping that which is in its heart bursts forth,
And its extremities are agitated with feeling and spirit.

It dances in the cage, desirous of reunion,
So that [even] sentient beings are moved when it sings.

Such are the souls of lovers, oh youth,
Desires propel them to the most sublime world.

Are we to force patience upon [souls] when they are enraptured?
Is one who has perceived the Quintessence able to be patient?

If you have not tasted the desire that [true] human beings have tasted,
Then by God, oh empty husk, do not defame us!

Concede to us what we advocate, for
When our desires overcome us we are likely to cry out loud.

Our hearts vibrate during sessions of invocation,
[And] when we cannot hide our ecstasies we lose control.

In the Divine Mystery are fine and subtle secrets
That perceptibly surround us. If only we could utter them!

Oh Distractor of Lovers, arise and openly proclaim!
Fill us to the brim and refresh us with the Name of the Beloved!

Because of our gratitude, preserve our secret from those who envy us,
And if Your eyes disapprove of something, then forgive us.

When we have become light-headed and carefree,
And the wine of Love intoxicates us, we are exposed.

Do not blame the drunkard for his state of drunkenness,
For in our drunkenness we have been absolved of responsibility.

فَفَرَّحَ بِالتَّغْرِيدِ مَا بِفُؤَادِهِ   فَتَضْطَرِبُ الأَعْضَاءُ فِي الحِسِّ وَالمَعْنَا
وَيَرْقُصُ فِي الأَقْفَاصِ شَوْقاً إِلَى اللِّقَا   فَتَهْتَزُّ أَرْبَابُ العُقُولِ إِذَا غَنَّا
كَذَلِكَ أَرْوَاحُ المُحِبِّينَ يَا فَتًى   تُهَزِّزُهَا الأَشْوَاقُ لِلْعَالَمِ الأَسْنَا
أَنُلْزِمُهَا بِالصَّبْرِ وَهِيَ مُشَوَّقَةٌ   وَهَلْ يَسْتَطِيعُ الصَّبْرَ مَنْ شَاهَدَ المَعْنَا
إِذَا لَمْ تَذُقْ مَا ذَاقَتِ النَّاسُ فِي الهَوَى   فَبِاللهِ يَا خَالِي الحَشَى لَا تُعَنِّفْنَا
وَسَلِّمْ لَنَا فِيمَا ادَّعَيْنَا لِأَنَّنَا   إِذَا غَلَبَتْ أَشْوَاقُنَا رُبَّمَا صِحْنَا
وَتَهْتَزُّ عِنْدَ الاِسْتِمَاعِ قُلُوبُنَا   إِذَا لَمْ نَجِدْ كَتْمَ المَوَاجِدِ بَرَحْنَا
وَفِي السِّرِّ أَسْرَارٌ دِقَاقٌ لَطِيفَةٌ   تُرَاوِدُ عَنَّا جَهْرَةً لَوْ بِهَا بُحْنَا
فَيَا حَادِيَ العُشَّاقِ قُمْ وَاحْدُ قَائِمًا   وَزَمْزِمْ لَنَا بِاسْمِ الحَبِيبِ وَرَوِّحْنَا
وَصُنْ سِرَّنَا فِي سُكْرِنَا عَنْ حَسُودِنَا   وَإِنْ أَنْكَرَتْ عَيْنَاكَ شَيْئاً فَسَامِحْنَا
فَإِنَّا إِذَا طِبْنَا وَطَابَتْ نُفُوسُنَا   وَخَامَرَنَا خَمْرُ الغَرَامِ تَهَتَّكْنَا
فَلَا تَلُمِ السَّكْرَانَ فِي حَالِ سُكْرِهِ   فَقَدْ رُفِعَ التَّكْلِيفُ فِي سُكْرِنَا عَنَّا

VII

QAṢĪDA IN *MĪM*[1]

RETURN to us the nights that have been lost to us,
And erase, by Your favor, that which has issued from us.

How much we have sinned, yet out of generosity You forgive [us];
How much we have erred, yet we still hope for Your good pardon!

Nothing but You have I—You are the recourse of my sorrow;
I have been ignorant, and possess nothing but Your indulgence.

Not for a single day have I turned toward anyone but You,
For in all the world I own nothing but Your favor.

How much respect I display in [my] love [for You]!
No friendship do I hope for, other than Your affection.

Were I to have a thousand tongues with which to express
Thanks to You, I would not stop thanking You for a single day.

1. The original of this poem can be found in manuscript Add. 7596 (folio 35), of the British Library, London.

قَصِيدَةٌ مِيمِيَّةٌ

رُدُّوا عَلَيْنَا لَيَالِينَا الَّتِي سَلَفَتْ — وَامْحُوا الَّذِي قَدْ جَرَى مِنَّا
فَكَمْ زَلَلْنَا وَأَنْتُمْ تَصْفَحُوا كَرَمًا — وَكَمْ أَسَأْنَا وَنَرْجُو حُسْنَ عَفْوِكُمُ
مَا لِي سِوَاكُمْ وَأَنْتُمْ حُزْنِي — وَقَدْ جَهِلْتُ وَمَا لِي غَيْرَ سَتْرِكُمُ
وَلَمْ أَمِلْ عَنْكُمْ يَوْمًا إِلَى أَحَدٍ — فَلَسْتُ فِي الْبَرِيَّةِ غَيْرَ فَضْلِكُمُ
وَكَمْ إِلَى شَرَفٍ فِي الْحُبِّ أُظْهِرُهُ — وَلَسْتُ أَرْجُو وِدَادًا غَيْرَ وُدِّكُمُ
لَوْ كَانَ أَلْفُ لِسَانٍ لِي أُبُثُّ بِهَا — شُكْرًا لَمْ أَقُمْ يَوْمًا بِشُكْرِكُمُ

VIII

QAṢĪDA IN *RĀ'*[1]

WHAT delight is there in life other than companionship with the
fuqarā'?
They are the sultans, lords, and princes.[2]

So befriend them and learn the ways of their assemblies,
And keep your obligations, even if they ignore you.

Profit from [your] time and participate always with them,
And know that [Divine] satisfaction distinguishes one who is present.

Make silence obligatory unless you are questioned, then say:
'No knowledge have I', and conceal yourself with ignorance.

Regard not any fault, but that acknowledged within yourself
As a manifest, clearly apparent fault, though it be concealed.

Lower your head and seek forgiveness without [apparent] cause,
And stand at the feet of Justice, making excuses [in your own behalf].

If a fault appears in you, acknowledge it, and direct
Your pleas toward that within you which comes from you.

Say: 'Your slaves are more worthy [than ourselves] of your forgiveness,
So excuse us and be kind to us, oh *fuqarā'*!'

By giving preference to others they are exalted, for it is their nature,
So do not fear that they will punish or harm you.

1. The Arabic texts of the following poems were most recently published in ᶜAbd al-Ḥalīm Maḥmūd, *Shaykh ash-shuyūkh Abū Madyan al-Ghawth: ḥayātuhu wa miᶜrājuhu ilā Allāh* (Cairo: Dār al-Maᶜārif, 1985). Although the translator of the present volume has not been able to find corroboratory examples of any of these poems in consulted manuscript collections, both their style and their content are consistent with other, verifiable works by Abū Madyan. The poems contained on pages 124 and 130–32 of the collection cited above, however, were not included in this volume because either their style or their vocabulary did not conform to previously known works of Abū Madyan or to common western Maghribi usage.

2. The attitudes toward *futuwwa* and *īthār* expressed in this poem may have been partly responsible for the charges filed against Abū Madyan by members of the Almohad élite. See Introduction, p. 15.

قَصِيدَةٌ رَائِيَّة

مَا لَذَّةُ العَيْشِ إِلَّا صُحْبَةُ الفُقَرَا   هُمُ السَّلَاطِينُ وَالسَّادَاتُ وَالأُمَرَا
فَاصْحَبْهُمُوا وَتَأَدَّبْ فِي مَجَالِسِهِم   وَخَلِّ حَظَّكَ مَهْمَا قَدَّمُوكَ وَرَا
وَاسْتَغْنِمِ الوَقْتَ وَاحْضُرْ دَائِمًا مَعَهُم   وَاعْلَمْ بِأَنَّ الرِّضَى يَخْتَصُّ مَنْ حَضَرَا
وَلَازِمِ الصَّمْتَ إِلَّا إِنْ سُئِلْتَ فَقُلْ   لَا عِلْمَ عِنْدِي وَكُنْ بِالجَهْلِ مُسْتَتِرَا
وَلَا تَرَ العَيْبَ إِلَّا فِيكَ مُعْتَقِدًا   عَيْبًا بَدَا بَيِّنًا لَكِنَّهُ اسْتَتَرَا
وَحُطَّ رَأْسَكَ وَاسْتَغْفِرْ بِلَا سَبَبٍ   وَقُمْ عَلَى قَدَمِ الإِنْصَافِ مُعْتَذِرَا
وَإِنْ بَدَا مِنْكَ عَيْبٌ فَاعْتَرِفْ وَأَقِمْ   وَجْهَ اعْتِذَارِكَ عَمَّا فِيكَ مِنْكَ جَرَى
وَقُلْ عُبَيْدُكُمُ أَوْلَى بِصَفْحِكُمُ   فَسَامِحُوا وَخُذُوا بِالرِّفْقِ يَا فُقَرَا
هُمْ بِالتَّفَضُّلِ أَوْلَى وَهْوَ شِيمَتُهُمْ   فَلَا تَخَفْ دَرَكًا مِنْهُم وَلَا ضَرَرَا

And in magnanimity toward the brothers be forever limitless,
Out of feeling or understanding, and avert your gaze if one of them
stumbles.

Observe the shaykh attentively in his states, for perhaps
A trace of his approval will be seen upon you.

Display earnestness and be eager in his service;
Perhaps he will be pleased, but beware lest you see annoyance.

For in his satisfaction is that of the Creator and obedience toward Him;
He has granted you His good pleasure, so beware lest you forsake it!

[Know] that the Way of the Folk is [now] decadent,
And that the state of one who preaches it today is as you see.

When shall I see [the true Folk of God], and how am I to have sight of them,
Or my ear hear news of them?

How can I or one like me dispute with them
Over spiritual experiences about which I am not familiar?

I love them, am courteous to them, and follow them
With my innermost soul—especially one person among them.

They are a folk noble in character; wherever they sit,
That place remains fragrant from their traces.

Sufism guides one quickly by means of their conduct;
A fitting harmony is theirs, delightful to my sight.

They are my loved ones, my family, who
Are among those who proudly hold up the Hems of Glory.

I am united with them still, brought together in God,
And through Him our transgressions are pardoned and forgiven.

So [may] blessings [be] upon the Chosen One, our Lord
Muḥammad, the best of those who fulfill their vows.

وبالتَّفَتِّي عَلَى الإِخْوانِ جُدْ أَبَداً ... حِسّاً وَمَعْنًى وغُضَّ الطَّرْفَ إِنْ عَثَرا

وراقِبِ الشَّيْخَ في أَحْوالِهِ فَعَسَى ... يَرَى عَلَيكَ مِنِ اسْتِحْسانِهِ أَثَرا

وقَدِّمِ الجِدَّ وانْهَضْ عِنْدَ خِدْمَتِهِ ... عَساهُ يَرْضَى وحاذِرْ أَنْ تَرَى ضَجَرا

فَفِي رِضاهُ رِضَى البارِي وطاعَتُهُ ... يَرْضَى عَلَيْكَ مِنكِها حَذِرا

[واعْلَمْ] بِأَنَّ طَرِيقَ القَوْمِ دارِسَةٌ ... وحالُ مَنْ يَدَّعِيها اليَوْمَ كَيْفَ تَرَى

مَتَى أَراهُمْ وأَنَّى لِي بِرُؤْيَتِهِمْ ... أَوْ تَسْمَعُ الأُذْنُ مِنِّي عَنْهُمُ خَبَرا

مَنْ لِي وأَنَّى لِمِثْلِي أَنْ يُزاحِمَهُمْ ... عَلَى مَوارِدَ لَمْ آلَفْ بِها كَدَرا

أُحِبُّهُمْ وأُدارِيهِمْ وأُوثِرُهُمْ ... بِمُهْجَتِي وخُصُوصاً مِنْهُمُ نَفَرا

قَوْمٌ كِرامُ السَّجايا حَيْثُما جَلَسُوا ... يَبْقَى المَكانُ عَلَى آثارِهِمْ عَطِرا

يَهْدِي التَّصَوُّفُ مِنْ أَخْلاقِهِمْ طَرَفاً ... حُسْنُ التَّآلُفِ مِنْهُمْ راقَنِي نَظَرا

هُمْ أَهْلُ وُدِّي وأَحْبابِي الَّذِينَ هُمُ ... مِمَّنْ يَجُرُّ ذُيُولَ العِزِّ مُفْتَخِرا

لا زالَ شَمْلِي بِهِمْ فِي اللهِ مُجْتَمِعاً ... وذَنْبُنا فِيهِ مَعْفُوّاً ومُغْتَفَرا

ثُمَّ الصَّلاةُ عَلَى المُخْتارِ سَيِّدِنا ... مُحَمَّدٍ خَيْرِ مَنْ أَوْفَى ومَنْ نَذَرا

IX

QAṢĪDA IN *BĀ'*

I HAVE stretched out my hand to You in every adversity,
And have found kindness from You in every affliction.

You are the recourse and reassurance of my seclusion—
Can it be impossible for hope to be a necessity?

So confirm my hope in You, oh Lord, and protect me,
From the malice of an enemy or the mistreatment of a friend.

You have already rescued me from the hazards of so many tribulations
That were locked deep within me between the bowels and the throat.

Neither strength have I, nor stratagem,
Save my poverty before the beautiful Bestower of Gifts.

Oh refuge of one oppressed when he calls upon Him,
Aid me, for my ways to salvation have all been blocked!

My hope in You is my principal and profit,
And my detachment from created things is the purest of my earnings.

Oh Charitable One! Despite what I have done, You are able
To forgive me for the occurrence and outcome of each sinful act.

Most surely I hope only for that which is Your nature to bestow,
Although I have erred often and am full of shortcomings.

And bless the Chosen One from the family of Hāshim,
The Intercessor of mankind in their severest afflictions.

قَصِيدَةٌ بَائِيَّة

إِلَيكَ مَدَدْتُ الكَفَّ فِي كُلِّ شِدَّةٍ ... وَمِنكَ وَجَدْتُ اللُّطْفَ فِي كُلِّ نَائِبِ

وَأَنْتَ مَلَاذِي وَالأَنَامُ بِمَعْزِلٍ ... وَهَلْ مُسْتَحِيلٌ فِي الرَّجَاءِ كَوَاجِبِ

فَحَقِّقْ رَجَائِي فِيكَ يَا رَبِّ وَاكْفِنِي ... شَمَاتَةَ عَدُوٍّ أَوْ إِسَاءَةَ صَاحِبِ

فَكَمْ كُرْبَةٍ تُنْجِنِي مِنْ غِمَارِهَا ... وَكَانَتْ شَجًى بَيْنَ الحَشَا وَالتَّرَائِبِ

فَلَا قُوَّةٌ عِنْدِي وَلَا لِي حِيلَةٌ ... سِوَى أَنَّ فَقْرِي لِجَمِيلِ المَوَاهِبِ

فَيَا مَلْجَأً لِمُضْطَرٍّ عِنْدَ دُعَائِهِ ... أَغِثْنِي فَقَدْ سُدَّتْ عَلَيَّ مَذَاهِبِي

رَجَاؤُكَ رَأْسُ المَالِ عِنْدِي وَرِبْحُهُ ... وَزُهْدِي فِي المَخْلُوقِ أَزْكَى

وَيَا مُحْسِنًا فِي مَا مَضَى أَنْتَ قَادِرٌ ... عَلَى اللُّطْفِ بِي فِي حَالِهِ وَالعَوَاقِبِ

وَإِنِّي لَأَرْجُو مِنْكَ مَا أَنْتَ أَهْلُهُ ... وَإِنْ كُنْتُ خَطَّاءً كَثِيرَ المَعَائِبِ

وَصَلِّ عَلَى المُخْتَارِ مِنْ آلِ هَاشِمٍ ... شَفِيعِ الوَرَى عِنْدَ اشْتِدَادِ النَّوَائِبِ

X

QAṢĪDA IN *LĀM*

SAY: 'ALLĀH!' and let go of existence with all it contains,
If you desire the attainment of perfection.

For everything other than God, were you to realize it,
Is nothing, whether in part or as a whole.

And know that you and all the worlds,
Were it not for Him, would be obliterated and destroyed.

As for the one who has no existence in and of himself,
Were it not for God, 'his' existence would be utterly impossible.

The gnostics have been annihilated—they perceive
Nothing but the Imperious, the Most Exalted.[1]

They see what is other than Him destroyed in actuality,
In the present, in the past, and in the future.

So look, either with your intellect or with your eye, do you see
Anything but an action among acts?

Examine the highest and lowest levels of existence
With a view that is supported by demonstrable proof,

And you will find that all which exists alludes to His Majesty
With the language of experience or the language of speech.

He is the Encompasser of all things, from the highest to
The lowest, and their Originator, beyond compare.

1. This verse and the one that follows are identical to verses contained in the *Treatise on Sufism* attributed to Abū Madyan's shaykh, Abū Yaᶜzā. See Appendix II.

قَصِيدَةٌ لامِيَّةٌ

اللهَ قُلْ وذَرِ الوُجُودَ وما حَوَى — إنْ كُنْتَ مُرْتَادًا بُلُوغَ كَمَالِ
فَالكُلُّ دُونَ اللهِ إنْ حَقَّقْتَهُ — عَدَمٌ على التَّفْصِيلِ والإجْمَالِ
واعْلَمْ بأنَّكَ والعَوالِمَ كُلَّها — لَوْلاهُ في مَحْوٍ وفي اضْمِحْلالِ
مَنْ لا وُجُودَ لِذاتِهِ مِنْ ذاتِهِ — فَوُجُودُهُ لَوْلاهُ عَيْنُ مُحالِ
فالعارِفُونَ فَنُوا ولَا يَشْهَدُوا — شَيْئًا سِوَى المُتَكَبِّرِ المُتَعالِ
ورَأَوْا سِواهُ على الحَقِيقَةِ هالِكًا — في الحالِ والماضِي والاِسْتِقْبالِ
فالْمَحْ بعَقْلِكَ أو بطَرْفِكَ هَلْ تَرَى — شَيْئًا سِوَى فِعْلٍ مِنَ الأَفْعالِ
وانْظُرْ إلى عُلْوِ الوُجُودِ وسُفْلِهِ — نَظَرًا يُؤَيِّدُهُ بالاِسْتِدْلالِ
تَجِدِ الجَمِيعَ يُشِيرُ نَحْوَ جَلالِهِ — بِلِسانِ حالٍ أوْ لِسانِ مَقالِ
هُوَ مُمْسِكُ الأشْياءِ مِنْ عُلْوٍ إلى — سُفْلٍ ومُبْدِعُها بغَيْرِ مِثالِ

XI

QAṢĪDA IN *LĀM*

THE Folk of Love were engrossed in the Beloved,
And in love for Him expended their souls.

They ruined everything that had enriched them, and preserved
What remained [with God]. How beautiful is that which they do!

They are preoccupied by neither the beauty of the world nor its finery,
Nor its fruits, its sweetness, or its garb.

They wander throughout existence in ecstasy and rapture,
And no quarter of the Earth is free of them—not even an empty ruin.

The Herald of Insight has called and awakened them,
How can they rest content when the fire of yearning is lit?

From the first of the night they have made their resolve,
And stay in the tents of the Beloved's protection.

Robes of honor are bestowed on them, so that they may bear
Intimacy with the breeze whose fragrance intoxicates.

They are the lovers—He brings them close, for they
Have never forgotten to serve the Incomparable Beloved.

Glory be to Him who favors them with nearness when they are actualized
In His love for them and arrive at their goal!

قصيدة لامية

أَهْلُ المحبَّةِ بالمحْبوبِ قَدْ شَغلوا | وفي محبَّتهِ أرواحُهُم بذلوا
وخرَّبوا كلَّ ما يَغني وقدْ عمَّروا | ما كانَ يَبقى فيا حُسْنَ الَّذي عَمِلوا
لمْ تُلْهِهِمْ زينة الدُّنيا وزُخْرُفُها | ولا جناها ولا حَلى ولا حُلَلُ
هاموا على الكوْنِ منْ وجْدٍ طَرِبٍ | وما استَقلَّ بهم رَبْعٌ ولا طَلَلُ
داعِي التّشوُّق ناداهم وأقْلَقَهُم | فكيف يَهْنوا ونارُ تَشْتَعِلُ
مِنْ أوَّلِ اللّيلِ قدْ سارَتْ عزائِمُهُم | وفي خِيامِ حِمى المحْبوبِ قدْ نَزَلوا
وافتْ لهم خِلَعُ التّشْريفِ يحمِلُها | عُرْفُ النّسيمِ الَّذي مِنْ نَشْرِهِ ثَمِلوا
هُمُ الأحِبَّةُ أَدْناهُم لأنَّهُمُ | عَنْ خِدْمَةِ الصَّمَدِ المحْبوبِ ما غفلوا
سُبْحانَ مَنْ خصَّهُم بالقُرْبِ حينَ قَضَوْا | في حُبِّهِ وعلى مَقْصودِهِم حَصَلوا

XII

QAṢĪDA IN *RĀ'*[1]

THROUGH you life is brought to every land you visit,
As if you were rain, falling on parcels of earth,

And the eye expects a pleasurable sight from you,
As if you were flowers in the eyes of mankind.

Your light guides the traveler toward sight of [his goal],
As if you were moons in the darkness of night.

God will not prevent any quarter of the Earth from receiving your visit,
Oh you who are remembered in the deepest hollows of every body and
heart!

1. This short poem describes the Muslim saints, or *awliyā' Allāh*, and the blessings their presence brings to the lands they visit and to those who follow them.

قصيدةٌ رائيّةٌ

تَحْيَا بِكُمْ كُلُّ أَرْضٍ تَنْزِلُونَ بِهَا   كَأَنَّكُمْ في بِقَاعِ الأَرْضِ أَمْطَارُ

وَتَشْتَهِي العَيْنُ فِيكُمْ مَنْظَرًا حَسَنًا   كَأَنَّكُمْ في عُيُونِ النَّاسِ أَزْهَارُ

وَنُورُكُمْ يَهْتَدِي السَّارِي لِرُؤْيَتِهِ   كَأَنَّ في ظَلامِ اللَّيْلِ أَقْمَارُ

لا أَوْحَشَ اللهُ رَبْعًا مِنْ زِيَارَتِكُمْ   يا مَنْ لَهُمْ في الحَشَا والقَلْبِ تِذْكَارُ

XIII

VERSES

(1)

WHEN you look with the eye of your intellect, you will not find
Anything but Him pictured in bodily forms.

Yet when you seek Reality from other than Him,
The transformation of your ignorance remains incomplete.

(2)

GOD, my Lord, I desire nothing but Him.
Is there, in all existence, anything living but God?

By means of the Divinity's essence are our bodies maintained.
Were it not for Him would anything else be found?

بَعْضُ الأَبْياتِ

(1)

فَإذا نَظَرْتَ بِعَيْنِ عَقْلِكَ لَمْ تَجِدْ   شَيْئًا سِواهُ على الذَّواتِ مُصَوَّرَا
وإذا طَلَبْتَ حَقِيقَةً مِنْ غَيْرِهِ   فَبِذَيْلِ جَهْلِكَ لا تَزالُ مُعَثَّرَا

(2)

اللهُ رَبِّي لا أُرِيدُ سِواهُ   هَلْ في الوُجُودِ الحَيِّ إلاَّ اللهُ
ذاتُ الإلهِ بِها قِوامُ ذَواتِنا   هَلْ كانَ يُوجَدُ غَيْرُهُ لَوْلاهُ

Appendix I

THE ODE IN *NŪN*

by ᶜAlī ibn Ismāᶜīl b. Ḥirzihim[1]

WHEN calamities befall you, cleave to us,
For we are generous, and our guest is never distressed.

Entrust yourself to us, and lodge in our quarter,
For we are a people among whom a visitor is never harmed.

If one who is troubled comes to us, complaining of his lot,
He quickly learns that he will attain his desire.

So whenever calamities and misfortunes befall you,
Flee to us and be sure to seek our noble presence.

If you desire eternal consideration,
Gain strength for yourself through God, and then through our high standing.

Even if you are not one of us, your love remains valid,
But the one who wins our love is granted felicity!

So seek and ask what you wish at our door,
For you will attain your desires and talents among us.

We grant and forbid to whom we wish, if we so desire;
Do you not see that the Deity aids us?

1. This poem is the only known extant work by Abū Madyan's *shaykh aṭ-ṭarīqa* (the shaykh from whom he took his Sufi *khirqa* and spiritual lineage), ᶜAlī ibn Ismāᶜīl b. Ḥirzihim, the famous 'Sīdī Ḥarāzim' of the city of Fez. The Arabic text of this poem can be found in al-ᶜAbbās ibn Ibrāhīm, *Kitāb al-iᶜlām bi man ḥalla Marrākush wa Aghmāt min al-aᶜlām* (Rabat: al-Maṭbaᶜa al-Malakiyya [Royal Printing House], 1980), (9), p. 54.

If our hierophany has disappeared from you beneath the earth,[2]
Our secret has not disappeared from you in the [world of] events.

It would be shameful for us to thwart a seeker
Of our presence; for what is excellence other than our excellence?

I am Ibn Ḥirzihim, in Fez is my fame,
Spiritual Axis of the western lands. He who visits us has won!

Be sincere, and hold fast to our rope,
For we are the Nurturers, and our army is never defeated![3]

Firmly adhere to visiting our tomb,
Humbly, and full of awe at our shrine.

Submit to us, and learn the covenants of our friendship,
And when calamities befall you, cleave to us!

2. The word *ṭūr* in the Arabic text of this poem refers to Mount Sinai (*Ṭūr Sīnīna*), as in Qur'ān, XCV [*at-Tīn*], 2. 'Hierophany', a term made famous by Mircea Eliade, refers to any geographical location or moment in time where the 'Wholly Other' is experienced. See Mircea Eliade, *Patterns in Comparative Religion* (New York: New American Library, 1974), pp. 3–14.

3. The word, 'nurturer' (*ghawth*, pl. *ghuyūth*), is commonly used in the Maghrib to refer to the paramount spiritual master of the age, and is a synonym for 'spiritual axis' (*quṭb*)—a term also employed by Ibn Ḥirzihim in this poem. In the North African folk tradition Shaykh Abū Madyan is often referred to as 'Abū Madyan the Nurturer'.

إنْ غَابَ عَنْكُمْ طُورُنَا تَحْتَ الثَّرَى   مَا غَابَ عَنْكُمْ فِي الحَوَادِثِ سِرُّنَا

عَارٌ عَلَيْنَا أَنْ نَخِيبَ قَاصِدًا   لَجْنَابِنَا مَا الفَضْلُ إلاَّ فَضْلُنَا

فَأَنَا إبْنُ حِرْزِهِمِ بِفَاسَ شُهْرَتِي   قُطْبُ المَغَارِبِ رَابِحٌ مَنْ زَارَنَا

كُنْ خَالِصًا مُتَمَسِّكًا بِجِبَالِنَا   نَحْنُ الغُيُوثُ وَلَيْسَ يَهْزِمُ جُنْدُنَا

وَاشْدُدْ يَدَيْكَ عَلَى زِيَارَةِ قَبْرِنَا   مُتَوَاضِعًا مُتَخَشِّعًا بِمَقَامِنَا

وَاخْضَعْ لَنَا وَاحْفَظْ عُهُودَ وِدَادِنَا   وَإذَا أَصَابَتْكَ الشَّدَائِدُ لُذْ بِنَا

Appendix II

A TREATISE ON SUFISM[1]

by Abū Yaʿzā Yalannūr ibn Maymūn ad-Dukkālī

KNOW that gnosis means 'knowledge of the state'. It is this that takes the one who possesses it out of himself, and is found in all parts of the heart, including its deepest corners. In all states the possessor of gnosis perceives his Lord in [the complementary Divine aspects of] Beauty and Glory:

I have seen Beauty, I have seen Glory,
My Lover and Beloved, in any case.

Yet the gnostics have been annihilated;
They perceive nothing but the Imperious, the Most Exalted.

They see what is other than Him destroyed in actuality,
In the present, in the past, and in the future.

The sun of the day sets by night, but the sun of the heart is never absent. One who perceives the interiors of vessels comprehends the secrets of the Divine Mysteries. But one who sees the Sun of the Beloved is absent from near or far, and finds nothing but the All-Hearing and the All-Answering.

It is impossible for one who sees Him to perceive anything apart from Him, for that which is other than Him does not see Him. The gnostic feels no sadness at realization. I have seen the Beloved with the eye of His heart, [and] by means of the hidden secret:

1. This short treatise appears to be the only extant work attributed to the famous 'Sīdī Būʿāzza', *shaykh at-tarbiyya* (spiritual master specializing in personal guidance) of Abū Madyan. The version reproduced here can be found as manuscript number 1019D of the Bibliothèque Générale in Rabat, Morocco. Since Abū Yaʿzā is known to have been an uneducated and monolingual Berber speaker, and hence untutored in the Arabic language, one must assume that this treatise, if it is indeed genuine, was set down in writing by the Shaykh's permanent companion and translator, who came from the city of Fez. Parts of this text also appear to have been attributed to Abū Madyan himself, and may include that listed under the same title in the Süleymaniye Library, Istanbul (Fatih, 5375/6, folios 88–92).

«رسالةٌ في التَّصوُّف»
لأبي يَعْزَى يَلَنور إبن مَيْمُون الدَّكَّالي

قال رضي‌الله : إعْلَمْ أنَّ المَعْرِفَةَ هي معرفةُ الحَالِ وهي التي تَأْخُذُ صاحِبَها عنهُ وتَكونُ في جَمِيعِ القَلْبِ وسُوَيْدَاهُ . فَيَشْهَدُ صاحِبُها مَوْلاهُ في كلِّ الأَحْوالِ في الجَمالِ والجَلالِ .

شَاهَدْتُ الجَمالَ شَاهَدْتُ الجَلالَ   حَبِيبِي ومَحبُوبِي عَلى كلِّ حَال

فَالعَارِفونَ فَنوا لَمَّ يَشْهَدُوا   شَيئًا سِوَى المُتَكَبِّرِ المُتَعَال

ورَأوْا سِواهُ على الحَقِيقَةِ هَالِكًا   في الحَالِ والمَاضِي والاسْتِقْبَال

شَمسُ النَّهارِ باللَّيلِ تَغْرُبُ وشَمسُ القُلوبِ لَيسَ لَها مَغِيبٌ ، مَن شَهِدَ باطِنَ الأَوَاني أَدْرَكَ أَسْرارَ المَعاني ، ومَن شَهِدَ شَمْسَ الحَبِيبِ غابَ عَنِ البَعيدِ والقَرِيبِ ، ولم يَجِدْ إلاّ السَّمِيعَ المُجِيب .

ومَن شَاهَدَهُ مُحالٌ أنْ يَشْهَدَ مَعَهُ سِواهُ لأنَّهُ لا يَراهُ غَيرُهُ . ولا غَمَّ عِندَ العارِفِ على التَّحْقِيقِ . شَاهَدْتُ الحَبِيبَ بِعَينِ قَلْبِه [و] بالسِّرِّ المُغِيب .

There is no god but God.

Oh wonder of wonders! How can existence prevail within nonexistence, and how can material creation be affirmed in the presence of One who is characterized by eternity?

Also, gnosis is a sun, and at the appearance of the sun the star holds no sway. For knowledge of the Truth is the perception of [God], and there is nothing other than Him in perceiving it, because it is impossible for you to perceive Him and perceive anything else with Him.

Were the light of certainty to dawn,
The existence of the universe would surely be concealed.

Thus when we say, out of weakness, inability, ignorance, error, poverty, ecstasy, or falsehood, that the 'sight' of a thing is part of gnosis, we have [apparently] affirmed existence in the company of nonexistence. Yet the two are never found together, for nonexistence is something that does not exist. Characterizations such as these do not [logically] follow, except in regard to the nonexistence which is the 'other' or 'others' for the gnostic.[2]

Say: 'Truth has come and falsehood has vanished. Verily falsehood was bound to vanish.'[3]

So where is the 'other' that is associated with error, poverty, inability, or ignorance for one who knows the Truth? He perceives Him in everything and becomes glorious in his error, rich in his poverty, knowledgeable in his ignorance, powerful in his weakness, and able in his helplessness.

2. The point made by Abū Yaʿzā in this passage is that descriptions of gnostic states in terms of physical attributes are mere figures of speech.
3. Qur'ān, XVII (*Banī Isrā'īl*), 81.

لا إِلَهَ إِلَّا اللهُ يَا عَجَبًا ! كَيْفَ يَظْفَرُ الوُجُودُ فِي العَدَمِ أَمْ كَيْفَ يَثْبُتُ الحَادِثُ مَعَ مَنْ لَهُ وَصْفُ القِدَمِ ؟

أَيْضًا المَعْرِفَةُ شَمْسٌ وَعِنْدَ ظُهُورِ الشَّمْسِ لا حُكْمَ لِلنَّجْمِ لِأَنَّ مَعْرِفَةَ الحَقِّ شُهُودُهُ وَشُهُودُهُ لَا يَكُونُ مَعَهُ غَيْرُهُ إِذْ مُحَالٌ لِأَنْ تَشْهَدَهُ وَتَشْهَدَ مَعَهُ سِوَاهُ .

لَوْ أَشْرَقَ نُورُ الإِيقَانِ   لَغَطَّ وُجُودُ الأَكْوَانِ .

وَإِذَا قُلْنَا بِرُؤْيَةِ شَيْءٍ مِنَ الضَّعْفِ أَوِ العَجْزِ أَوِ الجَهْلِ أَوِ الذُّلِّ أَوِ الفَقْرِ أَوِ الوَجْدِ أَوِ اللَّيْلِ أَوِ البَاطِلِ مَعَ المَعْرِفَةِ فَقَدْ أَثْبَتْنَا الوُجُودَ وَالعَدَمَ . وَهُمَا لَا يَجْتَمِعَانِ أَبَدًا لِأَنَّ العَدَمَ شَيْءٌ لَمْ يَكُنْ وَهَذِهِ الأَوْصَافُ لَا تَتَرَتَّبُ إِلَّا عَلَى العَدَمِ الَّذِي هُوَ الغَيْرُ وَالأَغْيَارُ عِنْدَ العَارِفِ .

﴿ قُلْ جَاءَ الحَقُّ وَزَهَقَ البَاطِلُ إِنَّ البَاطِلَ كَانَ زَهُوقًا ﴾

فَأَيْنَ الغَيْرُ الَّذِي يَتَرَتَّبُ عَلَيْهِ الذُّلُّ أَوِ الفَقْرُ أَوِ العَجْزُ أَوِ اللَّيْلُ أَوِ الجَهْلُ عِنْدَ مَنْ عَرَفَ الحَقَّ ؟ وَشَاهَدَهُ فِي كُلِّ شَيْءٍ وَرَجَعَ عَزِيزًا فِي ذُلِّهِ غَنِيًّا فِي فَقْرِهِ عَالِمًا فِي جَهْلِهِ قَوِيًّا فِي ضَعْفِهِ قَادِرًا فِي عَجْزِهِ ؟

Thus it is, so understand, may God have mercy on you, whether one is in the state of annihilation or eternal presence. When one is annihilated, he perceives no 'other', while one who is eternally present—who has arrived at the Eternal Presence—is safe from rupture and becomes eternally joyful in the state of attachment [to God]. It is in this sense that someone has said:

For one who is truthful in his call to love,
The lights are manifested from every side without concealment.

He goes about in . . . (gap in text)
And the veil is removed from him.

The states speak to him from every quarter,
And by means of them he comprehends with conscience and heart.

[They come to him] with secrets from their dominion,
And the [Divine] effusion comes to him from the world of the unseen.

Also, gnosis is strength and its opposite is weakness; gnosis is knowledge and its opposite is ignorance; gnosis is life and its opposite is death; gnosis is the sun and its opposite is darkness; gnosis is power through God and its opposite is helplessness. If any of these qualities were to appear, then the other would be negated.

Say: 'Truth has come and falsehood has vanished. Verily falsehood was bound to vanish.'

القَصِيدَةُ النُّونِيَّةُ

لِلشَّيْخِ عَلي بن اسماعيل بن حِرْزِهِم (سِيدِي علي حرازِم)

إذا أَصابَتْكَ الشَّدائِدُ لُذْ بنا — نحْنُ الكِرامُ ولَيس يَشْقَى ضَيْفُنا

والجَأْ إلَيْنا وانْزلَنَّ برُبْعِنا — إنّا أُناسٌ لا يُضامُ نزيلُنا

إنْ جاءَنا المَلْهُوفُ يَشْكُو ما به — يُبْشِرْ بأَنْ يحْظَى سَرِيعًا بالمُنَى

فإذا دهَتكَ شَدائِدُ ونَكائِبُ — فاهْرَبْ إلَيْنا واقْصُدَنَّ جنابَنا

وإذا أَردْتَ عِنايَةً أَزلِيَّةً — فتعزَّزَنْ باللهِ ثُمَّ بعِزِّنا

إنْ لم تكُنْ مِنّا فحُبُّكَ نافِعٌ — رُزِقَ السَّعادَةَ مَن يفوزُ بحُبِّنا

فاطْلُبْ وسَلْ عمّا تُريدُ ببابِنا — تجِدِ الأَمانِي والمَواهِبَ عِنْدَنا

نُعطِي ونَمْنَعُ إنْ أَرَدْنا مَن نَشا — أَوَما تَرَى أنَّ الإلَهَ أَمَدَّنا

وهكذا فافهمْ رحمكَ الله سواءً كانَ فانيًا أَوْ باقيًا . إذا كان الفاني لا يُشاهِدُ الغيرَ فَأَحْرَى الباقي مَن وَصَلَ البَقاءَ [و] أَمِنَ مِنَ الشّقاءِ صارَ دائِمًا مَسْرُورًا باللّقاءِ . وفي هذا المَعْنى قال بَعْضُهُم :

فَمَنْ كانَ في دَعْوى المحَبّةِ صادِقًا ... تَجَلّتْ لهُ الأَنْوارُ مِن غيرِ مَحْجَبِ
[فـيراح ــفي (كذا)] ... وَيَنْزاحُ عنه الحِجـابُ
تُخاطِبُهُ الأَحْوالُ مِن كلّ جانِبٍ ، ... فَيَفْهَمُ عَنْهـا بالضّمِيرِ وَبالْقَلْبِ
[وتأْتِيهِ] بالأَسْرارِ مِن مَلَكُوتِها ، ... فيأْتِي عَليهِ الفَيْضُ مِن عالمِ الغَيْبِ

وأَيضًا المَعْرفَةُ قُوّةٌ وضِدُّها ضَعْفٌ والمعرفةُ عِلْمٌ وضِدُّها جَهْلٌ والمعرفةُ حياةٌ وضِدُّها مَماتٌ والمعرفةُ شَمسٌ وضِدُّها ظُلْمَةٌ والمعرفة قُدْرَةٌ باللهِ وضِدُّها عَجْزٌ . وهَذهِ الأَوْصافُ مَهْما ظَهرَ أَحدُها بَطلَ الآخرُ .

﴿ قُلْ جاءَ الحَقُّ وزَهَقَ الباطِلُ إنّ الباطِلَ كانَ زَهُوقًا ﴾

Oh partaker of the Source! If you have been actualized, then doubt of the Essence will fall away from [your perception of] the [Divine] attributes, [for] in the [understanding of their] meanings there is no doubt. Once we have found knowledge, ignorance is transformed; once we have found strength, weakness is transformed; once we have found the Truth, we lose creation. And that is that.

How wonderful is this thing you say (and God knows best): 'In its absence is the "knowledge" of knowledge!' This is because the spiritual state is lifted from the slave at certain times so that the Truth may know him and sprinkle him with what He has bestowed upon him. What is asked of [the Sufi] at this moment in time is that he stop [his activity] out of proper conduct and not depart from the door until the veil is lifted from him and the Truth speaks to him intimately with the sweetest speech.

Oh God, our Lord, by the high rank of Your Chosen Prophet bless Your Beloved Muḥammad, the Generous and Chosen One, and bestow entry into the presence of the elect upon us and all Muslims. Praise be to God, sufficiency and peace.

يَا وَارِدَ الْعَيْنِ! إِنْ حَقَّقْتَ زَالَ شَكٌّ الذَّاتِ عَنِ الصِّفَاتِ مَا فِي الْمَعَانِ شَكٌّ. لَمَّا وَجَدْنَـا الْعِلْمَ ارْتَفَعَ الْجَهْلُ وَلَمَّا وَجَـدْنَا الْقُوَّةَ ارْتَفَعَ الضَّعْفُ وَلَمَّا وَجَدْنَا الْحَقَّ فَقَدْنَا الْخَلْقَ. وَالسَّلَام.

نَعَمَ هَذَا الْأَمْرُ الَّذِي تَقُولُ (وَاللهُ أَعْلَمُ) : «بِغَيْبِهِ مَعْرِفَةُ الْعِلْمِ»! وَذَلِكَ أَنَّ الْحَالَ قَدْ يُرْفَعُ عَنِ الْعَبْدِ فِي بَعْضِ الْأَوْقَاتِ لِيُعَرِّفَهُ الْحَقَّ وَذَرًّا مَا مَنَّ بِهِ عَلَيْهِ. فَالْمَطْلُوبُ مِنْهُ فِي هَذَا الْوَقْتِ أَنْ يَقِفَ بِأَدَبٍ وَلَا يَتَنَحَّى عَنِ الْبَابِ حَتَّى يُرْفَعَ عَنْهُ الْحِجَابُ وَيُنَاجِيَهُ الْحَقُّ بِلَذِيذِ الْخِطَابِ.

اللَّهُمَّ يَا مَوْلَانَا بِجَاهِ نَبِيكَ الْمُصْطَفَى صَلِّ عَلَى حَبِيبِكَ مُحَمَّدٍ صَاحِبِ الْجُودِ وَالْوَفَاءِ وَمُنَّ عَلَيْنَا بِالدُّخُولِ فِي حَضْرَةِ أَهْلِ الِاصْطِفَاءِ نَحْنُ وَجَمِيعَ الْمُسْلِمِينَ وَالْحَمْدُ للهِ وَكَفَى وَالسَّلَام.

Index of Names, Titles and Technical Terms